The Feeling Body

The Feeling Body

Affective Science Meets the Enactive Mind

Giovanna Colombetti

The MIT Press
Cambridge, Massachusetts
London, England

A mio padre,
e al ricordo di mia madre

First MIT Press paperback edition, 2017

This book was set in Stone Serif and Stone Sans by the MIT Press. Printed and bound in the United States of America.

Library of Congress Cataloging-in-Publication Data

Colombetti, Giovanna.
The feeling body : affective science meets the enactive mind / Giovanna Colombetti.
    pages   cm
Includes bibliographical references and index.
ISBN 978-0-262-01995-8 (hardcover : alk. paper), 978-0-262-53376-8 (pb.)
1. Emotions and cognition. 2. Affective neuroscience. 3. Philosophy of mind. I. Title.
BF531.C58   2013
128—dc23
2013016542

10 9 8 7 6 5 4 3

Contents

Acknowledgments   ix
Introduction   xiii

1   Primordial Affectivity   1

1.1   Reclaiming a Broader and Deeper Notion of Affectivity   1
1.2   Spinoza's Conatus: Striving as the Ground of All Affects   4
1.3   Enter the *Lived Body*: From Maine de Biran's Experience of Effort to Henry's "Interior Quivering"   7
1.4   Heidegger's Care and Moods, and Patočka's "Physiognomic Impressions"   11
1.5   Enactive Sense Making   15
1.6   Primordial Affectivity and Affective Science   20
1.7   Conclusion   24

2   The Emotions: Existing Accounts and Their Problems   25

2.1   Introduction   25
2.2   The Theory of Basic Emotions (BET)   26
2.3   Assessing Existing Criticisms of BET   29
2.4   The Arbitrariness of the Alleged Basic Emotions   36
2.5   The Problematic Unity/Disunity Debate   40
2.6   Alternatives to BET and Their Problems   46
2.7   Conclusion   52

3   Emotional Episodes as Dynamical Patterns   53

3.1   Introduction   53
3.2   Fundamental Concepts of Dynamical Systems Theory (DST)   54
3.3   Dynamical Affective Science   56
3.4   Implications for the Debate on the Nature of the Emotions   70
3.5   Discreteness and Boundaries   75
3.6   Moods   77
3.7   Conclusion   82

4   Reappraising Appraisal   83

4.1   Introduction   83
4.2   Beginnings   84
4.3   Downplaying the Body in the 1960s and 1970s   87
4.4   Appraisal Theory Today: The Body as a Mere Interactant   94
4.5   Eroding the Neural Boundaries between Cognition and Emotion   98
4.6   Enacting Appraisal   101
4.7   Phenomenological Connections   106
4.8   A (Brief) Comparison with Prinz's "Embodied Appraisal"   109
4.9   Conclusion   111

5   How the Body Feels in Emotion Experience   113

5.1   Introduction   113
5.2   A Taxonomy of Bodily Feeling   115
5.3   Conspicuous Bodily Feelings in Emotion Experience   118
5.4   The "Obscurely Felt" Body   122
5.5   Feeling Absorbed   128
5.6   Conclusion   132

6   Ideas for an Affective "Neuro-physio-phenomenology"   135

6.1   Introduction   135
6.2   Neurophenomenology in Theory and Practice   136
6.3   Neurophenomenology and the Study of Consciousness   139
6.4   Affective Neuroscience and Emotion Experience   143
6.5   Outline of an Affective Neuro-physio-phenomenological Method   148
6.6   Bodily Feelings and Emotion Experience   163
6.7   Conclusion   170

7   Feeling Others   171

7.1   Introduction   171
7.2   The Experience of the Other as a *Leib*   173
7.3   Perceiving Emotion in Expression   176
7.4   Impressive Others   179
7.5   Feeling Close   181
7.6   Sympathy   184
7.7   Doing as Others Do   187
7.8   Do We Mimic Others to Read Their Minds?   190
7.9   Mimicry as a Mechanism for Social Bonding   194
7.10   Beyond Strict Mimicry   198
7.11   Conclusion   201

Epilogue   203
Notes   205
References   229
Index   261

Acknowledgments

I began working on some of the ideas advanced in this book already during my Ph.D. dissertation. I thus owe a big intellectual debt to my supervisor, Andy Clark, for his many suggestions and his encouragement. I also benefited at the time from the interdisciplinary environment of COGS at Sussex University, and from a short but inspiring visit at Indiana University, where I attended Esther Thelen's seminars. Further impetus came from working as a postdoctoral fellow with Evan Thompson, whose vision has since then greatly influenced and inspired my work, and whom I want to thank also for introducing me to Asian philosophies and practices, as well as for his advice and support.

Several other people have contributed to the final shape of this book with useful comments, objections, clarifications, advice, or reading suggestions, for which I am grateful: Ken Aizawa, Rory Allen, Tony Atkinson, Luca Barlassina, Alfonso Caramazza, Erik Christensen, Jason Clark, Marco Colombetti, Vito Colombetti, Trami Dac, Jonathan Davies, Tia DeNora, Ezequiel Di Paolo, Barney Dunn, Marco Giunti, Paul Griffiths, Neil Harrison, Michael Hauskeller, Tony King, Kerrin Jacobs, Natalia Lawrence, Dorothée Legrand, Sabina Leonelli, Brian McLaughlin, Kevin Mulligan, Wayne Myrvold, Søren Overgaard, Federica Pacifico, Doria Polli, Simon Procter, Matthew Ratcliffe, Jim Russell, David Sander, Corrado Sinigaglia, Cristina Soriano, Steve Torrance, Íngrid Vendrell Ferran, Sven Walter, Mike Wheeler, Wendy Wilutzky, Kim Wright, Carlos Zednik, Adam Zeman. I also want to thank Willem Kuyken and Alison Evans of the Exeter Mood Disorders Centre for allowing me to attend the Postgraduate Certificate in Mindfulness-Based Cognitive Therapy in 2010–2011, and for what I learned from them and the other teachers (especially Christina Feldman and Jenny Wilks) and students. The discipline of mindfulness not only supported me in a difficult year but helped me shape some of the ideas for this book as well.

I also benefited from various visits at different research centers. In particular I thank Klaus Scherer for my visits to the Swiss Center for Affective Sciences in Geneva in 2010 and to its Summer School in 2011, and Dan Zahavi for my visit to the Center for Subjectivity Research in Copenhagen in 2011. I learned a lot from both of them and their collaborators. An especially intense visit was arranged by Achim Stephan at the Cognitive Science Institute in Osnabrück in 2012; I thank him for his support, his comments, the workshop on my manuscript, and the wine-tasting retreat in the Rhine Valley.

Particularly heartfelt gratitude goes to those who read and commented on whole draft chapters and greatly helped to improve them: Carl Craver, John Dupré, Julian Kiverstein, Joel Krueger, Tom Roberts, and all the postgraduate students in Osnabrück who read a whole draft of the manuscript and worked to provide comments and criticisms.

And finally, thanks to my family for being a perennial source of a variety of feelings—especially my mother, who left us unexpectedly while I was working on this book, too early to see what I have been up to all this time. The last thought goes to Brian Rappert, for our discussions and for gracefully dealing with the whole range of my affective spectrum throughout this journey.

This work has been funded by the European Research Council under the European Community's Seventh Framework Programme (FP7/2007–2013), project title "Emoting the Embodying Mind (EMOTER)," ERC grant agreement 240891.

Earlier versions of some of the arguments in this book can be found in the following works:

"Enactive Appraisal." *Phenomenology and the Cognitive Sciences* 6 (2007): 527–546.

"The Feeling Body: Towards an Enactive Approach to Emotion" (with E. Thompson). In *Developmental Perspectives on Embodiment and Consciousness*, ed. W. F. Overton, U. Müller, and J. L. Newman, 45–68. New York: Lawrence Erlbaum, 2008.

"From Affect Programs to Dynamical Discrete Emotions." *Philosophical Psychology* 22 (2009): 407–425.

"Reply to Barrett, Gendron, and Huang." *Philosophical Psychology* 22 (2009): 439–442.

"Enaction, Sense-Making, and Emotion." In *Enaction: Toward a New Paradigm for Cognitive Science*, ed. J. Stewart, O. Gapenne, and E. D. Di Paolo, 145–164. Cambridge, MA: MIT Press, 2010.

"Varieties of Pre-reflective Self-Awareness: Foreground and Background Bodily Feelings in Emotion Experience." *Inquiry* 54 (2011): 293–313.

Introduction

This book takes several ideas from the so-called *enactive* approach developed in cognitive science and philosophy of mind over the last twenty years or so and applies them specifically to the field of affective science. The result is both a further development of the enactive approach itself, by extending it to a further domain of inquiry, and a reconceptualization of various affective phenomena as they appear in affective science that, I think, does more justice to their complexity.

Affective science, to be sure, is not a field with clear boundaries. Like its close relative cognitive science, it is a research area in which multiple disciplines study a common object of interest—which in this case is "affect" or "affectivity," broadly understood to include related phenomena such as emotions, feelings, moods, and mood disorders. In a liberal interpretation, any theory or study that explores these phenomena can be seen as contributing to affective science. Not only psychology and neuroscience, then, but history, anthropology, ethology, sociology, computer science, political science, education, literature, and philosophy—just to mention some, and in no particular order—can be seen as disciplines making up the field. The more these disciplines cross-fertilize, the better are our chances of gaining an accurate understanding of affectivity, and thus of ourselves (as well as of other creatures). In this work, however, I focus primarily on the two disciplines that arguably have the most prominent role in the field, namely, experimental psychology and neuroscience. My goal is to bring a variety of "enactivist" ideas to bear on these two disciplines, in different ways. I see enactivism as a highly suitable framework for an account of affectivity that characterizes it as an essential dimension of the mind, as well as a rich source of ideas for how to conceptualize and study a variety of affective phenomena.

What, however, is enactivism? There are now various accounts that call themselves "enactive." The version of enactivism on which I draw in this book is the one originally articulated by Varela, Thompson, and Rosch (1991) and further elaborated more recently by Thompson (2007, 2011a, 2011b), as well as others (see, e.g., the collection of papers in Stewart, Gapenne, and Di Paolo 2010). It is a complex tapestry of several interrelated and mutually supporting ideas from different fields of inquiry, notably cognitive science, biology, and the philosophical tradition of phenomenology. As such, it is not a radically novel framework but a synthesis of various ideas (some older, some newer), one that keeps evolving by incorporating new empirical studies and theoretical perspectives. Enactivism explicitly traces its sources to various phenomenological and existential philosophies. Varela, Thompson, and Rosch (1991, xv) presented their approach specifically as a continuation of Merleau-Ponty's work, and further "phenomenological connections" (especially with Merleau-Ponty and Husserl, but not only) are discussed in more detail by Thompson (2007). Other important affinities can be found, for example, in the pragmatism of James and Dewey, Gestalt psychology, the cybernetic movement of the 1940s and 1950s, and ecological psychology (see also Di Paolo, Rohde, and De Jaegher 2010).

Because of this complexity, it is not easy to characterize the enactive approach briefly, and one always runs the risk of overlooking some important features. For the purposes of this introduction, I outline only some of enactivism's major ideas and themes, leaving the illustration of more specific points to individual chapters. I should also emphasize that I do not address *all* facets of the enactive approach in this book. Rather, I pull out from its tapestry those threads that I think are more relevant for affective science, and weave them further. For now I limit myself to the most visible strands and mention why I think they are promising for a study of affectivity.

One of the central ideas of enactivism is *embodiment*. According to it, the mind is not an immaterial Cartesian substance, a thinking thing, but neither (and more controversially) is the brain its minimally sufficient physical basis. Rather, the mind is enacted or brought forth by the living organism in virtue of its specific organization and its interaction with the world. Particularly significant for present purposes is that the body, in the enactive approach, is not just a sensorimotor system, namely, a physical system that links sensory inputs and motor actions. Enactivism importantly also emphasizes the wetter and bloodier *self-regulatory* dimension of embodiment, which includes the biochemical activity of metabolism, and more generally homeostatic (or better, homeodynamic) processes. The body of the enactive mind is thus not just the perceiving and acting body but the living body, and as such it includes, for example, the viscera, the circulatory system, the immune system, and the endocrine system. These dimensions of the body are all seen as contributing to the kind of mind one has (although, as I explain later, even unicellular organisms can be said to have a mind from the enactive perspective). Such a comprehensive notion of the body is especially relevant for a study of affectivity. In everyday life, affective phenomena such as emotions and moods come with a variety of bodily experiences, and others' bodily posture and facial expressions undoubtedly play a part in how we understand them when we are in their presence. Affective science has been confirming that several changes take place in expression, autonomic nervous system activity, and muscular tension when people undergo an emotion or are in a specific mood. So not only would it be restrictive to constrain the study of affective phenomena to the brain only (or even to claim that they *are* just brain processes), but a conception of the body that limits it to a sensorimotor system does not suffice for an account of these phenomena, either.[1]

Another central idea of the enactive approach is that the scientific study of the mind cannot ignore *lived experience*; rather, it has to take it seriously and develop adequate methods for its investigation. Adopting an enactive approach thus entails paying special attention to, and developing accurate descriptions of, this dimension of the mind. This is why Varela, Thompson, and Rosch (1991) engaged not just with the Western philosophical tradition of phenomenology but also with the Buddhist tradition of mindfulness meditation, which offers accounts of experience but also techniques for the first-person exploration of consciousness. This concern with lived experience is another feature of the enactive approach that I find particularly appealing for a study of affective phenomena. Emotions and moods can be complex experiences and as such deserve to be addressed with adequate descriptive and analytical tools. Enactivism provides such tools via its phenomenological connections and encourages the development of new ones. Compared to the study of the organism in its many physical (or better, living) aspects, the one of lived experience is much less advanced in affective science. So as part of taking an enactive perspective, I often call for more attention to this dimension and develop some phenomenological considerations myself.

Importantly, the enactive approach is not just interested in lived experience per se but maintains that phenomenological analyses should be part and parcel of the experimental investigation of the mind. The study of the organism as a living system and the study of the organism as a subject of experience are not independent but need each other and should aim to complement each other productively. More specifically, the scientific inquiry needs adequate descriptions of lived experience to make sense of brain and bodily activity; conversely, the study of the living organism can help to refine accounts of lived experience. This idea, as we shall see in more detail later in the book, fits broadly with recent attempts to "naturalize phenomenology," although it does not aim to reduce lived experience to descriptions of physical processes. In line with this enactivist theme, in the course of the book I often use phenomenological and empirical considerations about a variety of affective phenomena to support and illuminate one another (in addition to dedicating a whole chapter to the suggestion of augmenting current affective neuroscience with first- and second-person methods for the study of lived experience).

These ideas are related to the most radical-sounding theme of the enactive approach (one that can be traced to the philosophy of the organism of Hans Jonas, and to some extent further back to Aristotle), namely, the so-called thesis of the *deep continuity* of life and mind. Thompson (2007, ix) introduces it from the beginning as the main subject of his book, phrasing it as follows: "The organizational properties distinctive of mind are an enriched version of those fundamental to life" (see also Thompson 2011a). This formulation should not be read as implying that there are forms of life not rich enough to be "minded." Life, for the enactive approach, is in fact sufficient for mind (as we shall see in more detail in chapter 1). The thesis is then that the organizational properties of life are sufficient for mind, and enriched forms of mind are an enriched version of them. Mind did not appear at some point in evolution in a specific life-form but reaches down to the simplest organisms. Life is thus always "minded" or "mindful," and the richer a living form, the richer its mind. Importantly, the deep life-mind continuity thesis also entails that even in its richest forms, mind remains "life-like." Mind shares the organizational properties of life, and to understand the organizational properties of life is thus to make considerable progress toward understanding the mind as well.

This thesis is more than just another theme in the enactive approach; it is in fact what holds its many threads together—what grounds and justifies its ambitious striving for a synthesis of biological, neuroscientific, psychological, and phenomenological ideas, as well as its emphasis on self-organization, mutual influences and temporality, deep brain-body integration, bodily experience, and more (all topics to which I return in the course of the book). It also entails a very different conception of cognition from what is generally assumed in cognitive, as well as affective, science. The enactive conception, as I argue in the first chapter, importantly entails that cognition is, necessarily, always already affective (in a sense that I specify). So although in this book I end up discussing primarily the emotions (and, occasionally, moods) of the affective scientist, it is important to bear in mind that the enactive approach entails that there is no difference in kind between cognition and emotion. Rather, both cognition and emotion turn out to be instances of the relentless *sense-making* activity of the precarious living organism as it maintains itself via continuous processes of self-regulation and exchange with the environment. Sense making, as we shall see, is a central notion in the enactive approach, and I present it toward the beginning of the book to provide an overarching frame to the rest of the discussion.

The rest of the book otherwise focuses, primarily at least, on the more mundane phenomena that traditionally occupy the psychologists and neuroscientists of emotion—such as basic emotions, appraisals, bodily arousal, bodily feelings, emotion experience, and more. Sometimes I criticize how these phenomena are characterized in affective science; other times I propose alternative conceptualizations that are variously inspired by the enactive approach. Importantly, then, the aim of this work is not so much to defend the enactive approach by developing new arguments in addition to those already advanced in the relevant literature. Rather, I aim to bring enactive ideas to bear on a further set of phenomena that until now have been relatively neglected by enactivism itself, as well as more generally by the so-called embodied-embedded approach in the philosophy of cognitive science.[2]

Some readers will be unsympathetic to the enactive approach to start with and will thus want to question the very premises of some (if not all) of my arguments. But many of the ideas of this book can be taken on board even by those who do not endorse the whole enactivist package. Given the many themes that make up enactivism, I believe that, different worldviews notwithstanding, even the non- or anti-enactivist reader can find value in some of the specific ideas that I advance. Also, some of the lines I develop (e.g., the critique of basic emotions, the analyses of emotion experience, the discussion of empathy and mimicry) do not require taking any stance toward enactivism altogether. My main concern is first of all with affectivity and emotion, and I think of the enactive approach as a most suitable tool for what I want to say about them, as well as a rich source of ideas and inspiration for further elaborations. I have not found the same degree of intellectual affinity and the same resources in other frameworks. Yet if some readers will find independent value in some of the specific ideas about affectivity and emotion on offer, I shall not think my efforts have been in vain.

1 Primordial Affectivity

1.1 Reclaiming a Broader and Deeper Notion of Affectivity

Affective scientists, as their name implies, study affective phenomena. As we shall appreciate in more detail as the book unfolds, they focus especially on *emotion*, understood as a psychological faculty of its own, distinct from but also importantly linked to other faculties, such as perception, attention, memory, and so on. This emotional faculty manifests itself in a variety of different and primarily short-lived *emotions*—sadness, fear, happiness, guilt, pride, shame, and many others. Affective scientists also (although more rarely) study *moods*, which they see as differing from emotions mainly in intensity and duration, in particular as being less intense and longer lasting than emotions.[1]

I discuss several affective-scientific approaches in this book; however, the aim of this initial chapter is to emphasize that emotions and moods do not exhaust the realm of affectivity.[2] The emotions and moods of the affective scientist are usually temporary episodes that take place in an otherwise affect-free mind. They are, in other words, mere contingent happenings of the mind. Even when moods, unlike emotions, are (sometimes) said to be always present, they remain "surface" phenomena that could be taken away from the mind, while the mind would still be such. Affectivity as I understand it and discuss it in this chapter goes beyond such fleeting events: it is a broader phenomenon that permeates the mind, necessarily and not merely contingently. The mind, as embodied, is intrinsically or constitutively affective; you cannot take affectivity away from it and still have a mind. Affectivity as discussed in this chapter refers broadly to a *lack of indifference*, and rather a *sensibility* or *interest* for one's existence. The etymology of the term already points to this meaning: "affectivity" refers to the capacity or possibility to be "done something," to be "struck" or "influenced" (the term comes from the past participle of the Latin verb *afficio*, "to strike, to influence"—itself a compound of *ad*, "to," and *facio*, "to do"). This influence is not merely physical or mechanical (as when one says that the daily amount of sunlight affects the air temperature) but psychological. It refers to the capacity to be personally affected, to be "touched" in a meaningful way by what is affecting one. In this broad sense, it is not necessary to be in a specific emotion or mood to be in an affective state; one is affected when something merely strikes one as meaningful, relevant, or salient.

Drawing on the enactive approach, in this chapter I argue that affectivity thus understood depends on the organizational properties of life, such that all living systems—even the simplest ones—are affective; hence the term *primordial affectivity*. As we will see in detail later, according to the enactive approach, all living systems are *sense-making* systems, namely (and roughly for now), they inhabit a world that is significant for them, a world that they themselves enact or bring forth as the correlate of their needs and concerns. In the enactive approach, this activity of sense making is the mark of *cognition*. What I add to this idea is the point that the activity of sense making is simultaneously also *affective*. To clarify, the claim is not that all living systems, including the simplest ones, have emotions. The claim is rather that even the simplest living systems have a capacity to be sensitive to what matters to them, and in this sense they are affective. Nor is the claim that even the simplest living systems are conscious; rather, the simplest living systems already realize a relationship with themselves and the world in which they are situated that entails purposefulness and concern for their existence. But such purposefulness and concern need not be accompanied by consciousness; rather, they ought to be understood as properties of a specific organization that sets up an *asymmetry* between the living system and the rest of the world, which consists in a perspective or point of view from which the world acquires meaning. Once embedded in more complex organisms, this perspective will also (at some point, although when and how is not the present concern) exhibit awareness.

Affectivity thus characterized is not just broader but "deeper" than the emotions and moods of affective science, in the sense that it grounds them or makes them possible; in other words, without the primordial capacity to be affected, no specific emotions and moods would appear. The idea that affectivity is a broader and deeper phenomenon than distinct emotions or even moods can be found in various works in the philosophical tradition of phenomenology, but also before them. In the first part of this chapter, I introduce and discuss some of these works. I begin with Spinoza's notion of the *conatus*, which grounds all the emotions in a conative or motivational dimension of existence. I then move on to the notion of the *lived body*, as introduced in particular by Maine de Biran, who especially emphasized the active and effortful character of bodily subjectivity, arguably providing a phenomenological account of the conative dimension of existence. I also address Michel Henry's discussion of Maine de Biran, which endorses his characterization of the lived body while also making room in it for a dimension of *passivity*; passivity, for Henry, is required if we want to include affectivity in the sphere of bodily subjectivity. In addition, Henry himself points to an even deeper dimension of bodily subjectivity, which straddles the active–passive distinction and is arguably itself "affective" in the broad sense of sensitive and nonindifferent. I then consider Heidegger's conception of moods, which, unlike the moods of the affective scientist, are noncontingent, inescapable modes of existing that allow the world to matter in various ways. Finally I turn to Patočka's appropriation, as well as criticism, of Heidegger's treatment of moods, which links them back to Maine de Biran's notion of the lived body and sees them as manifestations of how the world impinges "physiognomically" on the bodily subject.

This historical overview will be brief. It is not meant to be exhaustive and to engage with scholarly debates; its more modest aim is to begin tracing the philosophical lineage of a notion of affectivity that is rarely if ever acknowledged in current scientific as well as philosophical accounts of emotion and mood (and one that could be traced in many more works).[3] With the exception of Heidegger, none of the philosophers I have mentioned feature, for example, in the recent seven-hundred-page *Oxford Handbook of Philosophy of Emotion* (Goldie 2010). In addition, the views I have chosen refer explicitly to the body (again with the exception of Heidegger, as discussed hereafter) and will thus allow me to clarify the sense in which primordial affectivity is a dimension of embodiment.

After this historical premise, I turn properly to the enactive approach, in particular to the notion of sense making as elaborated in recent discussions. I explain why this notion entails that all living systems are not only cognitive but also affective.[4] I also explain in which sense this notion can be seen as grounding the emotions of more complex organisms. Finally I turn to affective science itself, to qualify the claim that it relies on a relatively narrow and shallow notion of affectivity. As we shall see, there are exceptions to this claim. Some scientific accounts deviate from the mainstream approach and identify affective phenomena that go beyond emotions and moods and are intimately related with embodied existence. Such affective phenomena have various features in common with my notion of primordial affectivity; however, they still fall short of it in some respect or another, which will be useful to elucidate.

1.2 Spinoza's Conatus: Striving as the Ground of All Affects

Spinoza in his *Ethics* developed a rich account of the emotions ("affects" in his terminology) while also acknowledging a deeper conative or motivational dimension of existence. He maintained that all existence is intrinsically striving, that the "essence of everything," including nonliving things, is a conatus—an effort or endeavor to persevere in its being (see III.6 and III.7).[5] It was quite common in seventeenth- and eighteenth-century philosophy to employ the term "conatus" to refer to a thing's effort or striving toward what is advantageous for it. Spinoza himself had been influenced by Hobbes, who in *Leviathan* discussed an analogous phenomenon, claiming that all finite beings are driven by "a perpetuall and restlesse desire of Power after power" (Hobbes [1651] 1991, 70).

Spinoza's philosophy rejects several aspects of Cartesianism, including the idea that body (matter, extension) and mind (soul, thought) are two separate substances that interact causally at the level of the pineal gland.[6] Spinoza famously criticized this interactionist view, arguing that the mind, as an immaterial substance without extension and thus without surfaces, cannot causally affect and be affected by the material substance that is the body. He held instead that mind and body are two of the infinite attributes of the same divine Substance, God, which is also none other than Nature. These two attributes alone are known to us and constitute our nature. In human beings, the conatus thus has a mental and a bodily expression and as such is called "appetite" (*appetitus*). "Desire" (*cupiditas*) refers in particular to awareness or consciousness of one's appetite, but otherwise "there is no difference between appetite and desire" (III.9). Importantly, in Spinoza's ontology the two realms of body and mind are causally closed systems:

every bodily event follows from a bodily event, and every mental event follows from a mental event. Bodily and mental events thus do not interact causally; there is, however, a "parallelism" between them: "The order and connection of ideas is the same as the order and connection of things" (II.7). Every bodily event corresponds to a mental one; they are different expressions or modes of the same substance: "A mode of extension and the idea of that mode are one and the same thing expressed in two different ways" (II.7). Human behavior is thus not caused by mental activity; rather, it is the manifestation of the unfolding of the appetite, itself an aspect of the changing nature of God-Nature as it unfolds in its striving self-affirmation.[7]

One consequence of this view is that, as Spinoza explicitly pointed out, we do not first evaluate things and situations as good and desirable for us and subsequently strive for them; rather, it is our fundamental striving nature that determines what counts as good or bad for us: "We neither strive for, wish, seek, nor desire anything because we think it to be good, but, on the contrary, we adjudge a thing to be good because we strive for, wish, seek, or desire it" (III.9). This claim constitutes a reversal of the current widespread position according to which evaluations bring about desires and emotions (see chap. 4). As we shall see, this reversal is very much in line with the enactive approach, according to which what counts as good or bad for an organism is not detected by a disembodied cognitive-evaluative faculty; rather, it is the intrinsically purposive nature of the organism that enacts or brings forth what matters for its continuation.

Spinoza's characterization of the conatus is followed by an account of, in his terminology, the "affects," namely, "the affections of the body, by which the power of acting of the body itself is increased, diminished, helped, or hindered, together with the ideas of these affections" (III, definition 3). All affects spring from three "primary" ones, of which desire is one; the other two are joy (*laetitia*) and sorrow (*tristitia*), defined as the passions in which the mind (and the body with it) passes to a greater and lesser perfection respectively (III.11). All the other affects derive from these three, depending on the different "ideas" that accompany them.[8] For example, "*Love* is nothing but joy accompanied with the idea of an external cause, and *hatred* is nothing but sorrow with the accompanying idea of an external cause" (III.13); "*Hope* is nothing but unsteady joy, arising from the image of a future or past thing about whose issue we doubt. *Fear*, on the other hand, is an unsteady sorrow, arising from the image of a doubtful thing" (III.18); "*commiseration* ... we may define as sorrow which springs from another's loss. ... Love toward the person who has done good to another we shall call *favour* ... , whilst hatred towards him who has done evil to another we shall call *indignation*" (III.22).

Individual affects thus involve different "cognitions," to put it in contemporary terms. Spinoza's theory of the affects has in fact been characterized as cognitive by various commentators, which is accurate given that for Spinoza cognitions (ideas, concepts) play an important role in distinguishing different affects from one another. Yet far from being identified uniquely with ideas or images, in Spinoza the individual affects remain fundamentally appetitive, namely, based on the essentially conative nature of everything, which in humans takes the form of appetite and desire. Importantly, although Spinoza characterizes joy and sorrow as "primary," they themselves depend on the appetite; indeed, they are "species" of the appetite. In III.57 Spinoza writes that "desire is the very nature or essence of a person," and after reminding us of his characterization of the primary affects, he concludes that joy and sorrow are "indexes," so to speak, of how conducive external events are to one's self-affirming existence: "Joy and sorrow are passions by which the power of a person or his effort to persevere in his own being is increased or diminished, helped or limited. ... But by the effort to persevere in his own being, in so far as it is related at the same time to the mind and the body, we understand appetite and desire, ... and therefore joy and sorrow are desire or appetite in so far as the latter is increased, diminished, helped, or limited by external causes." Desire (conscious appetite) is thus "more primary" than joy and sorrow; these two affects would not be possible in a nonappetitive being. Because all other affects depend on desire, joy, and sorrow, we can conclude that for Spinoza they are all grounded in a primordial appetitive dimension.

This appetitive dimension is affective in the broad sense mentioned earlier: the striving being is not indifferent toward its own existence but rather endeavors to maintain it; its perspective is thus not neutral but interested and concerned. Moreover, the striving being needs to be open and sensitive to what is conducive to its continuation and what is not.[9] Thus we can see Spinoza's conatus as a dimension of affectivity that runs deeper than the affects. The affects are specific forms that this affective dimension takes depending on the mental activity that accompanies it.

Importantly also, both the appetite and the affects in Spinoza's account remain thoroughly *embodied*. The appetite, as we saw, is the form that the conatus takes in human beings, and has a bodily and a mental expression. Likewise for the affects. Although they are characterized as differing from one another in terms of the mental ideas they involve, they remain thoroughly "psychosomatic" events, because any idea for Spinoza is always accompanied by a specific mode of extension (that is, a bodily event).

1.3   Enter the *Lived Body*: From Maine de Biran's Experience of Effort to Henry's "Interior Quivering"

Spinoza thus grounds the affects in a primordial affective dimension and characterizes them as both mental and bodily. Yet something important is missing from his account, namely, a description of how the appetite, as well as the different affects, are also *experienced as bodily*. This is where Spinoza arguably remains Cartesian. Although mind and body in the *Ethics* are not two separate substances, they are nevertheless distinct attributes that can be conceived apart from each other. Now, Spinoza's conception of matter is quite unlike that of Descartes. As Hampshire (1951, 79–80) puts it, Spinoza's "was materialism with a difference, if only because the word 'matter' normally suggests something solid and inert, and no such notion of matter is to be found in his writings." Spinoza's matter, unlike Descartes's lifeless *res extensa*, is striving and self-maintaining; as an attribute of God-Nature, it is subject to the conatus and thus endeavors to persevere in its being (see also Jonas 1965). Yet Spinoza never mentions how matter, when instantiated as a human body, is experienced. Every change in the body is also a change in the mind, but aside from this parallelism, the activity of the body is not reflected or mirrored in consciousness. Instead the body quickly disappears from Spinoza's account of the emotions—not in the sense that they become "disembodied" (every emotion is always at the same time mental *and* bodily), but in the sense that they are analyzed solely in terms of the various ideas that accompany them, with no reference to bodily movements or bodily feelings.[10]

It is here that Spinoza remains Cartesian. Descartes, in his own account of the emotions (elaborated in the last of his works published in his lifetime, *The Passions of the Soul* [1649] 1989), characterized the emotions as passions or perceptions caused by bodily movements whose effects are felt in the mind. Among other things, he spent considerable time providing detailed descriptions of the different bodily changes causing the various emotions. Even so, these bodily changes remained mere *causal antecedents* of the emotions; they were not felt as part of the emotions (see also G. Hatfield 2007). The body in Descartes thus remained extrinsic to experience. Similarly, even if for Spinoza the body is constitutive of the emotions, it remains a silent, nonconscious material substrate. Neither in Descartes nor in Spinoza, then, do we find an account of the body as lived or experienced. The body is either the extrinsic cause or the silent parallel accompaniment of the mind. The emotions remain experientially disembodied in both accounts.

For an account of the body as lived and not just as extended, we need to turn to phenomenology. The notion of the lived body or, in German, *Leib*—namely, the body as it is experienced in the first person—is usually traced to Husserl's discussion in the second volume of the *Ideas* (Husserl [1952] 1989), where he distinguishes it from the notion of *Körper*, namely, the body under a physical description.[11] Merleau-Ponty is traditionally introduced as the philosopher who made the most room for the lived body in his phenomenology of perception (Merleau-Ponty [1945] 1962), in particular with his discussion of "motor intentionality" and "corporeal schema"—where the first notion refers to the body's implicit relatedness to the world, its concrete and practical "reaching out" to the world in its various activities, and the second, related notion refers to the implicit awareness I have of my body when orienting myself in the world.

Before Husserl and Merleau-Ponty, however, a less-known (at least in Anglo-American philosophy) French philosopher, Maine de Biran (1766–1824), had already provided an account of the body as "subjective."[12] Merleau-Ponty, who lectured on Biran (see Merleau-Ponty [1968] 2001), acknowledged (although with various qualifications) that he radically transformed the Cartesian *cogito* (thinking thing) by positing the body as necessary for it. Biran indeed rejected Descartes's characterization of subjectivity as a thinking substance separate from the body. For Biran, a proper analysis of consciousness reveals that subjectivity is given in experience, via an "immediate apperception," as a *force* manifested in effort and movement: "Because I think, I understand, I want, I act, I perceive my effort, I know that I act, I exist for myself as an individual force; therefore I am really and absolutely an acting force" (Maine de Biran 1841, 18; my translation). That

I exist as bodily is entailed by this phenomenological fact; my corporeity is immediately given to me in the effortful experience I have of myself as an acting force. Importantly, this experience of myself as a force is inextricably linked with the experience of the *resistance* that objects in the world offer to my explorations, most apparently my tactile ones, but not only. The experience of this barrier reveals to me at the same time my corporeal subjectivity, including its boundary.

Hence in Maine de Biran the body, rather than being an extended substance only causally related to the mind or a nonconscious material attribute, belongs to the I as an original phenomenological fact, indeed as the primary "fact of consciousness" that reveals to us our nature. Maine de Biran's body is lived, not just physical. It moves because it is intrinsically animated, not because it is directed by a mind extrinsic to it; and it is given as a phenomenological fact, not just as the causal antecedent or the silent accompaniment of mental activity.

As I read it, Biran's characterization of subjectivity as an active force complements, at the experiential level, Spinoza's view of the appetite as a primary bodily and mental phenomenon. It refers to a primordial experience of ourselves as striving bodily beings, which is constitutive of other experiences. Moreover, because of its emphasis on the experience of effort, compared to better-known phenomenologies of the body, Biran's arguably portrays a particularly *thick* or *full* lived body: he emphasizes its presence, its striving corporeality, as opposed to its transparency or self-forgetfulness in its dealings with the world (to use the terminology that I introduce in chap. 5, Biran's lived body comes with a high degree of *self-luminosity* or *self-intimation*).[13] This bodily thickness makes Biran's philosophy, I believe, particularly suitable for developing an account of affectivity in which the body does not just tacitly operate in the world but is also experienced in its visceral and kinesthetic dimensions as it does so (I explore the notion of the lived body and its place in emotion experience in chapter 5).

Yet we need to wait until Michel Henry (1965) to find Biran's account of the lived body properly applied to affectivity. Biran himself, as Henry points out, was prevented from doing so satisfactorily because of, once again, residual Cartesian influences on his own view of affectivity. On the one hand, Henry keenly defends Biran's characterization of subjectivity as effortful and corporeal; he even praises Biran for being the first philosopher able to overcome Descartes's mind–body dualism by refusing to reduce the body to mere lifeless extension. On the other hand, Henry finds various echoes of Descartes still lingering in Biran's philosophy, notably in his account of affectivity and other "passive" phenomena, such as sensation and imagination. Henry (1965, chap. 6) points out that, in characterizing subjectivity as effort, Biran limited it to an *active* force and was subsequently at pains to make room in it for the passive dimension of subjectivity. To the extent that affectivity also involves being affected (being "done something") and not just outward striving, in Biran it then had to fall outside the domain of subjectivity. In fact, Biran often relegated it to a modality of "organic life," characterized as purely physical or subconscious—namely, deprived of lived subjectivity. In this sense, Henry notes, Biran's account of affectivity and other passive phenomena is "strangely" like the account of Descartes in his treatise on the passions: they depend on (are brought about by) something that lies *beyond* the sphere of immanent subjectivity, namely, on mere extension.

Henry's own remedy is to view *both* passivity and activity as grounded in a deeper foundation of corporeal subjectivity, a more fundamental "power" (1965, 225) that is alive not just when one moves effortfully but also when one is passively influenced. Henry speaks here of a "latent tension" experienced in the body, which is the "essence" of feeling and affectivity, as well as of active motor effort; this tension is "the proper interior quivering of knowing" (le propre frémissement intérieur du savoir), where this knowing is "a life, not a dead knowing" (1965, 230). At this level of latent tension, which Henry also characterizes as "an origin," there is no room for an opposition between passivity and activity; rather, this level is the common root of both, the precondition of both.[14]

This bodily quivering is thus the most primordial level of subjectivity. Henry sees it as a *precondition* for the passive phenomenon of affectivity. Yet one can interpret it as itself already affective, in the sense of a source of meaning for the being in question; the quivering being is affected, that is, struck, touched, or moved by a sense, if minimal, of significance. This interpretation fits well also with what Henry says in other parts of his book about affectivity characterizing every experience: "Every thought is an affective thought. ... Every experience has its own tonality" (1965, 199), and "There is no room for distinguishing certain affective *Erlebnisse* [lived experiences] from allegedly nonaffective ones, but all our experiences, *as they are our different ways of living*, carry in themselves that which is precisely the primary character of every life and of every experience, and which we call here, for want of a better term, an affective tonality" (200; my translation, my italics; German in original). This passage suggests that affectivity for Henry is not restricted to a passive phenomenon underpinned by a more fundamental level of "tension" or "power" but is itself, as "the primary character of every life," this more fundamental level.[15]

1.4   Heidegger's Care and Moods, and Patočka's "Physiognomic Impressions"

Another author who can be regarded as endorsing the view that there is a deeper and more primordial level of affectivity than individual emotions is Heidegger—though his account pertains explicitly to human existence only and in this respect does not support the enactive claim (discussed in the next section) that all living beings are affective. However, we can draw important parallels between his account of care and moods in *Being and Time* ([1926] 1996) and the present notion of primordial affectivity, which should become clearer as both are expounded.

Heidegger in *Being and Time* famously uses the term *Dasein* (usually translated as "being-there") to refer to human existence. Dasein is, most fundamentally, that for which its existence is an issue. Dasein is purposeful and goal oriented; it is "projected" toward its realization. As Heidegger also puts it, Dasein is fundamentally (necessarily, constitutionally) characterized by *care* (*Sorge*) for its activities and projects. One of the three inextricable constituents of care is what Heidegger calls, with a neologism, *Befindlichkeit*—a term notoriously difficult to translate into English.[16] The reflexive verb *sich befinden*, from which it comes, literally means "to find oneself," "to be" in a certain state, and is used in two different ways: to answer the question "where are you?" by saying, for example, "Ich befinde mich in der Uni" (I am at the university), and to answer the question "how are you?" by saying, for example, "Ich befinde mich gut" (I'm fine). *Befindlichkeit* thus refers at the same time to "where" and "how" one finds oneself.[17]

To say that one of the ingredients of care is *Befindlichkeit* is to say that, as concerned with its existence, Dasein always necessarily finds itself in one way or another. These different ways in which Dasein finds itself are its *moods*, namely, specific ways in which it is *attuned* to the world (the German term for mood here is *Stimmung*; the verb *stimmen* also means "to tune," as in "to tune a piano"). Heidegger discusses different moods in *Being and Time* and other works. Most famously, he discusses the anxiety (*Angst*) we find ourselves in when we contemplate our finite nature, our being-toward-death.

Crucially for Heidegger, *we cannot escape* our moods, because our existence is never care free; we are always attuned to the world in one way or another. Even indifference, or better "everydayness," is itself a mood. Likewise for the allegedly disinterested theoretical attitude of science, which is itself a specific mode of being attuned to the world. In other words, Heideggerian moods are not interruptions of an otherwise moodless mind but are constitutive of human existence. In this sense they are quite unlike the moods of affective science, which are longer lasting than the emotions, but nevertheless still contingent states of mind—mere colorations or "accompanying phenomena," as Heidegger put it ([1926] 1996, 135). This point applies also to scientific accounts that claim that moods, unlike emotions, are always present, albeit in an attenuated form (e.g., Davidson 1994; D. Watson and Clark 1994). In these accounts, mood remains a surface phenomenon, something that "colors" the mind all the time but only happens to do so; arguably in these accounts mood could be taken away from the mind, but the mind would still be there. For Heidegger, on the other hand, moods are fundamental, inescapable modes of being in the world that necessarily characterize our existence; it is not possible for Dasein not to be in a mood.

Also, whereas in affective science moods are usually characterized as specific feelings, namely, subjective experiences with distinctive qualities (e.g., of elation, irritability, anxiety), Heidegger emphasizes that moods are not private states of mind but modes of being in the world: "Being attuned is not initially related to something psychical, it is itself not an inner condition which then in some mysterious way reaches out and leaves its mark on things and persons"; rather, "Mood assails. It comes neither from 'without' nor from 'within,' but rises from being-in-the-world itself as a mode of that being" (Heidegger [1926] 1996, 129). Thus *Angst*, for example, is analyzed in terms of how one encounters the world; in this specific attunement, the world takes on the character of "complete insignificance" (174), its objects lose their familiarity, its context of practical meanings collapses onto itself.

Importantly, Heidegger's moods are necessary conditions for anything to matter to us. A detached, purely contemplative stance cannot disclose anything relevant for Dasein. It is mood that constitutes the world as meaningful, and different moods disclose different meanings. Being in a fearful mood, for example, discloses the world as threatening. A detached, purely contemplative stance would not be able to do so: "Pure beholding, even if it penetrated into the innermost core of the being of something objectively present, would never be able to discover anything like what is threatening" ([1926] 1996, 130). As Guignon (2003, 183) puts it, in Heidegger's account "there is a reciprocal relationship between our purposive agency and the practical contexts in which we find ourselves. Our goals, interests, and needs structure the ways in which things will *count* for us in the context" (recall Spinoza's point that we do not first evaluate things as good or bad for us and then strive for them; rather, it is our striving nature that determines what counts as good or bad for us). This disclosive role is "primordial," at least in the context of Dasein: "The possibilities of disclosure belonging to cognition fall short of the primordial disclosure of moods in which Dasein is brought before its being as the there" (Heidegger [1926] 1996, 131), namely, in which Dasein faces its own existence for what it is.

In spite of this acknowledgment of the primordial character of moods, unlike the authors discussed earlier, Heidegger does not address the relationship between affectivity and the body. In fact, his account, as others have remarked, is strangely "disembodied," in the sense that it does not mention the body at all when characterizing moods.[18] Yet an interesting proposal to synthesize Heidegger's account of moods with Maine de Biran's account of the lived body has been provided by the Czech phenomenologist Jan Patočka (1907–1977). Patočka ([1995] 1998)[19] endorses Heidegger's view of mood as a fundamental trait of our existence but also explicitly criticizes him for failing to note and discuss mood's bodily character. Patočka then returns to Biran to emphasize the active, effortful, and thus corporeal character of subjectivity. Patočka talks of the "energy" and "primordial dynamism" (e.g., 40–46) that characterize our bodily subjectivity, and at the same time our orientation and projection toward the world, which we live as a correlate of this dynamism. In addition, he particularly emphasizes the affective or moodlike nature of our corporeal existence. As he puts it, the corporeal self always has an "emotional localization" (47).

This emotional localization is experienced as bodily: "Mood constrains or encourages us. We grasp it corporeally, we feel it in our dynamism" (79). Yet far from being only an experience of one's body, mood is always also an experience of how one finds oneself in the world, namely, of one's situatedness. In mood, Patočka says, the world "makes a certain impression on us," and the quality of this impression is corporeal, "physiognomic": "The ceiling presses upon us, the sky is leaden, the air is heavy, the surroundings are boring" (132–134). In other words, in mood we experience our surroundings in distinctive ways, which depend on how those surroundings impinge on or impress our body. The body here does not disappear; it is not passed over or forgotten in one's dealings with the world. Rather, the body is present in experience and contributes to the quality of how we are attuned to the world. Specifically, the way in which one finds oneself in the world in different moods or attunements has an experiential counterpart, which is thoroughly corporeal (it is a "physiognomic impression"); indeed, the world is given to experience as a specific mode of bodily affection (in chap. 5, I develop this idea further with the notion of "background bodily feelings" in emotion experience).[20]

Patočka's proposal also goes beyond Heidegger's restriction of affectivity to human existence. His account grants that not just adult humans but "animals and children" as well experience the primordial dynamism of their bodies, and accordingly the world as impressing on them. As he writes, "human sensibility, must be in principle other than that of animals and children. It must be more flexible, richer, and have a tendency to objectify itself in the perceptible world of objects. ... Something fundamental, though, remains the same; ... the elementary protofact of *harmony with the world* is the same for humans, children, animals" (133; italics in original). Shortly thereafter, he adds that there is a "more elementary ground" to Dasein's existence, which is shared also by animals and children, namely, "the world as an empathy of a kind." As I understand it, Patočka's point here is that animals and children are not able to reflectively and actively take up projects to determine the course of their existence; however, they can still experience and make sense of the world—yet tacitly, from an entirely immersed and nonmediated perspective, by "feeling it in" via a direct "empathetic understanding" (an idea Patočka borrows from Herder) that does not require thought and reflection. If this is the case, however, children and animals must also have moods, which they experience corporeally as different ways in which the world impresses itself on them.

1.5   Enactive Sense Making

The views presented so far apply at different levels—for example, Spino-za's conatus pertains to *all* existence, whereas Heidegger's moods concern human existence only. In this sense they identify different phenomena, and I do not intend to suggest otherwise. Yet they have something in common, which is why I have presented them here together: they all acknowledge a dimension of existence that, as I see it, is affective—that is, meaningful, relevant, or salient for the agent at stake—without or before being bounded into distinct emotions; in addition, this dimension grounds other forms of mentality, namely, it makes them possible.

I turn now to the enactive approach, to show that it provides a biological as well as phenomenological framework for the idea of a primordial dimen-sion of affectivity. In particular, from an enactive perspective, primordial affectivity is neither restricted to the human case, nor extended to all exist-ing things, but pertains specifically to *living* systems in virtue of their orga-nization. The enactive notion of *sense making* in particular, which refers to the capacity of all living systems to enact a meaningful world from a point of view, lends itself naturally to being interpreted in this way—or so I shall suggest.

In a nutshell, according to the enactive approach, all living systems are sense-making systems in virtue of their *autonomous* and *adaptive* nature.[21] Following Varela (1979), Thompson (2007, 44) defines an autonomous sys-tem formally as one whose constituent processes "(i) recursively depend on each other for their generation and their realization as a network, (ii) con-stitute the system as a unity in whatever domain they exist, and (iii) deter-mine a domain of possible interactions with the environment." These three criteria characterize autonomous systems as *operationally closed*. Operational closure refers to a specific kind of organization in which the results of the operations performed by the constituents of the system remain within the system itself. Crucially, operational closure does not imply that the system is completely self-enclosed and sealed against the environment. On the contrary, for the physical realization of autonomy, the operationally closed network needs to be *thermodynamically open*, namely, able to continuously swap matter and energy with the environment, to regulate its self-generat-ing activity, as well as its exchanges with the environment. Operational clo-sure, as the term indicates, thus refers not to material or energetic isolation but to a specific mode of functional relatedness among the components of a system that makes the system autonomous. An important qualification is that autonomous systems constitute and maintain their identity under *precarious conditions*. In other words, their constituent systems not only sustain themselves as a network but also would not be able to sustain themselves individually (they would extinguish) *unless* they were organized in such a network (Di Paolo 2009, 16).

The paradigm and best-known example of an autonomous system is the living cell. Its component processes are chemical, and their interrelation takes the form of a self-producing metabolic network that also produces its semipermeable membrane; this network constitutes the system as a unity in the biochemical domain and determines a domain of interactions with the world. This form of self-generating autonomy at the molecular level has been characterized as *autopoietic* (Maturana and Varela 1980). Thus an autopoietic system is a particular kind of autonomous system. Whereas all autopoietic systems are autonomous, not all autonomous systems are autopoietic: complex living systems such as multicellular metazoan systems, nervous systems, insect colonies, and so on, are operationally closed but do not possess a clear semipermeable membrane.[22]

Importantly, autonomous systems are *inherently purposeful*, in the sense that they generate ends or purposes within themselves (see esp. Thompson 2007, chap. 6). In brief, this is because an autonomous system is at the same time both the cause and effect, and the means and end, of itself: the activity of each component causally influences the activity of all the others (and is thus causally influenced by them); in addition, these causal influences are the means to the self-maintenance of the system, and at the same time its purpose.[23]

Combined with *adaptivity*, autonomy generates sense making, namely, the system's activity of assessing the environment as more or less conducive to its continuation. Autopoietic autonomy by itself entails only a crude, all-or-nothing assessment: the system only appreciates that its condition is either good or bad as it survives or disintegrates, respectively. An adaptive autonomous system, however, brings forth a graded scale of values. To put it succinctly (see Di Paolo 2005 for the original extended discussion), an adaptive autonomous system is one that monitors and regulates itself with respect to its conditions of viability in its environment and improves its situation when needed. To take a much-cited example, think of a motile bacterium that, to maintain itself, swims toward higher concentrations of sugar and away from noxious substances. In doing so, it evaluates its viability with respect to its environment in various degrees. This graded assessment or evaluation—which, importantly, is not carried out by a separate homunculus within the system but takes place implicitly as a function of the organization of the system—is what in the enactive approach is called "sense making."

Sense making thus characterized necessarily entails a *point of view* from which the system and the environment are evaluated. The adaptive autonomous system is not just a unity of interrelations among processes but a *perspective* on the world that generates meaning and norms for itself, a locus of *inwardness*: "The key here is to realize that because there is an individuality that finds itself produced by itself it is *ipso facto* a locus of sensation and agency, a living impulse always already in relation with its world" (Weber and Varela 2002, 117). As Jonas ([1966] 2001) already put it, living organisms *transcend* the material that realizes them: they are living in virtue of their organization, which enables them to differentiate themselves from the inanimate world. This differentiation implies the appearance of inwardness and selfhood: "There is inwardness or subjectivity involved in this transcendence, imbuing all the encounters occasioned in its horizon with the quality of felt selfhood, however faint its voice" (Jonas [1966] 2001, 84).[24]

The enactive notion of sense making is also intimately related to the one of *Umwelt* (literally, "world around"), in Uexküll's ([1934] 2010) sense of the environment as experienced or lived from the organism's perspective. For a living system to be a sense-making system is to live in a world that is always an Umwelt, namely, an environment that has a specific significance or value for it. Take again the example of motile bacteria swimming in a sugar gradient. These cells tumble about until they hit an orientation that increases their exposure to sugar and subsequently swim toward the highest concentration of sugar, which is good for them because of how their metabolism chemically realizes their autonomous organization (Thompson and Stapleton 2009, 24–25). The important point is that the sugar gradient, for the bacteria, is not just a neutral physiochemical world but an Umwelt with a specific range of values for them: sugar is good, more sugar is better, less sugar is worse, noxious substance is bad, and so on. As Thompson and Stapleton put it, this example illustrates that "even the simplest organisms regulate their interactions with the world in such a way that they transform the world into a place of salience, meaning, and value—into an environment (*Umwelt*) in the proper biological sense of the term. This transformation of the world into an environment happens through the organism's sense-making activity" (25).

Now, a fundamental tenet of the enactive approach is that all living systems are *cognitive* systems (life is sufficient for cognition). "Cognition" in this context ought to be understood broadly, to refer to "behavior or conduct in relation to meaning and norms that the system itself enacts or brings forth on the basis of its autonomy" (Thompson 2007, 126). The enactive claim, then, is that all living systems are cognitive in the sense that, in virtue of their adaptive autonomous organization, they behave according to meaning and norms that they themselves bring forth (generate) in interaction with the world. Note that this claim is tantamount to saying that living systems are sense-making systems. Cognition, in other words, is the activity of sense making.

This is clearly a very different characterization of cognition from the one typically adopted, more or less explicitly, in cognitive science. Cognition as sense making does not require a central executive system that represents facts about the world, reasons about them, and generates rules for action. Cognition from an enactive perspective is, rather, the capacity to enact or bring forth a world of sense, namely, an Umwelt that has a special significance for the organism enacting it. That this is a cognitive relation of the organism to the world can also be appreciated by noticing that it implies a *discerning* perspective on the part of the organism—one from which the organism discriminates or distinguishes what is good for itself from what is bad, in various degrees ("to discern" literally means "to cut off, to divide").[25]

For present purposes, what I want to emphasize now is that the enactive characterization of cognition as sense making entails that cognition is simultaneously also *affective*. This claim is not explicit in the enactive approach, but I think it follows naturally from the various points just summarized. First, as we have just seen, the sense-making living system is inherently purposeful; it aims at maintaining its unity and conditions of viability. Its autonomous organization makes it into a system that continuously aims or endeavors to be itself and as such is "concerned" about its continuation (as often put in Weber and Varela 2002, following Jonas [1966] 2001); in this sense, we can say that the living system also "cares" about its existence, to use Heidegger's term.[26] Second, we have also seen that sense-making systems are adaptive, that is, they monitor and regulate themselves with respect to their conditions of viability. To do so, they must be able to discern what in the world is suitable for their continuation, and what is not. This is a cognitive-discriminative capacity, and at the same time an affective-evaluative one that requires the living system to be affected or struck by the suitability of an event for its own purposes. Third, the notion of Umwelt is also thoroughly affective. The Umwelt is the world as it strikes the living system as relevant for its purposes. It is not a flat landscape of neutrality but a world of significance tailored to the living being that enacts it. As such, the Umwelt represents what the living system sees as relevant or salient, what matters to it and what it cares about. These points are all interconnected. Immanent purposefulness and care are required to discriminate what matters to the organism; at the same time, the world takes on significance and value precisely in relation to what the organism is concerned about and striving for—there is no meaningful environment for the indifferent, nonmotivated being.

To clarify, these considerations are not meant to imply that all living systems, including the simplest ones such as bacteria and other microorganisms, can have different emotions. The idea is, rather, that primordial affectivity is a source of meaning that grounds (makes possible) the richer and differentiated forms of sense making in more complex organisms, such as the emotions of animals and human beings—including what are often characterized as the "cognitive" or "highly cognitive" human emotions (such as guilt, romantic love, resentment, and so on). This is a version of the thesis of the deep continuity of life and mind, which, as mentioned in the introduction, lies at the core of the enactive approach. According to this thesis, as we saw, mind shares the organizational properties of life, and richer forms of mind depend on richer forms of life. The idea, then, is that the richer and more differentiated emotions that one finds in animal and human lives are enrichments of the primordial capacity to be sensitive to the world.

Nor is the notion of primordial affectivity meant to imply that even the simplest living systems are conscious. According to the enactive approach, the continuity of mind and life is admittedly also *phenomenological* (Thompson 2007, 129; 2011a; 2011b). What this means, however, is not that consciousness, not even in some minimal nonreflective form, is present in all forms of life. Rather, the idea here is that the autonomous and adaptive organization of living systems sets up an *asymmetry* between them and the rest of the world, such that living systems realize a perspective or point of view from which the world acquires meaning for them, and not vice versa. Thus a kind of "inwardness" is present already in the simplest living systems, and the suggestion is that, as it is realized in more complex organisms, this inwardness becomes a conscious perspective.[27]

1.6   Primordial Affectivity and Affective Science

Before concluding this chapter, I want to qualify my initial claim that affective science works with a narrower conception of affectivity than the one articulated here. As mentioned (and as discussed in more detail in the next chapter), the emotions of the affective scientist are short-lived episodes. As such they have relatively clear-cut boundaries, and between them there is no emotion. Other affective phenomena that are sometimes (although rarely) mentioned in affective science are moods, usually considered less intense and longer lived than emotions. Yet moods do not appear to be better candidates for primordial affectivity; like the emotions, moods are temporary perturbations of an otherwise neutral, nonaffective mind. Even if moods last longer than emotions (or may be always present, as some have proposed), still the assumption appears to be that moods are not constitutive of the mind but merely contingent superficial colorations.

There are, however, some exceptions. A few scientists have advanced theoretical constructs that go beyond affectivity narrowly conceived. These constructs come close to the phenomenon I am interested in; however, as we shall see, they still fall short of it in some respects.

One such construct is the idea of *core affect* proposed by James Russell (e.g., Russell 2003). Core affect is an ever-present "primitive" and "raw" feeling constituted by a certain degree of hedonic tone or valence (pleasantness or unpleasantness) and felt arousal.[28] It does not depend on language and becomes part of different emotions via a process of "psychological construction" (more about this idea in the next chapter). It is a ubiquitous feeling of how the organism is faring, an assessment of its condition. Thus, like primordial affectivity, it is pervasive and exceeds individual emotions. Note, however, that it remains a "neurophysiological state" (Russell 2003, 148), and its relationship to the organism seems to be solely one of conscious detection or representation of it. Core affect is a "consciously accessible" neurophysiological state (148) that represents whether the organism is drowsy, alert, in pain, and so on. Primordial affectivity as I have characterized it, however, is not meant to depend on the nervous system alone. Rather, it is enacted by the whole organism, and indeed even by organisms that lack a nervous system. Second, primordial affectivity, as we saw, is at the same time the bringing forth of a world of significance, an Umwelt. Core affect, on the other hand, remains limited to a perception of how the organism is faring. Third, core affect is a feeling, a conscious experience, whereas, as we saw, primordial affectivity need not be conscious. Finally, core affect remains distinct from cognition. It can influence it and be influenced by it but is by itself noncognitive. Hence core affect, unlike primordial affectivity, is not conceptualized in terms of a simultaneously cognitive-affective phenomenon.

Another interesting construct is the idea of *vitality affects* proposed by Stern (1985, 53–61). These are mainly proprioceptive and kinesthetic experiences imbued with affective qualities, such as feelings of muscular tension, contraction, and resistance, or of ease of movement, fluidity, and unobstruction, which come with a degree of felt arousal and changes in hedonic tone accompanying shifts in bodily dynamics. These vitality affects also come to the fore in bodily expressive forms of art such as dance, where bodily movements often convey extremely specific qualities—of energy, explosiveness, lightness, heaviness, frenzy, tranquility, and so on (see also Sheets-Johnstone 1999; 2009, discussed in chap. 5). Other examples include being touched in specific ways, as when one is comforted by being patted on the shoulders—a gesture that has a soothing quality and characteristic rhythm; importantly, the same vitality affect can be conveyed in a different modality, for example, by the repetition of the words "there, there," which has a similar rhythm. Vitality affects as Stern characterizes them are not "regular affects" but rather "noncategorical" feelings with fuzzy boundaries, for which there are no distinctive labels. Unlike regular affects that come and go, vitality affects are ever present (Stern 1985, 54) and appear to be intrinsic to our bodily existence. As such, although they are most apparent in the prelinguistic experiential world of infants (Stern's primary focus), they are presumably still present in adult experience and will come to the fore in some activities more than others.

The notion of vitality affects does not belong to "mainstream" affective science; for example, it does not feature in the recent *Oxford Companion to Emotion and the Affective Sciences* (Sander and Scherer 2009). Yet as Stern

(1985, 55) himself emphasizes, vitality affects "are definitely feelings and belong to the domain of affective experience." He does not explain why he considers them affective; however, in the present framework, they are clearly such: they involve changes of the organism, which are experienced in the form of proprioceptive and kinesthetic feelings meaningful to the subject. As Patočka would put it, they are manifestations of the organism's primordial dynamism, at the same time implying a capacity to be corporeally sensitive to the world (Henry's "interior quivering"). Aside from this bodily dimension, however, vitality affects fall short of primordial affectivity for the same reasons that core affect also does. Unlike primordial affectivity, and like core affect, vitality affects are not conceptualized as affective as well as cognitive sense-making phenomena; they are primarily feelings of one's body. Also, like core affect, vitality affects are feelings, whereas primordial affectivity need not be so. Finally, although we can assume that the category applies also to animals, Stern (1985) remains silent on this point; and in any case, the fact that vitality affects are feelings implies that only organisms capable of conscious experiences will enjoy them. The notion of primordial affectivity adds to this account the idea that affectivity is a property of the organization of living systems and as such appears even before the simplest forms of consciousness.

An account that comes especially close to the present notion of primordial affectivity has been proposed by Antonio Damasio. Damasio (2003) in particular relates his views of the workings of brain and body in emotion to Spinoza's account of the mind–body relation and the affects, endorsing his claim that emotions are modifications of the body, and the ideas of these modifications. Importantly for present purposes, Damasio (2003, 31–34) characterizes the emotions as the branches of a tree, whose lowest part of the trunk consists of basic organismic self-regulatory processes (metabolism, homeostasis) shared by all living systems. Whereas a human emotion is "a complex collection of chemical neural responses forming a distinctive pattern" (53), simple emotional responses are present in all living organisms, including, for example, the unicellular paramecium, whose activities consist in swimming away from danger (too much heat, too many vibrations) and toward nutrients. "The events I am describing in a brainless creature already contain the essence of the process of emotion that we humans have" (41). Damasio thus acknowledges a deep level of self-regulatory processes that count as "affective" in the sense that they reflect life's adaptivity and concern for itself (see also Damasio 2010, chap. 2, for a discussion of life, self-regulation, and biological value). His conception of emotion is clearly broader than the one typically assumed in affective science and converges with the enactive claim that metabolism and homeostasis, as basic life-sustaining processes, are deeply continuous with mentality and constitutive of a level of existence that can already be seen as affective. In addition, Damasio identifies a category of *background emotions*, which does not correspond to any of the emotion categories of the affective scientist but exceeds them; background emotions are manifested in, for example, energy or enthusiasm in one's attitude, "subtle malaise or excitement, edginess or tranquility" (2003, 43). Background emotions depend on the ongoing self-regulatory activity of the organism and as such are ubiquitous and intrinsic to embodied life.[29]

Although it is common nowadays to regard emotions and moods as affecting and being affected by the organism's self-regulatory processes, the idea that brainless creatures can be characterized as having emotion is not particularly prominent among affective scientists—quite the opposite. Emotions are usually regarded as requiring relatively complex organisms. For example, another eminent affective neuroscientist, Jaak Panksepp, posits a number of "primary" emotional systems in both human and animal brains, but only in the mammalian brain (see, e.g., Panksepp 1998a, 2005). Walter Freeman, whose views I present in more detail later in the book, sees the limbic system as the primary source of emotion (affectivity, in my terminology); however, in so doing, he limits it to organisms with a limbic system. From the present perspective, what these accounts overlook is that the fundamental processes of life regulation that enable organisms to maintain themselves are already, in a primordial sense, meaning generating and thus affective. Although only mammals may be able to display a variety of emotions, simpler organisms already live in a meaningful world in virtue of their capacity of being struck or influenced by what matters to them.

It should be noted, however, that, unlike the enactive approach, Damasio does not go as far as claiming that brainless creatures enact a world of significance and are in this sense already cognitive. More generally, cognition and emotion remain distinct in Damasio's framework, with emotion importantly cooperating with cognition to achieve intelligent behavior and rationality. In his "somatic marker hypothesis," for example, emotion in the form of somatic states is characterized as cooperating with cognition to enable advantageous decisions (Damasio 1994). The hypothesis, roughly,[30] proposes that cognition by itself, as realized by various "higher" cortical areas, is not sufficient for making good decisions; the various possible outcomes of a decision also need to be associated with a somatic state (an emotion). Thus Damasio retains a separation between emotion and cognition, with emotion identified with bodily activity (and as such present in all organisms) and cognition as a more complex dimension of the mind, achieved by organisms provided with a nervous system, and more specifically a cortex. From the present perspective, on the other hand, cognition, like emotion, is already present at the level of sense making.

1.7 Conclusion

This excursus into the affective roots of the mind has served to provide a background for the arguments of the rest of the book. From now on, I will be concerned primarily with views and experimental work in current affective science; however, every now and then, it will be useful to come back to this primordial dimension, to ground the phenomena under analysis back in their source and remind ourselves that the emotions studied by affective scientists are not the only repositories of affectivity.

It is time now, however, to turn to affective science "proper," and to discuss some of its most influential conceptions of emotions in more detail.

2 The Emotions: Existing Accounts and Their Problems

2.1 Introduction

The primary object of study of affective science is not affectivity as characterized in the previous chapter but relatively short-lived and bounded episodes during which specific feelings are experienced, and specific changes in one's body and behavior become apparent. These episodes are what affective scientists usually refer to as the *emotions*. To some extent, this use of the term overlaps with the folk psychological one; in my experience, when you ask someone who has never really given the matter much thought what emotions are, he or she will often answer by giving examples of relatively short-lived episodes, such as a fit of anger or a pang of jealousy.

In this and the following chapter, I address the question of how we should conceptualize these episodes. I often use the term *emotional episodes* in place of "emotions," to make it clear that I am concerned with occurrent events. This qualification is needed because, as Goldie (2000) emphasizes, the English folk psychological conception of emotion is broader than the scientific one and includes phenomena that are not episodic, such as enduring dispositions or longer-lasting feelings (think of lifelong love).[1] Although I say something about longer-lasting affective phenomena such as moods in the next chapter, I am overall primarily concerned here with short-lived occurrent events. It is these phenomena I have in mind when I use the term "emotions."

There are several scientific accounts of the emotions, and little agreement among them. I am dissatisfied with most of them, as this particularly critical chapter shows. Whereas the next chapter provides more constructive arguments, here I explain why I think that the most influential accounts of the emotions provided in affective science are problematic. Ultimately my aim here is to pave the way for the more positive view of the next chapter, where I present and discuss what I think is a more plausible account—one that is also consistent with the enactive approach. In this chapter, however, I leave the enactive approach aside and focus instead on mainstream scientific frameworks.

I begin by illustrating the main tenets of what is arguably *the* most influential paradigm in affective science: the theory of basic emotions (BET from now on). Before drawing attention to what I consider BET's most serious shortcomings, I discuss some existing criticisms of it that I think miss their mark. To clarify, the aim of this discussion is *not* to support BET but to try to put some order in an increasingly complex debate by pointing to arguments raised against BET that I think are misguided. The main problem with BET, in my view, is that it has fostered the impression that empirical evidence points to the existence of a small number of basic emotions—when, in fact, the process that has led to this view, as I show, is fraught with arbitrariness. Yet this view not only persists but is self-reinforcing, as affective scientists tend to conceptualize and investigate the alleged "basic" emotions differently from the "nonbasic" ones. A related problem regards the relationship between alleged basic and nonbasic emotions: if only a few emotions are basic, then how do they relate to the nonbasic ones? I criticize both the proposal that basic emotions are *building blocks* of nonbasic ones (a version of what is known as the *unity thesis*) and the proposal that basic emotions are entirely distinct from nonbasic ones (the *disunity thesis*). My conclusion ultimately is that affective scientists would be better off dropping the notion of basic emotions. Toward the end of the chapter, I turn to the most influential alternatives to BET—the *psychological constructionist* and the *componential* approaches—and also highlight what I think are their own limitations.

2.2 The Theory of Basic Emotions (BET)

According to BET, at least some emotions are basic; that is, they are genetically determined sets of instructions called *affect programs* that, once activated, generate a series of distinctive changes in the brain, as well as in behavior, expression (typically facial, but also vocal and bodily), and physiology or autonomic nervous system (ANS) activity.[2] The term "affect program" was introduced by Sylvan Tomkins (1962, 144): "By innate affect programs we refer to what is inherited as a subcortical structure which can instruct and control a variety of muscles and glands to respond with unique patterns of rate and duration of activity characteristic of a given affect." The term was then taken up by others; according to Paul Ekman (1980a, 82), for example, "The term *affect program* refers to a mechanism that stores the patterns for these complex organized responses, and which when set off directs their occurrence."

The responses set off by affect programs are considered to be the same for each basic emotion in all populations. Early evidence for this claim came from various cross-cultural studies conducted in the 1960s and 1970s, which typically involved taking pictures of an actor expressing different emotions, and asking people from different countries to say which emotions these pictures expressed. When subjects had to answer by matching the pictures with pregiven emotion labels, a high degree of agreement was found in their responses, even when subjects came from distant countries (such as the United States, Brazil, Japan, New Guinea, Borneo, and more; see Ekman, Sorenson, and Friesen 1969; Izard 1968, 1969). The now famous study by Ekman and Friesen (1971) in particular found high levels of agreement even among the Fore in New Guinea—a preliterate people who at the time had had minimal or no visual contact with Westerners. In this study, in each trial the experimenters showed participants (both adults and children) a set of three pictures of emotional facial expressions; each picture represented the expression of one of six emotions (fear, anger, happiness, sadness, disgust, and surprise). At the same time, participants listened to a very short story designed to represent one of these emotions (the stories were very simple scenarios, such as "her friends have come and she is happy" and "she is looking at something that smells very bad"). After each story, participants were asked to point to the picture of the facial expression that best fitted the emotion described in the story. Results showed that Fore subjects matched stories and pictures in the same way as Western subjects. The only significant difference was that the Fore did not distinguish between fear and surprise, which Ekman and Friesen explained, rather hastily, with reference to the prevalence of surprising frightening events in the life of the Fore.

Since then, the six facial expressions used in this study have been regarded as distinctive of basic emotions and present in all cultures (pancultural), with the later addition of contempt (Ekman and Friesen 1986; Ekman and Heider 1988). Ekman, Levenson, and Friesen (1983) also provided evidence for their physiological differentiation. The facial expressions used by Ekman and Friesen are still extensively used in the laboratory as experimental stimuli and as indicators of basic emotions. Psychologists and neuroscientists are also busy looking for patterns of neural, behavioral, and autonomic activity distinctive of each basic emotion, and for patterns of neural activity correlated with the recognition of basic emotions in others. Basic emotions in BET are often also characterized as *discrete*, although what this means is not particularly clear (I discuss the issue of discreteness in more detail in the next chapter).

Importantly, BET sees basic emotions as *adaptations* selected by evolution because they enabled our ancestors to cope with "fundamental life tasks" (Ekman 1999, 46).[3] Basic emotions in addition are taken to be initiated by automatic appraisals or "auto appraisals" (Ekman 2003) that mark the beginning of the emotional episode, which is typically short-lived and subsides as its various manifestations terminate. Ekman (1999, 56) has provided a list of the characteristics "which distinguish basic emotions from one another and from other affective phenomena":

1. Distinctive universal signals
2. Distinctive physiology
3. Automatic appraisal, tuned to:
4. Distinctive universals in antecedent events
5. Distinctive appearance developmentally
6. Presence in other primates
7. Quick onset
8. Brief duration
9. Unbidden occurrence
10. Distinctive thoughts, memories images
11. Distinctive subjective experience[4]

Basic emotions, once activated, cannot be interrupted. However, their outputs can be "masked" as a consequence of acquired *display rules*, namely, "conventions, norms and habits that develop regarding the management of emotional responses. A display rule specifies who can show what emotion to whom, and when" (Ekman 1980a, 87). Individuals learn how to regulate their expression and behavior, so that these "can become so well learned that they operate automatically and are called forth when the affect program is set off" (89). A much-cited study in this context is Ekman 1971, which found that Japanese subjects, when they are aware that they are being observed while watching distressing movies, smile more than American subjects; nevertheless, as shown by slowed-down movies of their facial expressions, Japanese subjects still manifest distress before putting on the smile.

BET is not the first theory to posit some emotions as primary or fundamental. The Stoics already distinguished four basic types or species of emotion (Brennan 2003). In seventeenth- and eighteenth-century philosophy, it was also common to distinguish between simple and complex emotions. Descartes and Spinoza both suggested that some emotions are more primitive than others; so did Malebranche, Hume, Locke, and others (see Schmitter 2010). Note, however, that BET differs fundamentally from these early proposals because it posits basic emotions as *biologically* basic. Previous proposals primarily distinguished the emotions into simple and complex ones mainly on the basis of *psychological* considerations, such as the complexity of their cognitive antecedents or components. They also usually saw simple emotions as *parts* of complex ones; indeed, positing simple emotions was one way to explain the complex ones. BET, on the other hand, characterizes basic emotions primarily in terms of the changes they bring about in the organism, and their character of adaptations. In this sense, BET is different also from more recent accounts that aim at identifying *conceptually* basic emotion categories. A conceptually basic emotion category is one that occupies a privileged position in a conceptual taxonomy, for instance, by being learned first in development, by being produced more quickly by adults in various laboratory settings, by being designated by shorter names, and so on (e.g., Fehr and Russell 1984). As Scarantino and Griffiths (2011) rightly emphasize, the notion of biologically basic emotions is orthogonal to the one of conceptually basic emotions, as well as to the one of psychologically basic emotions—which, among other things, implies that evidence that some emotions are, for example, conceptually basic cannot be used to claim that they are also biologically or psychologically basic, and vice versa (see also Ortony and Turner 1990).

2.3   Assessing Existing Criticisms of BET

Several criticisms have been raised against BET. Although, as will become clearer in the next section, I think that BET is indeed problematic and the notion of "basic" emotions should be abandoned, I also think that many of its criticisms miss their mark.

First, it follows from the last point of the previous section that BET cannot be rejected on the basis of arguments from cross-cultural linguistic differences. We know from linguistic and anthropological evidence that the English terms for basic emotions do not have equivalents in all languages: the English term "fear," for example, appears to have no equivalent in Ifalukian, Utku, and Pintupi; the term "sadness" has no equivalent in Tahitian; likewise for "disgust" in Polish, Ifalukian, and Chewong (Russell 1991; see also Wierzbicka 1999). Yet this evidence does not imply that fear, sadness, and disgust *do not exist* in these cultures. Russell (1991, 440) remarks that "it is puzzling why a language would fail to provide a single word for an important, salient, discrete, and possibly innate category of experience—if such exists." However, as he also quickly acknowledges, "one must recognize that the existence of basic emotions does not entail nor is entailed by the existence of universal categories for understanding emotions. There is no guarantee that human beings have got the matter right" (441).

Indeed, languages have their own life, so to speak; they are influenced by sociocultural norms, and their terms can change their meanings more or less subtly over time as a function of use and changes in social practices. Linguists are familiar with the phenomenon of *lexical lacunae*, namely, the lack of words corresponding to concepts for which other languages have one or more words. Yet importantly linguists also acknowledge that lexical lacunae may be an index that certain phenomena are *hypo-cognized* (Levy 1984) in a culture, that is, relatively unattended and little valued, rather than nonexistent (see Ogarkova, forthcoming). In addition, it is important not to overlook that lexical lacunae refer specifically to missing one-word equivalents, and not to the impossibility of expressing and understanding the phenomena for which these terms are missing. In translation, lexical lacunae can often be replaced with multiword expressions; it is also often possible to find words that, in the given context, are suitable substitutes for the missing ones (again, see Ogarkova, forthcoming). Absence of an emotion term thus does not necessarily indicate absence of the corresponding emotion. Indeed, BET supporters usually emphasize that affect programs have nothing to do with language. Ekman has reiterated various times that he is primarily interested in facial expression, and more generally emotion, rather than emotion words. According to BET, affect programs exist and are activated irrespective of their labels (to emphasize this language independence, Panksepp [2005], for example, indicates brain systems for basic emotions with capital letters, such as RAGE, FEAR, PLAY), and there is no expectation that one-term words for them will exist in all languages.

This is not to deny that language can influence and change our emotions. Indeed, as I have argued elsewhere, language can do many things to our feelings (Colombetti 2009), including contributing to the construction of culture-specific emotional niches. As we saw in the previous chapter, organisms are open to the world and can change their structure in response to changes in the world; language, like other cultural artifacts, can impinge on this malleable structure to mold our emotional repertoire in different ways (and the next chapter will particularly emphasize the variability and context dependency of the emotions). Yet for the time being, the point is just that arguments from cross-cultural linguistic differences do not undermine the claim (supported by empirical evidence) that some organismic features recur reliably across cultures and languages in comparable situations. There appear to be similarities in emotional manifestations across populations that are resistant to linguistic practices.

A second criticism of BET that I think misses its mark addresses the forced-choice methodology of the early experiments on the recognition of posed facial expressions. We saw that in Ekman and Friesen's (1971) study, subjects had to match one of three facial expressions with a pregiven scenario; they were thus not allowed freely to label or describe the facial expressions portrayed in the pictures. In his critique, Russell (1994) points out that previous studies that had not adopted this forced-choice method found that subjects gave very different responses, including responses that did not involve emotional labeling at all (e.g., Frijda 1953). Studies that explicitly asked subjects to label expressions with emotion words found more agreement, but only by grouping different responses together as belonging to the same emotion cluster (for example, in Izard 1971 responses such as "distress," "loneliness," "pain," "pity," and "worry" were considered correct for the expression of sadness; see Russell 1994).

These findings are certainly interesting and suggest that we do not read specific emotions straightforwardly "out" from faces. Yet they are not damning for BET. Supporters of BET could respond that, indeed, emotion recognition never happens entirely out of context, as a readout from the face. The face provides important clues, but not the only ones that subjects rely on when they attribute emotions in everyday interactions; hence it is not surprising that when no response options are provided in an experimental setting, subjects are not very good at recognizing expressions and come up with different interpretations (for recent evidence that context influences perception of facial expressions, see Barrett and Kensinger 2010). This concession does not warrant the radical conclusion that facial expressions do not play any role in how emotions are attributed to others, and the rejection of BET's main tenet that at least some emotions are expressed panculturally in the face in the same way. Such a conclusion would need to be supported by evidence that BET's basic emotions are expressed by facial expressions that are differently judged in different cultures, as well as by evidence that they are produced differently in different cultures. To my knowledge, no such evidence has been provided.

A third criticism that has been raised against BET accuses it of overlooking and downplaying the rich variety of the emotions, in particular their context sensitivity (e.g., Russell 2003; Barrett 2006a). In BET, this criticism implies, the affect programs appear to be very much like the keys of a keyboard: when the key "anger" is pressed, a set of anger-specific changes occurs in the organism; when "fear" is pressed, fear-specific changes occur, and so on. Yet, the criticism continues, we clearly manifest anger, fear, happiness, and so on, in many different ways, depending on the situation we are in. Thus when angry I may bare my teeth and frown (as in BET's prototypical facial expression of anger), but I may also smile (e.g., with sarcasm); when happy I may jump for joy and laugh but also cry; when scared I may retreat but also respond aggressively; and so on (see also Ortony and Turner 1990). In other words, this criticism challenges the view that a one-to-one correspondence exists between BET's basic emotions and their manifestations.

It is certainly true that we manifest sadness, anger, happiness, and so on, in different ways; the question, however, is whether this is fatal for BET, specifically for its claim that at least some emotions are manifested panculturally in the same way. Note first that BET accommodates behavioral variability by appealing to display rules (as in the case of the sarcastic expression I put on when I am angry, instead of punching my adversary in the face). Also, supporters of BET could insist, in some cases at least, that some seemingly nondistinctive expressions *are* in fact distinctive of basic emotions. For example, they could insist that when an Olympic champion cries on the podium, she is *not* in fact "crying for joy"; rather, as long as she cries and manifests sadness, she *is* sad (maybe because she is remembering past efforts and sacrifices to achieve this result; maybe her body is releasing accumulated tension in the form of crying, which makes her feel sad, and so on). Or they could appeal (as in fact they do) to the possibility that affect programs *blend* and thus produce mixed expressions and manifestations.

Moreover, Ekman has recently conceded that affect programs are not closed but *open* (from Mayr 1974); namely, they can be modified in the course of life as a consequence of the organism's interactions with the environment (Ekman 2003; Ekman and Cordaro 2011). So even if affect programs, once activated, cannot be interrupted, still they may change over one's lifetime, by including instructions for blocking the occurrence of some of their manifestations. The openness of affect programs is an important concession to the role of learning and culture in modifying basic emotions; however, BET can endorse it without giving up the claim that we and other animals are biologically prepared to manifest at least some emotions in specific ways, and that these manifestations appear to be stable across contexts.

Finally, consider also that Ekman and collaborators specify that basic emotion categories refer to emotion *families*. Each family is organized around a theme, which is "comprised of the characteristics unique to that family" and is "influenced phylogenetically" (Ekman and Cordaro 2011, 365); variations on the theme are the product of social influences and learning. This claim is problematic in that it does not clarify how one is to distinguish the theme from the variations: is frustration a variation of anger, or vice versa? And if one finds pancultural elements in both frustration and anger, should one conclude that the latter are themes of two distinct families? For present purposes, however, what matters is that BET recognizes that basic emotion categories should not be taken to imply a strict one-to-one correspondence between an affect program, understood as an internal cause, and its outputs (although variability within a family remains constrained by the theme).

A fourth criticism of BET points out that affective scientists have had difficulty identifying distinctive brain and autonomic response patterns that occur reliably in situations allegedly activating affect programs. Barrett (2006a) points out that meta-analyses of a large number of studies have failed to reveal reliable one-to-one correspondences between alleged basic emotions, and neural as well as autonomic activity (Phan et al. 2002; Murphy, Nimmo-Smith, and Lawrence 2003; Cacioppo et al. 2000). Barrett takes the results of these works to provide further evidence that BET is wrong; if it were correct, distinct and reliably recurrent neural and ANS patterns for each basic emotion should have been detected.

The authors of the meta-analyses of brain studies mentioned by Barrett, however, interpret their results as more supportive of BET than she does (although not as conclusive). The main reason is that such results do in fact show *some* consistency in brain activity for a few emotions. Phan et al. (2002) looked at the results of fifty-five PET and fMRI studies of five emotions in humans (fear, anger, disgust, happiness, and sadness) and found that in 60 percent of the studies looking at fear, activation in the amygdala was significant compared to activation in other areas; they also found that 60 percent of the studies looking at disgust significantly engaged the basal ganglia, and 46 percent of the studies looking at sadness significantly engaged the subcallosal cingulate. Murphy, Nimmo-Smith, and Lawrence (2003), for their part, looked at 106 PET and fMRI studies and found that in 40 percent of the studies looking at fear, activation in the amygdala was significant compared to activation in other areas; this percentage increased to over 60 percent when they looked at a subset of fear studies that had used only facial expressions as stimuli. They also found that in 70 percent of the studies of disgust, insula and globus pallidus (a component of the basal ganglia) activation was comparatively significant, and lateral OFC (orbitofrontal cortex) activation was significant "in a higher proportion of studies of anger, relative to other emotions" (225). Unlike Phan et al., they did not find that sadness and happiness co-occurred with significant activation in distinct brain areas. In their view, differences in their results were attributable to the different number of experiments they took into consideration, as well as to the fact that only their analysis looked at experiments with carefully controlled neutral control conditions.[5]

Now, these results are certainly not very clean, and admittedly there are limitations to the meta-analytic method—not least that studies that fail to find significant activations are usually not published and thus do not make it into the analyses in the first place. The authors of the mentioned meta-analyses themselves acknowledge these limitations and also provide suggestions for further methodological improvements. Yet, discrepancies aside, it seems to me that one cannot overlook the fact that *some* recurrent activation of the same area or areas was found across studies for more than one emotion, largely consistently also with neuropsychological evidence from lesion studies. Murphy, Nimmo-Smith, and Lawrence (2003) mention some of these studies—for example, lesions to the amygdala have been found to disrupt the recognition of fear signals, as well as the acquisition and expression of fear response; similarly for the basal ganglia, insula, and disgust (for a review of amygdala and anterior insula lesion studies, see Calder, Lawrence, and Young 2001), and for the orbitofrontal cortex and anger. To which we can add evidence from animal studies, which have revealed that electrical brain stimulation of distinct areas can induce specific behaviors such as laughter, seeking, and aggression (Panksepp 1998a, 2005). Finally, a variety of chemical substances such as norepinephrine, serotonin, dopamine, vasopressin, oxytocin, and others, are associated with different behaviors and experiences (see Panksepp 2007 for a review of this evidence specifically in response to Barrett 2006a).

In addition, a more recent meta-analysis has confirmed and refined previous findings. Vytal and Hamann (2010) focused on eighty-three neuroimaging studies (PET and fMRI) published from 1993 to 2008 and used a different statistical method to analyze their results, called ALE (activation likelihood estimate). ALE preserves the three-dimensional spatial information of the original activations and generates statistical maps of significant brain activations across multiples studies. Vytal and Hamann identified significantly consistent and discriminable patterns of brain activation for happiness, sadness, fear, anger, and disgust, which overlapped considerably with those identified (partially) in the previous meta-analyses. Moreover, they were able to further differentiate between the emotions for which previous meta-analyses could not find distinct patterns. Specifically, even when they included only the studies used by Murphy, Nimmo-Smith, and Lawrence (2003) in their analysis, they were able to show differentiation between happiness and sadness.[6]

As for ANS activity, in a recent meta-analysis of 134 studies that looked at direction (increase or decrease) of several autonomic variables (such as heart rate, skin conductance level, finger temperature, diastolic and systolic blood pressure, respiration rate, and so on), Kreibig (2010) found what she interprets as "considerable specificity." The emotions she looked at (fourteen overall) were not just the alleged affect programs but also emotions such as affection, amusement, pride, relief, embarrassment, and suspense. Because she looked at many dimensions of arousal, the results of her analysis cannot be summarized briefly. In some cases she found that the same emotion ought to be divided into two subforms whose ANS activity recurs relatively consistently across studies. For example, she found that disgust toward polluting or contaminating stimuli (such as pictures of dirty toilets or cockroaches) is associated with different ANS activity compared with disgust toward stimuli like mutilation, injury, and blood (see also Harrison et al. 2010), and that sadness differs in ANS activity depending on whether it involves crying or not.

In sum, the results of existing meta-analyses do not indicate total lack of patterning and emotion specificity. Existing evidence remains consistent with the claim that a number of emotions come in relatively recurrent patterns of neural and ANS activity. Importantly, as we shall see in the next chapter, this stability need not imply that neural and autonomic patterns are products of prewired affect programs. Yet it indicates that "there is something" in, or better "of," the organism, which remains relatively stable for at least some emotions (versus, as we shall see, the radical claim that emotions are not "entities").

More generally, this section has argued that BET cannot be dismissed by pointing to cross-cultural linguistic differences, differences in attribution on the basis of facial expressions, and variability in behavioral, neural, and autonomic manifestations. True, BET has had to weaken or adjust some of its assumptions to make room for these differences (and the adjustments are sometimes very ad hoc). But the take-home message remains that in spite of all the undeniable variability, there still seems to be something that recurs reliably and manifests some degree of stability or robustness across contexts.

2.4   The Arbitrariness of the Alleged Basic Emotions

In my view, the main problem with BET is that it has fostered the conviction, now widespread in affective science, that available evidence supports the existence of a small number of pancultural emotions with characteristic manifestations (typically Ekman and Friesen's first "basic" six, with some minor differences), and accordingly also the existence of several emotions that are not pancultural and do not have any distinctive organismic traits. As we are about to see, the process that has led to this conviction is fraught with arbitrariness.

Note first that the view that only *some* emotions are "basic" is not Ekman's, at least not anymore. In recent papers, he has emphasized that "all emotions are basic," and he "does not allow for non-basic emotions" (e.g., Ekman 1994, 1999, 2003; Ekman and Cordaro 2011).[7] He presents this view explicitly as a hypothesis that needs to be further investigated empirically, with the aim of finding distinctive and pancultural expressions, and autonomic and neural mechanisms, for different emotions. Ekman and Cordaro (2011) specifically suggest that ten "enjoyable emotions" (sensory pleasures, amusement, relief, excitement, wonder, ecstasy, schadenfreude, rejoicing, Yiddish *Naches*, and Italian *fiero*—the last two are variations of pride), as well as guilt, shame, embarrassment, envy, and familial compassion, may be pancultural and associated with distinct autonomic profiles. The reason for the claim that "all emotions are basic" is that Ekman does not endorse what we can call the *building-block view* of the emotions, according to which some emotions are components of others. Unfortunately, however, the term "basic emotions" strongly suggests such a view. It is not surprising, then, that Ekman has tried to distance himself from the term, recommending, for example, that "the adjective 'basic' should not be the issue" (Ekman 1999, 57). Rather, the main issue for him is the pancultural character of the emotions, and their character of adaptations. In this sense, his view is similar to the one of the evolutionary psychologists Cosmides and Tooby (2000), according to which all emotions are adaptations to recurring situations, namely, mechanisms evolved to take advantage of the structure of situations that were common in the past of our ancestors.[8] Note also that the expression "basic emotions" appeared only gradually in the writings of Ekman and collaborators. Neither basic nor primary emotions are mentioned by Ekman and Friesen (1971), who were solely concerned with showing constants across cultures in the facial expression of emotion; there is also little reference to primary or basic emotions in Ekman and Friesen 1975 and Ekman 1980a.

Irrespective of Ekman's current stance, however, BET has acquired a life of its own, and the received view in affective science today is that only some emotions are basic, whereas others are not. In a recent special issue of *Emotion Review* dedicated to basic emotions, all defenders of BET other than Ekman and Cordaro (2011) endorse the view that basic emotions are a subset of the emotions: Izard (2011, 372) distinguishes between *first-order emotions* (which require minimal cognitive antecedents) and *emotion schemas* (which involve complex interactions between feelings and cognitive processes) and claims that "first-order emotion feelings may serve as building blocks for many, though by no means all, other emotions"; Levenson (2011, 379) claims that "only a subset of discrete emotions is basic" and suggests that basic emotions may be "building blocks" of more complex ones; and Panksepp and Watt (2011, 389) similarly claim that *primary-process* emotions are probably "building blocks for higher emotions such as guilt, hatred, loneliness; that is, emotions molded by cognitive attributions."

This view may well have been encouraged by Ekman and collaborators themselves, at least initially. As one reads in Ekman (1980b, 137; my italics), for example, in his view he and Friesen had "isolated and demonstrated *the basic set* of universal facial expressions of emotion." Yet the early studies *did not* support this statement, because they investigated only six emotions (all of which were subsequently characterized as basic). Moreover, those six emotions had not been chosen by Ekman and Friesen on the basis of a clear rationale. Rather, the process whereby they have come to be seen as "the basic ones" was quite arbitrary. This process goes back to Tomkins (1962, 1963), who, on the basis of his reading of Darwin ([1872] 2007), hypothesized the existence of *nine primary affects*, so called in his work by analogy with the "primary drives" of thirst, hunger, sexual desire, and pain. Tomkins's nine primary affects were surprise-startle, interest-excitement, enjoyment-joy, anger-rage, distress-anguish, fear-terror, shame-humiliation, disgust, and "dissmell," or response to unpleasant smells (the first term of each pair denotes the mild version of the affect, the second the more intense). Now, contrary to what is almost invariably implied in papers and talks about BET, this list did *not* come from Darwin. In fact, Darwin ([1872] 2007) never suggested that some emotions are primary or basic. He illustrated and discussed the expressions of a large number of emotions as manifested in different human cultures and even in animals, including emotions that never made it into Tomkins's list—such as sense of impotence, contempt, wonder, guilt, pride, and more. Darwin meticulously noted facial and bodily expressions for each of these emotions, from apparently pancultural to more culture-specific ones. On the basis of reports and pictures from correspondents in various parts of the globe, he observed, among other things, that shrugging the shoulders in impotence, sneering in contempt, and averting the gaze in guilt appear to occur panculturally.

So why did Tomkins propose those nine affects as primary? I could not find any valid justification for this choice, only some vague considerations, such as that the nine primary affects are "the primary motives of human beings" (1962, 111–112). No argument was given, however, as to why these affects are "primary motives," and no explanation provided to clarify the relationship between motivation and alleged nonprimary emotions: are nonprimary emotions not "primary motives," and if so, why not?

Note also that whereas Darwin had described facial, as well as vocal and bodily, expressions associated with different emotions, Tomkins decided to identify the face as "the primary seat of affect." This choice was once again not supported by a clear justification. Tomkins (1962, 205) says in this respect only that "the face expresses affect, both to others, and to the self, via feedback, which is more rapid and more complex than any stimulation of which the slower moving visceral organs are capable." It remains unclear, however, why rapidity and complexity of feedback should suffice for establishing the "seat of affect"; slower changes in the viscera may (and, as we now know, do) also bring about changes in emotion experience and behavior.

Ekman and Friesen (1971) thus started from an already arbitrary list. From it, they selected six emotions for their study, leaving out interest-excitement, distress-anguish, and dissmell. Why? I could not find any explanation for this decision in their work. The arbitrary character of this choice was confirmed to me at the 2011 meeting of the International Society for Research on Emotion (ISRE) in Kyoto. There Phoebe Ellsworth, who had collaborated with Ekman and Friesen in the 1970s and had been involved in the selection of the stimuli for their experiments, gave a talk in which she explained that their original aim had indeed been to study all of Tomkins's nine affects. Eventually, however, they had ended up studying only a subset of them because they could not sample enough pictures for nine facial expressions that satisfied their criteria (namely, the pictures had to be of different individuals, both males and females, and be known to elicit high agreement among American subjects).

In light of this process, one should be wary of the claim that only a few emotions are basic or, rather, that only a few emotions have distinctive manifestations and are expressed panculturally in the same way. There is just not enough evidence for this claim. True, there is not much evidence either for the claim that emotions other than the alleged six (more or less) basic ones have distinctive traits that also appear cross-culturally. However, this is precisely because of the widespread conviction that only a few emotions are basic. The conviction that emotions such as jealousy, shame, envy, love, and so on, are not basic and thus do not have distinctive manifestations has discouraged the study of their neural, behavioral, and bodily features, in the same as well as in different cultures (which, incidentally, also represents a marked departure from Darwin's approach, as he included observing and describing both pancultural and culture-specific expressions of emotion). We thus know little about the physiology, expression, and brain processes of emotions other than the alleged basic ones, which reinforces the conviction that only some emotions have distinctive and pancultural features. Importantly, this trend is changing, although slowly. Research on pride, for example, has revealed that expressions of pride are reliably discriminated from expressions of happiness, even by four-year-old children (Tracy, Robins, and Lagattuta 2005). Research on shame in humans and primates suggests that it is accompanied by patterned ANS activity, characteristic neural activity, and possibly a distinctive facial expression (see J. Clark 2010).

This story, in my view, far from suggesting—as Ekman would—that all emotions may be basic, indicates that the notion of "basic" emotions is redundant and misleading, and affective scientists would be better off if they dropped it. They could still look for pancultural and stable features of emotional manifestations, however, without any obligation to classify them as "basic" and thus to draw a dividing line between different kinds of emotions. Rather, as Darwin did, they could happily carry out research on both pancultural similarities and cross-cultural differences, with the aim to provide, first, accurate descriptions of what changes in which context and what stays the same, and then explanations of why this is so, without the need to posit any invariant building block (I reiterate this point in the next chapter, in the context of more constructive arguments).

2.5   The Problematic Unity/Disunity Debate

Getting rid of the notion of basic emotions would also eliminate the need to explain how alleged basic emotions relate to nonbasic ones. This need so far has generated accounts that in my view are problematic, in various ways.

We have already seen that, according to many supporters of BET, basic emotions are building blocks of nonbasic ones, namely, constitutive parts of them. This view is a version of what has been dubbed in the philosophy of emotion the *unity thesis* (see Prinz 2004b), so called because it claims that basic and nonbasic emotions are nevertheless unified under the broader natural category of "emotion." Unlike the unity thesis, the *disunity thesis* (Prinz 2004b) claims that basic and nonbasic emotions are profoundly different; basic emotions are not parts of nonbasic ones, the two form two distinct phenomena for which separate theories need to be developed, and the category of "emotion" should be split accordingly. Now, because both theses endorse the view that only some emotions are basic, they are already problematic: as we saw, no conclusive evidence supports this claim. In addition, both theses have difficulties of their own, which are useful to consider in some detail.

Supporters of the building-block view have proposed two main "unifying" mechanisms (see also Griffiths 1997; Prinz 2004b): *blending* and what I shall call *cognitive elicitation*. According to Plutchik (2001), for example, eight primary emotions are organized in a circle in a specific order (i.e., joy, acceptance, fear, surprise, sadness, disgust, anger, anticipation) and blend like colors to form primary, secondary, and tertiary dyads. For example, joy and acceptance, which are contiguous on the circle, blend to form the primary dyad of love; acceptance and fear blend into the primary dyad of submission; fear and surprise blend into the primary dyad of awe; and so on. Joy and fear, which are separated by one emotion on the circle, form a secondary dyad and blend into guilt. Joy and surprise, which are separated by two emotions on the circle, constitute a tertiary dyad and blend into delight (for the whole range of possible combinations, see Plutchik 2001). According to Damasio (1994), on the other hand, primary emotions engage deeper and older brain areas in the limbic system and are activated automatically without the intervention of the cortex.[9] The automatic fear response that many animals exhibit in front of predators, for example, is a primary emotion. When mechanisms for primary emotions are elicited cortically, they give rise to secondary emotions, as in the case of fear elicited by deliberation (rather than automatically). Damasio's (1994) framework is consistent with LeDoux's (1996) model of the double pathway for the elicitation of fear. According to it, primary fear is elicited entirely subcortically, by stimuli that enter the sensory thalamus and feed directly into the amygdala via a "quick and dirty" pathway (supporting evidence shows that cats and rats whose cortical components of the auditory system have been damaged still exhibit fear conditioning to auditory stimuli). Secondary or "cognitive" fear occurs when the amygdala is activated via the cortex, along a slower pathway that typically involves deliberation.

Both proposed unifying mechanisms are problematic. Most apparently, in Plutchik's model it is not clear whether the various dyads are merely mixtures of basic emotions or involve some extra component. Mere blending does not seem sufficient to account for the resulting emotions. Phenomenologically, love is certainly not merely a blend of joy and acceptance, for example, and guilt is not a blend of joy and fear. In addition, both love and guilt involve different thoughts, different action tendencies, and different behavioral manifestations from those of their alleged components, and so on.

Damasio's way of drawing the distinction between primary and secondary emotions (and LeDoux's related double-pathway model) is also problematic, although in a different way. It is based on an increasingly controversial view of the brain (although arguably still an influential one), according to which emotion and cognition are neurally distinct, with emotion residing in the deeper areas of the brain, and cognition depending primarily on the higher areas. Yet as we shall see in more detail in chapter 4, it does not seem possible to parse the brain into lower emotional and higher cognitive areas; rather, cognition and emotion overlap and are distributed over the whole brain (Lewis 2005; Pessoa 2008). Also, deeper brain areas are intimately interconnected with cortical ones; they are modulated by, and in turn modulate, cortical activity at various stages. The amygdala, for example, is influenced by activity in the visual cortex and at the same time modulates how it responds to visual stimuli. In addition, subcortical areas can process stimuli not just coarsely but in a detailed way (see Adolphs and Pessoa 2010).

Another building-block version of the unity thesis has been advanced by Prinz (2004b). According to him, all emotions are *embodied appraisals*, namely, perceptions of bodily changes that have the function of tracking or representing specific properties in the environment, such as danger, insult, and so on (following Lazarus 2001, Prinz calls these *core relational themes*; see also chap. 4). Basic emotions have been naturally selected to represent a limited set of core relational themes. Nonbasic emotions are either blends of basic emotions or basic emotions (or blends thereof) *recalibrated* in development so as to represent new themes. For example, schadenfreude, according to Prinz, is a recalibrated nonbasic emotion constituted by the perception of bodily changes distinctive of joy (a basic emotion), which have come to represent the new theme of "others' suffering."

There is, however, no empirical evidence for the view that some emotions involve the "same" bodily changes of others. Indeed, this is an empirical question that cannot be answered a priori. In addition, Prinz's account is phenomenologically perplexing in that it entails that recalibrated emotions must feel like the basic emotions of which they are recalibrations. Prinz follows James (1884, [1890] 1950) in claiming that a felt emotion is the perception of the bodily changes that occur during it. But then, because recalibrated emotions and the basic emotions of which they are recalibrations are supposed to involve the same bodily changes, they must also feel the same. Indeed, Prinz (2005, 19) suggests that guilt feels like sadness, "indignation feels like anger, disappointment feels like sadness, awe has an element of surprise, contempt has an element of disgust, pride feels like a kind of joy, exhilaration feels like a blend of fear and joy, and jealousy feels like a blend of anger, disgust, and fear." Yet it is plainly not the case that we experience only a limited number of basic feelings that remain the same in different contexts (including when they are brought about by judgments not previously associated with them, as in the case of recalibrated emotions). In my experience, guilt feels very different from sadness, in terms of bodily sensations, thoughts, perceived opportunities, and so on. Likewise for exhilaration and fear, jealousy and disgust, and so on.[10]

What about the disunity thesis? It has most notably been defended by Griffiths (1997), according to whom basic emotions are modular structures homologous to structures in nonhuman animals, whereas "higher cognitive emotions" are complex, uniquely human emotions, not homologous to states in other species. (Homology in comparative biology refers to shared descent from a common ancestor and is typically contrasted with analogy. Homologous traits have similar structure, whereas analogous traits have only superficial resemblance. For example, the human hand and the whale's flipper are homologous: they both descend from the tetrapod's limbs, as shown by their similar bone structure. The wings of the bat and of the bird, on the other hand, are only analogous: they are superficially similar and both enable flying, but they do not come from a common ancestor.) Because of this fundamental difference, according to Griffiths, basic and higher cognitive emotions do not form a unified class, and affective scientists should drop the category of "emotion" to replace it with at least two distinct ones, for which distinct theories should be elaborated.

Note first that in proposing the disunity thesis, Griffiths was mainly motivated by negative considerations, particularly the problematic nature of building-block views such as Plutchik's and Damasio's. Yet rejecting unity altogether is not the only alternative to the building-block view (as we will see in more detail in the next chapter). The major problem with the disunity thesis, in my view, is that it does not sit well with what we know about the brain. Basic emotions are for Griffiths (1997) *modules* in Fodor's (1983) sense: they are inescapable, opaque to our cognitive processes and awareness, and most importantly *informationally encapsulated*, namely, they "cannot access all the information stored in other cognitive systems, and … can store information that contradicts that other information" (Griffiths 1997, 93). Basic emotions are embedded in the deeper and older limbic system; if they were integrated within cortical systems, Griffiths argues, they would lose their rapidity and with it their selective advantage. This account is broadly consistent with some current affective neuroscientific ones, according to which a small number of "primary-process emotions" are situated in ancient subcortical areas of the brain. Evidence for these mechanisms has been provided by artificially activating subcortical circuits in animal brains (e.g., Panksepp 1998a; Panksepp and Watt 2011).

Note first, however, that automatic elicitation and informational encapsulation need not be supported by dedicated subcortical structures. They may also be supported by cortical structures, or integrated cortical-subcortical ones, as a result of the organism's interactions with the environment over development. We know, for instance, that fear conditioning can be induced in decorticated rats (LeDoux 1996). However, we also know that in nondecorticated animals, the cortex does play a role in fear conditioning. For example, Schneidermann et al. (1974) exposed nondecorticated rabbits to two tones, one of which was associated with an electrical shock; accordingly, rabbits started to exhibit fear conditioning to that tone. However, when the experimenters lesioned the auditory cortex of the rabbits, they exhibited fear conditioning to *both* tones (see LeDoux 1996, 161). This result suggests that even in the case of automatic fear responses to a conditioned stimulus, the cortex is involved; in particular, it contributes to discriminating the conditioned stimulus from non-conditioned ones. Without cortex, such discrimination does not occur. As Hardcastle (1999, 242) puts it, "It takes both the cortex and the amygdala, working together, to create fear in intact rabbits"; the intact brain appears to take advantage of its complexity and exploit all its resources, so that "without cortex, you get one neuronal configuration; with cortex, you get another" (243).

More problematic is Griffiths's characterization of higher cognitive emotions. He does not say anything about their neural substrate, and in fact he declares that he "cannot do much more than gesture" (1997, 91) at what he means by higher cognitive processes. In his account, however, higher cognitive emotions do not include basic emotions. Even when emotions such as fear, anger, sadness, and so on, are triggered by cognitive processes (which Griffiths thinks is possible, see p. 92), these do not involve basic emotions; rather, they are very different emotions that require different explanations. This account implies lack of overlap between brain areas for basic emotions, and brain areas for higher cognitive emotions. Here is where what we know about the brain suggests otherwise. As mentioned earlier, we know that the brain is highly integrated across older and newer structures. So even if some older structures may in some contexts underpin mandatory responses blind to declarative knowledge, this does not mean that they are *always* isolated from other parts of the brain. The amygdala, for example, is located in older subcortical parts of the brain and has reliably been found active in quick-and-dirty fear responses. However, it is also known to be a "hub" that projects widely to both cortical and other subcortical areas (Pessoa 2010). Consider also the phenomenon of *vertical integration*, which refers to dense bidirectional connectivity and reciprocal control between regions distributed along the whole neuraxis (Tucker, Derryberry, and Luu 2000). This indicates that structures that underpin mandatory and encapsulated responses are not necessarily insulated from the rest of the brain. More specifically this implies that older neural areas for basic emotions are not necessarily insulated from neural mechanisms underpinning the higher cognitive emotions. The higher cognitive emotions may involve parts of, or even all, neural mechanisms for basic emotions by integrating them into different neural patterns (incidentally, the idea that deeper and evolutionarily older brain structures participate with more recent ones to support new emotions or new functions of the same emotion is now widespread in affective neuroscience).

Griffiths (1997, 103–104) rejects the idea that higher cognitive emotions can come to include basic emotions by eliciting them through cortical activation because, he claims, no empirical evidence supports it. I agree that no evidence points to the existence of nonemotional cognitive appraisal processes taking place in the cortex that bring about emotional responses in lower parts of the brain (see chap. 4). Evidence does suggest, however, that the cortex is integrated with subcortical areas in such a way that if those areas are disrupted, cognitive activity is also impaired. Take, for example, the ventral tegmental area, located in the basal ganglia beneath the cortex; this area contains dopamine and projects richly to the prefrontal cortex, to the point that damage to the basal ganglia impairs the development of the cortex and leads to mental retardation (Quartz and Sejnowski 2002, 91). Another example is that congenital and early damage to the amygdala disrupts the capacity to understand others, such as the capacity to detect tactless or ironic comments and to interpret nonliteral utterances (Shaw et al. 2004). Also, inhibition of the noradrenergic system of the amygdala disrupts the capacity to form long-term memory (Ferry, Roozendaal, and McGaugh 1999). These results strongly suggest that parts of the brain involved in "higher cognitive emotions" are not distinct and separate from those involved in basic emotions, although, of course, more evidence is needed about the neural activity underpinning them.

In sum, then, distinguishing basic from nonbasic emotions has created a need to account for how these two classes of emotions relate to each other. Proposed accounts, however, I have argued, are problematic—which should count as another reason to drop the notion of basic emotions. To anticipate, in the next chapter I defend a view of *all* emotions as complex dynamical patterns of brain and bodily events, which could be seen as a version of the unity thesis, according to which, however, there are no emotions that are building blocks of others.

2.6 Alternatives to BET and Their Problems

BET is arguably the most influential framework in affective science, but it is not the only game in town. Alternatives have been proposed, which, however, I believe, have difficulties of their own. I discuss here in particular two of the most influential alternatives to BET and explain why I think they are problematic. These are the *psychological constructionist* models proposed by James Russell and by Lisa Barrett, and the *component process* model proposed by Klaus Scherer.

According to both Russell and Barrett, all emotions have something in common; more precisely, they all vary along a small number of dimensions—hence the characterization of their models as "dimensional." Their models explain the occurrence of emotional episodes in a very different way from BET.[11] According to both, crucially emotions are not organismic "entities." There are no basic emotions in the sense of genetically prede-termined internal causes of behavior, feeling, and so on. There are, at best, *prototypical* emotional episodes that recur relatively reliably across contexts and cultures. These episodes, however, are *psychological constructions* just as any other emotional episode, including nonprototypical ones. In other words, they are assemblies of a variety of psychological components. Those components include, most fundamentally, what Russell has called *core affect*, namely (as we saw in the previous chapter), a degree of felt arousal and affect valence:

[Core affect is] that neurophysiological state consciously accessible as the simplest raw (nonreflective) feelings evident in moods and emotions. ... At a given moment, the conscious experience (the raw feeling) is a single integral blend of two dimensions. ... The horizontal dimension, pleasure–displeasure, ranges from one extreme (e.g., ago-ny) through a neutral point (adaptation level) to its opposite extreme (e.g., ecstasy). The feeling is an assessment of one's current condition. The vertical dimension, arous-al, ranges from sleep, then drowsiness, through various stages of alertness to frenetic excitement. The feeling is one's sense of mobilization and energy. (Russell 2003, 148)

In Russell's model, core affect is always present and is independent from language and categorization. It is "primitive, universal and simple" (148). Core affect is already affective, but in an emotional episode it is typically "loosely linked" (Russell 2005, 38) to other psychological components such as appraisal (the evaluation of a situation in relation to one's own needs or goals), specific subjective quality (feelings of fear, shame, etc.), action tendencies, meta-awareness, and others. The details of these components need not concern us here. The important point is that for Russell, how these components generate an emotional episode is not a matter of biology, so to speak, but depends on available "mental scripts": "The set of events picked out by the English word *fear* is not a biologically given category. Indeed, the present analysis predicts that there is no neural circuit, peptide, or other biological marker that is unique to fear. ... Instead, to categorize is to note a resemblance between observed components and a mental repre-sentation, which is here thought of as a mental script" (Russell 2003, 151). In other words, perceiving an emotion in oneself and others depends on the existence of a mental script for that emotion. The mental script enables one to see or pick out a coherent set of properties in the organism (experi-ence included). The mental script includes language-dependent emotion categories (fear, anger, shame, etc.) and also "specifies a temporally ordered and causally linked sequence of subevents" (164).

Barrett's "conceptual act model" is similar. It denies the existence of basic affect programs, posits the dimension of valence as "a basic building block of emotional life" (Barrett 2006c), and denies that the emotions are "biological entities" independent of language and categorization. This model particularly emphasizes that "emotions are not biologically given, but are constructed via the process of categorization" (Barrett 2006b, 27). It is categorization that parses what are at best weakly correlated component processes into different items; categorization makes us experience our own emotions as distinct feelings, and it also "shapes" our perception of other people's states.

I find these proposals unconvincing, primarily because they are too radically dismissive of any role of the "biological" in emotional episodes.[12] It is right, I think, that mental scripts and language-dependent concepts play a role in categorizing features of a situation as distinctive of a specific emotion. After all, we become familiar with the vocabulary of emotion by association with situations that are described to us as characteristic of specific emotions. In this view, recognizing emotions is a matter of matching an acquired script with the features of a perceived event (see also the discussion of *paradigm scenarios* in De Sousa 1987, which he characterizes as criteria that enable us to make sense of our and others' emotional responses). Moreover, different languages are likely to parse perceived events in different ways.

Yet Russell and Barrett (and the latter seemingly more than the former) attribute *more* to mental scripts and concepts than a role in categorization; namely, they see them as "constructing" emotional episodes, by imposing structure where they claim to be none, or very little at most. Thus Barrett (2006a, 47) complains that "many of the most influential models in our science assume that emotions are biological categories imposed by nature, so that emotion categories are recognized, rather than constructed, by the human mind."[13]

But as we saw earlier, evidence for language-independent recurrent patterns in emotional episodes is compelling and cannot be dismissed altogether. It does not seem plausible to write off any role of biological influences in structuring our emotional behavior, physiology, and expressivity, and to deny that emotions are entities in the sense of relatively stable patterns of brain and bodily (including behavioral and expressive) processes. Also, after all, when it comes to everyday face-to-face encounters with others, mutual understanding relies largely on attributions of specific emotions on the basis of facial, vocal, and bodily configurations (see also chap. 7); and we respond consistently to art portraying emotions via facial expressions, postures, movements, vocal expressions, and music (of course, there are always exceptions, nuances, and idiosyncrasies). Barrett would probably respond that the perception of emotions in others is enabled by language-dependent concepts (see Barrett 2006b). However, animals and infants respond reliably to others' attitudes without or before acquiring such concepts. Existing evidence does not support the claim that language *enables* emotion perception altogether. Interesting experiments have shown that priming information about specific emotions—for example, by having subjects read scenarios representing different emotions—influences how subjects categorize facial expressions; specifically ambiguous or neutral faces tend to be interpreted as expressing the primed emotion, and nonambiguous expressions are also influenced by the priming process (e.g., Trope 1986; Carroll and Russell 1996). These results, however, are not inconsistent with the claim that people produce distinctive facial expressions for emotion. Another study has shown that repeating an emotion word thirty times interferes with the categorization of facial expressions by slowing it down and making it less accurate (Lindquist et al. 2006). Again, however, pace Lindquist et al., this result is far from supporting the claim that "language *forms* the emotional reality that we experience" (135; my italics).[14]

Importantly, acknowledging this point does not commit one to endorsing BET's claim that basic emotions are genetically predetermined affect programs. In the next chapter, I argue for an alternative view of the emotions that *does* posit the existence of coherent patterns of the organism and yet does not assume that emotions are "internal causal entities" or "stored patterns" that somehow bring about tightly connected outcomes. This alternative, as we will see, endorses the claim that emotions are variable and context dependent; at the same time, it explicitly addresses the question of how coherent emotional episodes "come to be," so to speak, and does so by reference to principles of organization that are widespread in nature and do not appeal to internal causes to explain patterned phenomena.

Another alternative to BET is the component process model (CPM), pioneered by Klaus Scherer (see Scherer 2009 for a recent overview). Its main contrast with BET is that it denies that patterned emotional episodes are the output of innate affect programs. It also denies that there are basic emotions in the sense of emotions that enter other emotions as components. All emotions, in the CPM, are characterized as "patterns of synchronization" of five component subsystems driven by the cognitive-evaluative process of appraisal (itself a component of the emotion system). Besides appraisal, the other component subsystems are autonomic physiology, action tendencies, motor expression, and feeling. More specifically, the appraisal subsystem itself is divided into four distinct subprocesses that appraise different aspects of an event and accordingly causally induce different changes in the other emotional components. These four appraisal subprocesses evaluate, respectively, the personal relevance of an event (does this event affect me directly?), its implications (how will this event affect my well-being and goals?), the subject's coping potential (how well can I cope with this event?), and the normative significance of the event (how does this event relate to my values and norms?). In addition, each of these appraisal subprocesses is divided into a number of "stimulus evaluation checks" (SECs), each of which exerts a specific effect on other subprocesses within the emotional episode (ANS, expressions, etc.).[15] For example, the "relevance" appraisal subprocess has an SEC for novelty, one for intrinsic pleasantness, and one for goal relevance; the "coping" appraisal subprocess has an SEC for control, one for power, and one for adjustment. A further central assumption of this model is that the various appraisal subprocesses and their SECs occur sequentially. Thus the implications of an event are evaluated after appraisal of its relevance has been completed; the subject's coping potential in turn is evaluated after the event's implications have been taken into account; and the event's normative significance is evaluated last. More specifically, during the evaluation of relevance, novelty will be evaluated before intrinsic pleasantness, which in turn will be evaluated before goal relevance, and so on.

The CPM predicts that different sequences of SECs will have different effects on the various emotional subprocesses, thus generating emotional episodes that will display a variety of different autonomic, motor, expressive, and feeling aspects. Given the high number of SECs, many combinations of these aspects will be possible. Some combinations will thus resemble the basic configurations predicted by BET (Scherer calls these *modal emotions*), yet importantly there will be many other configurations, corresponding to episodes of shame, guilt, expectancy, relief, and so on. Moreover, the CPM does not predict that there will be *one* distinctive configuration for each emotion category; rather, there will be different configurations for shame, jealousy, pride, and so on, and even configurations for which English does not have a label, but that still count as emotional episodes.

This model is similar to Russell's and Barrett's in that it characterizes emotional episodes as arrangements of component processes that do not come in preestablished packages elicited by the activation of hard-wired programs; rather, component processes "fluctuate," so to speak, relatively independently and can mix in various ways, thus giving rise to a range of different emotional episodes. However, the component process model does not claim that categorization is required to "bind" the components together into an emotional episode. The components, rather, combine into a configuration as a consequence of the changes brought about in the emotion system by the various SECs, which continuously scan the environment.

This approach does not suffer from the difficulties of the psychological constructionist models. Also, it importantly emphasizes the temporal and episodic nature of the emotions, the rich interactivity between the various emotional component subsystems, as well as the complexity, variability, and context dependency of the emotions. It is a particularly sophisticated model that precisely specifies the mechanisms whereby emotional episodes come about.

However, some aspects of this model remain perplexing. For one, it seems unlikely that specific components such as individual facial muscle actions (called "action units," or AUs, in the literature) or dimensions of autonomic arousal are guided by distinct appraisal subprocesses, or even sub-subprocesses such as SECs. Admittedly this is partly an empirical question. Scherer and collaborators are engaged in a large project to test it in the lab, and some interesting results have already been generated. Scherer and Ellgring (2007), for example, have shown that actors rarely produce BET's prototypical facial expressions. Moreover, they found that the facial expressions produced could be predicted by the model's associations between specific action units and specific SECs. For example, the model predicts that AUs 1 and 2 (inner and outer brow raised) occur more in relation to novelty and lack of control; consistent with this prediction, the actor study showed that these AUs are indeed used mostly in emotions of panic, fear, anxiety, and despair.

Arguably, however, because individual muscles usually work not in isolation but as part of larger configurations, it seems possible that whereas some AUs may depend on specific appraisals, others may just activate together and form a pattern as a function of muscular synergies. I discuss some relevant evidence in the next chapter. For now the point is that it appears more natural, that is, more in line with principles of biological organization, to allow the organism to generate emotional episodes without the pervasive guidance and control of an army of appraisal checks. Organisms are highly complex and interconnected systems, such that changes in one part typically modify the rest of the system. The CPM admits of interactivity among components within the emotion system, but it ultimately reiterates the *driving* role of the appraisal process in guiding the changes that occur in the organism. As we saw, it also hypothesizes that the various SECs occur *sequentially* in a specific order. The model thus leaves little if any room for biological self-organization and complex reciprocal influences among different organismic processes. We will look more in detail at these phenomena and their role in affectivity in the next chapter.

2.7 Conclusion

The debate about the nature of the emotions is complex and difficult to navigate. In this chapter, I reviewed and discussed some of the most influential accounts. After assessing what I consider misguided criticisms of BET, I pointed to a major problem with the theory, namely, the arbitrariness of the process that has led to the widespread view that evidence supports the existence of a small number of basic emotions. I also criticized related influential accounts of the relation between alleged basic and nonbasic emotions, such as various building-block views of basic emotions, and the disunity thesis—ultimately suggesting that it would be better to drop the notion of "basic" emotions altogether. Then I turned to proposed alternatives to BET and found problems with them, too. In particular I argued that the psychological constructionist models are too radical in their rejection of the idea that emotional episodes are biological events and that they come in recurrent organismic patterns, whereas the CPM, although sophisticated and detailed, appears artificially overcomplicated and overlooks principles of biological organization.

In the next chapter, I put forth more constructive arguments to depict a different account of the emotions that, I believe, overcomes the difficulties of existing approaches and fits better with accepted principles of biological organization.

3 Emotional Episodes as Dynamical Patterns

3.1 Introduction

The best way to conceptualize emotional episodes, I believe, is as *dynamical patterns*. More precisely, emotional episodes should be understood as self-organizing patterns of the organism, best described with the conceptual tools of dynamical systems theory (DST). DST is a branch of mathematics used to model a variety of complex temporal phenomena. In the mind sciences, it has been used to model a variety of cognitive phenomena. This "dynamical cognitive science," as Wheeler (2005) aptly calls it, is importantly related to the enactive approach. It can be seen as a precursor of it, with roots in cybernetics (see Pickering 2010), although it became more influential in cognitive science only in the mid-1990s with the publication of works such as Thelen and Smith 1994, Kelso 1995, and Port and van Gelder 1995.

The enactive approach takes from dynamical cognitive science the view that cognition is a *temporal* phenomenon. It is particularly sympathetic to what Thompson (2007, 10) calls *embodied dynamicism*, namely, the view that cognitive systems are not just temporal but also embodied and situated, involving "multiple simultaneous interactions" of brain, body, and world (van Gelder and Port 1995, 23). Indeed, the very notion of autonomy, which (as we saw in chap. 1) in the enactive approach captures a crucial property of living systems, refers to a network of processes that influence one another over time and in so doing generate and maintain the unity of the network. As we shall see in more detail shortly, this kind of mutually influencing relationship is precisely what can usefully be captured by DST.

In addition, the enactive approach has also begun to draw on what I will call, by analogy with dynamical cognitive science, *dynamical affective science*, namely, the application of dynamical systems concepts to affective and emotional phenomena (see Thompson 2007, chap. 12; Colombetti 2007; Colombetti and Thompson 2008). The aim of this chapter is, in brief, to focus on this approach in detail, and to show that it provides a valuable alternative to the theories of emotion discussed in the previous chapter. After introducing some fundamental conceptual tools of DST, I distinguish three strands within the dynamical systems approach in affective science, highlight their distinctive claims, and eventually reconstruct a character-ization of emotional episodes consistent with all of them. I then move on to spell out the implications that such a characterization has for the debate on the nature of the emotions illustrated in the previous chapter. I also dis-cuss the implications of a dynamical systems characterization of emotional episodes for further issues in affective science, such as the purported dis-creteness of emotions, and the relationship between emotions and moods.

3.2 Fundamental Concepts of Dynamical Systems Theory (DST)

DST is a branch of mathematics that describes the temporal evolution of dynamical systems, namely, systems that change over time.[1] What changes over time is called the *state* of the system. Describing the temporal evolu-tion of a dynamical system requires one first to provide a number of *state variables* that describe the state of the system at a given time. Next, one needs to provide a rule of evolution that describes how the values of the state variables change over time. When the system changes continuously over time, this rule takes the form of differential equations (systems that evolve in discrete steps do not need differential equations; difference equa-tions will do). Given the state variables of the system, it is possible to rep-resent all possible states of the system geometrically as a *state space*, such that each point of the state space corresponds to a state of the system. As the system changes its state over time, it moves from one point of the state space to another, tracing a curve in it that is called a *trajectory*. The set of all possible trajectories of a system is its *phase portrait*. Points or regions in the state space toward which the system's trajectories tend to converge are called *attractors*. When a system is in a region of the state space such that it will evolve into a particular attractor, that region is the attractor's *basin of attraction*. Points or regions in the state space from which the system's trajectories are deflected are called *repellors*, and the overall layout of attrac-tors and repellors in the state space is referred to as its *topology*. A *bifurcation* or *phase transition* occurs when the phase portrait undergoes a qualitative change as a consequence of small changes in the value of parameters affecting the behavior of the system (see hereafter for the notion of "control parameter"), yielding a new topology.

Two or more dynamical systems are said to be *coupled* when they reciprocally influence and constrain their behavior over time, such that they can be modeled as one system. The phenomenon is often illustrated with the example of wall-mounted pendulums (A. Clark 2001). If allowed to oscillate freely, two pendulums hanging on the same wall will tend to swing-synchronize as time passes, via the vibrations of the wall. The movement of one pendulum causes vibrations of a certain frequency that influence the movement of the other pendulum, and vice versa. In DST this is mathematically captured by a set of two differential equations (one for each pendulum) in which the evolution of each pendulum's behavior is factored into the equation of the other. The example of the wall-mounted pendulums also illustrates the phenomenon of *entrainment*, which occurs when two or more coupled dynamical systems become synchronized, either via a process of mutual influences or as one system adapts its motions to those of the other(s).

Another important concept from DST is *self-organization*. Self-organization refers to the capacity of a complex system to generate and maintain structured order within itself by way of mutual influences among its components. Autonomous systems, as defined in chapter 1, are paradigmatic self-organizing systems: they are generated and maintained in virtue of the influences that their constituent processes exert on one another. In DST, an example often used to illustrate self-organization is the Rayleigh-Bénard instability (see Kelso 1995). When liquid is poured into a pan and heat applied from below, rolling motions ("convection rolls") in the liquid appear that constrain (or, as it is sometimes said, *enslave*; see Haken 1977) the range of possible behaviors of the liquid's molecules. The amplitude of the convection rolls is known as a *collective variable*; namely, its value reflects the result of the mutual interactions of the various components of the system (the liquid's molecules, in this case). It is also referred to as an *order parameter*, because it reduces the degrees of freedom of the liquid molecules and constrains them into an ordered pattern. Importantly, nothing "controls" or "directs" the appearance of the convection rolls. The heat applied to the pan in the Rayleigh-Bénard instability is sometimes characterized as a *control parameter*, namely, a factor that influences the state of the system without being affected by it; aside from this influence, however, the heat does not control the system in the sense of "instructing" how it should behave or of "monitoring" its evolution. Rather, the Rayleigh-Bénard instability instantiates what some call a process of *circular causality* (Haken 1977): the initial disposition of the liquid's molecules and the temperature of the heat source applied to the pan influence the direction of motion and the amplitude of the convection rolls; at the same time, the appearance of convection rolls influences the behavior of the liquid's molecules by locking them into a certain range of motion.[2]

It is also useful to think of self-organization in terms of *first-* and *second-order constraints* (Juarrero 1999, 140–144; Thompson 2007, 424–425). First-order constraints refer to the influences that a system's components exert on one another. In the Rayleigh-Bénard instability, the reciprocal influences among the molecules of liquid instantiate first-order constraints. Second-order constraints refer to the global influence that macrolevel patterns or *forms* exert on the system's components; in the Rayleigh-Bénard instability, the convection rolls provide second-order constraints as overarching patterns that enslave the behavior of the liquid's molecules.

Finally, the term *emergence* is often used to refer to the appearance of interesting behavior in systems where several components influence one another reciprocally and via circular causality (see A. Clark 2001, 113–114). This notion of emergence, which I adopt here, does not commit one to the further, stronger claim that entirely new ontological properties appear from the interaction of components that do not themselves possess them (see, e.g., Bitbol 2007 for a discussion and criticism of this notion of emergence). As will become clearer shortly, in this chapter I am concerned not with ontological properties but with patterns of brain and bodily activity that appear in emotional episodes as instances of the organism's self-organizing activity.[3]

3.3 Dynamical Affective Science

DST has been adopted in different disciplines to model various physical, biological, ecological, and social systems—such as lasers, ant colonies, bird flocking, climate changes, economic behavior, and many more. As mentioned earlier, cognitive scientists have also adopted DST to model a range of cognitive phenomena. Several works already discuss the dynamical systems approach in cognitive science,[4] so I shall not illustrate it in any detail

here. I shall only mention that, in emphasizing the temporal character
of cognition, dynamical cognitive scientists typically take issue with the
view—widespread in more "standard" cognitive science—that cognition
is made up of static and context-free structures, and explaining cognition
is a matter of explaining how these structures can "represent" knowledge
and "control" or prescribe intelligent behavior. Explaining cognition,
dynamicists assert, is rather a matter of explaining how brain, body, and
world constrain one another to achieve adaptive behavior, and this kind
of explanation need not make any reference to internal representations. To
be sure, whether dynamical cognitive science can do without *any* kind of
representations at all is a debated issue, as is the more general question of
whether dynamical cognitive science is incompatible with, or rather complements, standard cognitive science (see discussions in, e.g., A. Clark 1997;
Wheeler 2005; Shapiro 2011). As I see it, from an enactive perspective, it is
possible to regard various aspects of dynamical systems (states, attractors,
trajectories, etc.) as having some kind of representational status, and this
may be useful for various purposes; however, one should keep in mind
that to do so is to take the system as *heteronomous* rather than autonomous
(Varela 1979; Thompson 2007, 49–51), namely, as characterized by inputs
and outputs, and by a transference of information from the inside to the
outside (and vice versa). When applied to cognitive systems, this perspective thus obscures their autonomous character, and the related point that
a cognitive system generates or enacts meaning in virtue of its organization. As Thompson (2007, 51) remarks, "For the enactive approach it is the
autonomy perspective on natural cognitive agents that remains the reference point for understanding mind and life, not a predefined input-output
task structure."[5]

In any case, I need not dwell on this debate here. For my aims, the value
of DST lies primarily in that it provides conceptual tools enabling a characterization of emotional episodes as self-organizing patterns of the organism.
As such, as we shall see, emotional episodes are context dependent, flexible,
and "loosely assembled" and yet can also display stability across contexts—
which has important implications for the debate about the nature of the
emotions discussed in the previous chapter.

To show this, I turn now to the dynamical systems approach in affective
science. Compared to dynamical cognitive science, this approach is relatively less known. One reason is perhaps the relative neglect of emotion in
cognitive science. Another reason is probably its predominantly discursive

and qualitative character. Whereas dynamical cognitive science has produced at least a few quantitative models that lend themselves to relatively detailed scrutiny and assessment (see Thelen et al. 2001; R. D. Beer 2003), dynamical approaches in affective science mainly just offer abstract dynamical qualitative descriptions of emotional phenomena, at disparate levels, advancing quite general hypotheses about their emergent character.

In spite of its undeniably discursive and speculative character, I think that the dynamical systems approach to emotion has much to recommend and should not be dismissed too quickly. Note first that existing accounts of emotions are not, by comparison, particularly strong mathematically and quantitatively. Quite the contrary, qualitative psychological modeling prevails in emotion theory. Moreover, my primary concern here is theoretical; the question I set up to examine is "what is the best way to conceptualize the emotions?" and from this perspective, the conceptual resources made available by dynamical systems theory are, I believe, particularly useful to overcoming the difficulties of existing accounts (discussed in the previous chapter).

In the following sections, I distinguish three strands of work within dynamical affective science. One strand emphasizes the role of *coordinative structures* and *preferential linkages* among muscles in the production of emotional expressions. Emotional expressions are seen not as the output of internal, pregiven instructions (BET's affect programs) but as the outcome of synergistic processes of mutual constraints among muscles. The second strand draws on work on brain plasticity and coherence to call attention to processes of *neural self-organization* in the stabilization of brain structures underpinning emotional episodes. The third strand applies principles of dynamical systems theory to *interpersonal relations*, and specifically to the emergence of patterns of emotional behavior between two or more agents. In spite of their (very) different levels of description, these three strands are compatible in that they all characterize the organism as complex, self-organizing, open, and plastic, realizing emotional episodes that are softly assembled, context dependent, and highly variable, yet patterned and recurrent.

3.3.1 Coordinative Muscular Structures

The dynamical systems approach to emotion expression can be traced to Peter Wolff's work on the development of emotional expression in infants (smiling and crying in particular). Adopting an ethological method, Wolff

(1987) observed twenty-two infants at home in their first month of life to make out their expressive repertoire and also informally manipulated their activities to examine the conditions that give rise to specific behaviors. These observations highlighted the variability of infant emotional expressions in relation to objects and people, showing that they rarely correspond to the prototypical configurations posited by BET. They also showed that infant expressions, even if variable, still come in a limited number of combinations of components and are relatively resistant to perturbation; in addition, they are discontinuous (i.e., they do not gradually change as stimulation gradually increases) and vary depending on the infant's state at the time of stimulation. According to Wolff, these observations were better accounted for by a dynamical systems account, rather than by a "central program" view entailing all possible responses being generated and controlled by internal rules (see also Camras and Witherington 2005).

Drawing on this work, Fogel and Thelen (1987) reinterpreted existing evidence on the expression of emotion in infants from a dynamical systems perspective. They focused on patterns of crying and smiling and on how these change in the course of the first year of life. Rather than viewing these changes as driven by transformations in brain structures taking place at predetermined developmental stages, they proposed viewing them as emergent from the mutual influences of a variety of bodily and environmental processes developing at different timescales. Take crying, for example. Wolff (1967) had already identified different types of cry, which appear at different moments during the course of the first year of life. He noted that two types of cry are present at birth: *rhythmical cry* and *pain cry* (so called because it is manifested in response to painful stimulation). Each is characterized by a distinctive breathing pattern in which expiration, inspiration, and the pauses between them all have a precise duration. Around the second month, a qualitatively different type of cry appears, the *irregular* or *fussy cry*, which becomes increasingly complicated during the first year of life, with variations in vocal intensity, bilabial friction noises, and squealing. Infants vary the auditory features of the cry depending on their goals and on the caregiver's responses to them. At nine months, the cry is less persistent and more punctuated by pauses, during which the infant checks the cry's effects on the caregiver. Soon afterward the cry becomes incorporated into a "demand behavior" that includes referential gestures of hands and arms. In infants older than one year, crying begins and declines more slowly, with more variations in the middle.

Fogel and Thelen's specific dynamical proposal is to view these changes as induced by control parameters that *themselves shift* as the organism develops and changes, and in response to the different behaviors that such changes make possible, and that affect development in turn (recall that the notion of control parameter does not imply a controller; "control parameters" here refers to intervening factors that affect the way the system self-organizes). Changes in the respiratory apparatus, for example, can be seen as control parameters for the appearance of fussy crying. Subsequent changes in patterns of crying may be due to the development of the oral musculature, itself dependent on experiences of feeding and oral exploration. The development of speech articulators may be another source of change, while itself being influenced by the infant's linguistic context. Similarly for the emergence of other skills, such as head turning, hand-to-mouth behavior and kicking, joint attention, and responsiveness to the caregiver. These are seen not as outputs of neural programs but as depending on the reciprocal influences of brain, bodily, and environmental processes; they are constrained by neural and muscular dynamics present at birth, but they change as the organism grows, and as the infant's interactional dynamics with the environment, including other people, also change and develop.

These theoretical considerations have found some support more recently in experimental work conducted by Linda Camras and colleagues, which has shown that infant facial expressions of emotion can be assembled dynamically from the realization of just one or a few of their components (e.g., brow raise, open mouth), and they can also be shaped in different ways by head lifts and tilts. Thus, for example, opening the mouth for oral exploration induces brow raising and eye widening, which are features of the surprise expression (Michel, Camras, and Sullivan 1992; Camras, Lambrecht, and Michel 1996). Structural synergies of this kind also explain, in Camras's view, the frequent occurrence in infants of "unexpected" emotional facial expressions, namely, expressions occurring in contexts where the corresponding emotion would ordinarily not be manifested (Camras 2000).

Note that like the component process model (CPM) we saw in the previous chapter, this approach acknowledges the possibility that changes in distinctive expressive features subserve specific functions; brow raising, for example, may be related to the presence of a novel stimulus that requires increased attention. Unlike the CPM, however, the dynamical approach does not claim that *each* muscle movement is driven by a distinct appraisal process. Rather, the rest of the face "takes care of itself," so to speak, in virtue of existing muscular constraints. It is important to emphasize the difference between the dynamical and the component process approach here, because the latter has sometimes also been presented as dynamical. Scherer (2000) in particular uses various dynamical systems concepts to describe the CPM, suggesting, for example, that the activity of the appraisal subsystem can be seen as triggering processes of mutual constraints, entrainment, and synchronization across the whole organism, and as directing the organism toward a variety of attractors. Scherer and Ellgring (2007) similarly write that, according to the CPM, "emotions have an *emergent* character based on the interaction of different components driven by the appraisal of an eliciting event" (115; italics in original), and "facial movements cumulatively combine in a dynamic fashion" (117). In spite of these claims, however, the CPM clearly inclines toward viewing all or most of the changes occurring during an emotional episode as *driven* by appraisal processes and thus does not leave room for genuine self-organization among the various components of the emotion system. Pace its emphasis on the interactivity of the various emotion subsystems, the CPM primarily aims to identify the causal antecedents (in the form of stimulus evaluations checks or SECs; see previous chapter) of all or most changes occurring in the organism in an emotional episode. These causal antecedents determine, in a sequential and piecemeal fashion (recall that the various SECs are supposed to follow one another sequentially), the activity of the other emotional subsystems (autonomic arousal, expression, motor activity, etc.). These subsystems thus do not really self-organize but obey the driving appraisal factor (see also the next chapter). As Camras and Witherington (2005, 336) also comment, in Scherer's model "the appraisal component both sets in motion relations with other components and responds to feedback from other components in an effort to 'guide' adaptation to a given context. Thus, the appraisal component of the system ends up assuming central executive properties; it is not by any means an encapsulated central executive, but it does operate as a monitoring system for the organization of other system."

The difference in approach is also apparent in their chosen methodology for the study of expression. According to Scherer, the main task is to identify the SECs that guide individual muscle movements (action units). According to Camras, the study of the development of emotional behavior ought to proceed following the method proposed by Thelen and Smith (1994). The experimenters first need to establish which phenomena to describe with collective variables. Then they need to identify which attractors characterize the system's behavior, map their evolution, and determine when the system changes from one attractor to another. Then they need to identify which factors may function as control parameters for the appearance and evolution of the charted phenomena, and eventually verify their hypothesis via experimental manipulations (Camras and Witherington 2005).

Note that the view that an emotional expression is not dictated by an affect program but is a coordinative structure need not apply only to infant expressions. Adult expressions are more stable than infant ones, namely, less variable and subject to perturbations. In dynamical systems terms, adult expressions can be characterized as relatively recurrent and fixed patterns whose specific shape has been carved in development as certain structures occurred more frequently, thus establishing specific basins of attraction in the topology of the "facial expression state space." This implies, among other things, that adult expressions remain open to modifications in the rest of the organism that occur as life progresses, as well as to interactions with others. Our organism does not stop changing as we reach adulthood, and our facial expressions vary as a function of new muscular synergies. In addition, as we will see in section 3.3.3 and in chapter 7, our expressivity is largely influenced by our concrete interactions with others.

Also, the view that an emotional expression is not dictated by an affect program but is rather a coordinative structure need not apply only to *facial* expressions, either. Little research has been conducted on the rest of the body, yet there are no reasons why dynamical systems principles could not be applied beyond facial expressions—quite the contrary. Complex synergies characterize the somatic (musculoskeletal) system, and emotional episodes are likely to entrain it into specific configurations that depend on external as well as internal constraints. As more data are gathered about bodily postures and gestures in emotion expression (it is only very recently that affective scientists have begun to code the actions of the body; see Dael, Mortillaro, and Scherer 2012), it may become possible to identify control parameters that influence the structure and dynamics of the expressive emotional body in context, and to plot the value of related collective variables reflecting the mutual influences of different parts of the body.

3.3.2 Neural Self-Organization

Dynamical systems principles have also been used to account for the organization as well as the development of neural systems underpinning emotion. One proposal, by Freeman (1999, 2000), is that evolutionarily older structures in the limbic system typically associated with emotion are self-organizing and constitute the *intentional core* of the living organism.[6] Freeman (2000, 214) actually identifies emotion with "the intention to act in the near future." Any analysis of the organism's behavior, he argues, ought to begin from this endogenous intentional activity, which motivates the organism into action. Freeman contrasts this view, which he characterizes as "activist-pragmatist," with the "passivist-cognitivist" view, according to which behavior is the output of a sequence of information-processing steps: in the first step, sensory stimulation provides information that goes from the sensory receptors to perceptual representations in the thalamus and sensory cortex; from there it is transmitted to the frontal lobes and motor cortex, where it is further processed before being passed on to the muscles to initiate action. Freeman criticizes this account for failing to integrate the activity of the limbic system into the process, which in his view is necessary to motivate action. Moreover, he rejects the sequential character of this account, emphasizing instead that brain activity involves primarily reciprocal influences between areas and processes that are complexly interconnected. The entorhinal cortex in particular (a major part of the limbic system) "not only receives and combines input from all of the primary sensory areas in the cerebral hemisphere; it also sends its output back again to all of them, after its previous activity has been integrated over time in the hippocampus" (2000, 221). From this perspective, it is misleading to see sensory stimulation as the initial step of a sequence that leads to perception and action; rather, sensory stimulation reaches a brain that is already motivated and action oriented and uses information about the world to modulate motor activity relative to its intentional orientation. There is, strictly speaking, no first cause in this process; rather, sensory stimulation impinges on ongoing mutually influencing neural processes, modifying their trajectories. Emotion, in this account, is thus integral to both perception and action. As goal-oriented intentionality, emotion involves premotor activity corresponding to action preparation and sustains actual motor action as this unfolds; at the same time, the ongoing character of emotion renders perception always more or less salient relative to the brain's intentionality.

Emotion is not a distinct step in a perception-action sequence, or a distinct representation added at some point to the sequence; emotion is rather an inescapable, pervasive dimension of brain activity on which sensory information impinges and from which action progresses.

This account is consistent with the so-called dynamic sensorimotor approach, which emphasizes the reciprocal constitution of action and perception (Hurley 1998; O'Regan and Noë 2001; Noë 2004). This approach acknowledges the embodied and active nature of the mind, and in particular it reconceptualizes perception in terms of embodied action. As Noë (2004, 1) puts it, "Perception is a way of acting. ... It is something we do." The idea, in a nutshell, is that perception cannot be reduced to the representation of sensory information within dedicated brain areas (this is what Freeman calls the "passivist-cognitivist" view). Rather, perception needs to be understood in the context of the organism's continuous active engagements with the world, and of its related "knowledge of sensorimotor contingencies." This term refers to the implicit knowledge that the organism, as embodied and active, possesses about how perception varies as a function of movement (see O'Regan and Noë 2001). When moving forward, for example, it expects that the optic flow pattern on the retina will expand; on the contrary, when moving backward, it expects that the optic flow pattern will contract (different perceptual modalities, such as touch and hearing, are characterized by different contingency rules). According to the dynamical sensorimotor approach, sensory information thus impinges on an active organism that is already furnished with knowledge and expectations about how the world changes in relation to movement; perceiving is, then, better characterized as the exercise of this practical knowledge, rather than the representation of sensory information in a dedicated part of the brain.

Freeman's account is not just consistent with this approach to perception, however; it importantly complements and enriches it by underscoring its affective dimension. The dynamic sensorimotor approach does not address either emotion or affectivity more generally; it portrays perception as something that the organism does, but is silent about the affective-motivational dimension of this doing, in particular its endogenous intentional orientation and, relatedly, the salient nature of percepts. In Freeman's account, on the other hand, emotion is explicitly embedded within the sensorimotor activity of the organism and pervades it thoroughly.

Note, however, that, to use the terminology introduced so far, Freeman's is best seen as a dynamical account of affectivity, and not of specific emotional episodes. As such, it pertains only secondarily to our present concern, namely, the question of how to conceptualize the emotions. A more relevant account here has been provided by Lewis (2005) and more recently by Lewis and Liu (2011). According to Lewis (2005), an emotional episode is a "cognition-emotion amalgam," or better an *emotional interpretation* that temporarily integrates neural processes widely distributed across the whole brain. This integration takes place via different mechanisms involving nonlinear influences among neural components, where "nonlinear influences" include (i) reciprocal or recursive relations characterized by multiple feedback cycles, such that cause–effect relations are multidirectional; and (ii) cause–effect relations where effects do not follow from causes in a linear way but "may be exponential, subject to threshold effects, and/or sensitive to damping or amplifying effects from other system components" (Lewis 2005, 173). The influences that Lewis mentions are positive feedback (which occurs when a change in the activity of a component system feeds back to it and amplifies the change), negative feedback (which occurs when an excitatory influence from one component system to the other is responded to with an inhibitory one, and stabilization or continuous oscillation ensues), entrainment of other systems into patterns of stability, and circular causality between different levels of the same system. According to Lewis, an emotional episode begins with a triggering event that initiates a process of reciprocal influences between various neural systems subsuming a variety of functions, such as attention, evaluation, bodily arousal, and action tendencies. An initial phase of self-amplification through positive feedback is followed by self-stabilization through negative feedback and entrainment, which leads to an orderly, coherent, and complex large-scale pattern corresponding, at the psychological level of description, to an emotional interpretation—namely, to a state that is at the same time a cognitive interpretation of the personal significance of the triggering event, and an emotional state. In sum, an emotional episode for Lewis corresponds to a large-scale, self-organizing, complex process that constrains or "enslaves" neural activity typically associated with cognitive and emotional processes into a temporarily stable structure, via various types of nonlinear influences.

I will say more about Lewis's (2005) account and the relationship between cognition and emotion in the next chapter, where I discuss specifically the notion of appraisal. For the moment, simply note the application of dynamical systems concepts at the level of neural self-organization to describe the emergence of specific emotional episodes. This account is different from, but not incompatible with, Freeman's. It can be seen as providing a specific account of the "microdevelopment" of an emotional episode within the broader superordinate context of endogenous intentionality that Freeman talks about (see also Thompson 2007, chap. 12).

The most relevant neurodynamical approach to emotion for present purposes is a recent paper by Lewis and Liu (2011), which explicitly addresses the debate between BET and the constructionist/conceptual act approach we saw earlier in the book. Lewis and Liu offer an account specifically of the development of brain structures underpinning different emotions. In their view, emotions, including BET's basic ones, are neither underpinned by "prespecified structures" nor entirely constructed psychologically or via conceptual acts. Rather, all emotions (i.e., the basic and nonbasic ones; note that Lewis and Liu do not drop the distinction) are subsumed by neural structures whose ontogenetic unfolding is shaped by forces that operate at different timescales. Hence the newborn brain is furnished with a few systems implementing primitive emotional functions, resulting from selective pressures at the evolutionary scale. Importantly, these systems are not rigid modules but open, flexible structures influenced by organism-environment encounters. As the infant interacts with the environment (including active and responsive others), the process of exponential synaptic growing (synaptogenesis) that occurs early in development is accompanied by a process of synaptic pruning in which some neural associations are established at the expense of others, fostering the relative stabilization of some emotional responses over time.[7] Caregivers significantly contribute to this process by encouraging certain responses and deterring others; social norms and encounters with other people further contribute to consolidating some emotional habits and brain structures with them. Eventually, an individual emotional episode is thus underpinned by a neural pattern whose shape is influenced by the local context, as well as having been molded by evolutionary and developmental forces.

3.3.3 Interpersonal Dynamics

Yet another domain of emotion theory to which dynamical systems principles have been applied is interpersonal relations. As we saw, in their discussion of crying and smiling, Fogel and Thelen (1987) already hinted at the role that interacting with others has on emotion expression. Patterns of crying, for example, change during the first year of life as infants develop the capacity to track the caregiver's responses to them. Crying also becomes incorporated into a more general "demand behavior" in which its various aspects are coordinated with other behaviors to obtain a response from the caregiver. On the basis of these and similar considerations, Fogel et al. (1992) proposed a "social process theory" of emotion in which they particularly emphasized the role of social context in shaping and organizing the emotional responses of infants. In later work, Fogel and colleagues have applied dynamical systems concepts to mother-infant interactions, identifying different patterns of dyadic coordination and their dependence on previous interactions (see Hsu and Fogel 2003; Lavelli and Fogel 2005). Most relevant for present purposes, in their study of smiles in six- to twelve-month-olds, Fogel et al. (2006) describe how different types of smiles are produced in different contexts, including interactions with different people. Four different types of smile are identified: *simple* smiles, with raised lip corners and no other facial action; BET's prototypical *Duchenne* smiles, with raised lip corners and raised cheeks; *play* smiles, characterized by a dropped jaw and also called "open mouth smile" or "gaping smile"; and so-called *duplay* smiles, involving raised lip corners, raised cheeks, and dropped jaw. Most smiles in the first weeks of age are endogenous; that is, they occur primarily during REM sleep and during transitions from waking to sleep. Smiles in social interactions appear at about two months, together with the ability to maintain eye contact and visual attention for a longer time. Between two and six months, different smiles appear in relation to various forms of sensory stimulation and in different contexts. Duchenne smiles, for example, are more likely than non-Duchenne smiles when mothers smile at infants, in speechlike nondistress vocalizations, and when infants gaze at their mothers in face-to-face play. After ten months, Duchenne smiles are more likely when infants greet their mothers after a brief separation, and non-Duchenne smiles more likely when they greet strangers. In addition, Fogel et al. found that infant smiles differ in kind, duration, and amplitude in different social games (tickle versus peekaboo), and in different phases of the games (setup versus climax). They conclude that simple smiles, Duchenne smiles, and duplay smiles have different functions, with simple smiles reflecting a background of enjoyment and maintaining the participants' mutual engagement, and Duchenne and duplay smiles reflecting an experience of buildup and completion of shared participation.

This work interestingly suggests a process of mutual coregulation and emotional attunement between infant and mother, in which the expression of emotion plays an important role in communicating and maintaining reciprocal engagement. In particular, in the mother-infant interaction, emotional expression in each interactant appears to be subtly dependent on the other's expression, such that we may consider the dyad a coupled system.[8] Fogel et al. (2006, 472) even claim that "rather than viewing each person's emotion as ... separate from each other, [dynamical systems theory] suggests that the other person's action is one component of emotion, which 'belongs' to the relationship system and not just the system within the skin boundary of the individual alone." From this perspective, emotional episodes can span two or even more organisms (see also Krueger, forthcoming, for the suggestion that emotions, in some cases at least, can be seen as "socially extended").

Granic (2000) similarly emphasizes that parent-child relations are best characterized by continuous reciprocal influences that lead to recurrent patterns of interaction that are difficult to undo once stabilized. This process is not driven by any one of the individuals involved but rather self-organizes as individuals respond to one another moment by moment and gradually sculpt a landscape of preferred modes of interaction. Aggressive parent-child relations, Granic argues, provide a good illustration of this process. These relations manifest recurrent patterns of reciprocal hostility ("coercive attractors") into which participants are "pulled," often without conscious intention or control. Such patterns are gradually carved in the course of several interactions over time. A mother prone to depression, for example, is more likely to appraise her child as particularly difficult or obstructive and to intrude in the child's behavior with frequent criticisms and disapprovals (Patterson 1982). This attitude in turn is likely to induce defensive and uncooperative behavior in the child, including aggressive attitudes such as yelling and arguing; the child is also likely to evaluate the mother as uncooperative and obstructive. The outcome is a complementary relationship in which each partner is a source of anger and frustration for the other, and the target of aggressive behavior. Importantly, these patterns are not deliberately established by the participants; rather, they take the forms they have in virtue of moment-to-moment affective-behavioral reciprocities that lead to the establishment of relational structures in which participants are, as they themselves report, out of control. Patterson (1982) observes that many of the parents of aggressive parent-child dyads are otherwise mild mannered and nonaggressive and are themselves puzzled by the hostility they display toward their children, which often includes aggressive shouting and physical beating (see Granic 2000).

From a dynamical systems perspective, however, one should also keep in mind that coupled systems such as parent-child dyads and spouses remain open and context dependent; the way the parts of these systems influence one another always depends on a variety of factors inside and outside them, and thus changes can always occur that will modify their coupling. Laible and Thompson (2000) argue that to explain the development of an infant's emotional style uniquely in terms of her relation to the primary caregiver, as attachment theory does, for example, is restrictive. Attachment theory notably explains the development of secure and insecure patterns of attachment primarily with reference to the mother's sensitivity and responsiveness to the infant. As Laible and Thompson point out, the idea that different patterns of behavior form as a consequence of previous interactions, and indeed that their development is constrained by them, is very much consistent with a dynamical systems approach. However, from the dynamical systems point of view, various factors *beyond* the primary caregiver can act as control parameters, such as other family members and affectively salient people. Moreover, these factors are themselves changeable; they vary over time, thus contributing to shifting modalities and styles of interpersonal coupling. This dynamical perspective importantly appears to fit the data better than merely dyadic attachment models. As Laible and Thompson point out, there is mixed evidence for the claim that the style of early mother-infant interactions predicts specific patterns of attachment; rather, attachment security appears to vary as family circumstances do. More empirical research is needed, however, to establish more precisely how factors other than the relationship to the primary caregiver affect attachment styles.

3.3.4 In Sum: Dynamical Emotional Episodes

The accounts just presented differ primarily in that they apply at very different levels of description of the organism—from neural structures, to facial and bodily expressions, to interpersonal relations. Yet overall they provide, I believe, a distinctive and coherent conceptualization of emotional episodes. Putting their insights together and drawing on the terminology introduced earlier, we can recapitulate by saying that, from a dynamical systems perspective, emotional episodes correspond to specific self-organizing forms or second-order constraints—*emotion forms*, as I shall call them—that recruit or entrain various processes (neural, muscular, autonomic, etc.) into highly integrated configurations or patterns. Reciprocal interactions among these various processes correspond to first-order constraints. Events in the organism and environment can influence the self-organization of the emotion form by acting as control parameters, although precisely which events play this role, and in which context, is not known (yet). Importantly, an organism can become coupled to another one (or other ones) via continuous reciprocal influences. In this case, we can talk of emotion forms instantiated by two (or more) organisms together in their coupling, with attractors that pull all organisms simultaneously into a specific interactive pattern.

Emotional episodes thus conceptualized can be highly variable, because the processes constituting them can organize themselves in different ways (by analogy, the convection rolls appearing in the Rayleigh-Bénard instability can vary in how the liquid's molecules organize themselves; the human organism is, of course, more complex and thus has many more possibilities of self-organization). Yet at the same time, the range of their possible variations is constrained by the topology of the state space, which is both evolutionarily and developmentally shaped. Regions of stability (attractors) within the state space pull variously constituted emotion forms toward or away from them. The presence of these regions guarantees relative stability in spite of variations, and the capacity of various processes (neural, muscular, etc.) to influence and constrain one another allows stability to be achieved in various ways.

3.4   Implications for the Debate on the Nature of the Emotions

This conceptualization has various implications for the debate on the nature of the emotions that we considered in the previous chapter. For one, it makes the notion of an internal affect program for coordinated responses redundant.[9] Dynamical emotion forms exhibit distinctive configurations not because they are outputs of internal instructions but because they result from a history of mutual influences between evolutionary and developmental factors that shape the organism in a certain way. As a bonus, this view makes all emotional episodes, including those usually associated with basic emotions, into open and flexible structures sensitive to local conditions, which naturally accounts for their variability and context dependence; there is no need in this view to posit acquired display rules for each deviation from BET's prototypical expressions. The variability found in infant expressions, especially very young ones who would not have had the chance to acquire display rules yet, is clearly a problem for BET. Yet even in adult expressions, it is more natural to posit emotional systems that are flexible from the beginning, rather than adding several ad hoc rules for each variant expression, neural or autonomic pattern, or behavior. Likewise, a dynamical conceptualization does not require each aspect of the emotional episode to be driven by a distinct appraisal process (as in the component process model). It does not necessarily reject the view that the brain and bodily processes recruited in emotional episodes may have specific functions (e.g., detecting novelty in the environment, preparing to attack), but it does not imply that this ought to be the case for *all* the components of an emotional episode, and that all these components must be preceded by a dedicated appraisal check. More in line with principles of physiological organization, it posits that existing physical constraints among components contribute to the form of emotional episodes, such that these components are not individually "led" or "driven" but collectively channeled into a specific pattern.

Another important aspect of this conceptualization is that it does not deny that biology plays a role in shaping emotion forms, and therefore it does not suffer from the difficulties of the psychological constructionist models highlighted in the previous chapter. Dynamical emotional episodes are not outputs of genetically determined affect programs, but this does not mean that genetic factors play no part in their formation. Rather, the idea is that genes are just *some* of the causal factors that contribute to shaping emotion forms over time. The ontogeny of the "emotional topology" of the organism is affected by genetic as well as environmental constraints. Genes contribute to setting up such a topology always in interaction with other factors variously distributed over brain, body, and world. We are far from being able to understand more specifically what makes certain emotional manifestations more stable across cultures than others; however, for present purposes, the aim is just to emphasize that a dynamical systems perspective enables a characterization of emotional episodes that does not force them into being *either* outputs of genetically determined programs *or* acts of categorization driven by linguistic concepts unrelated to our biological organization.[10]

What about the very notion of "basic" emotions? The suggested dynamical conceptualization applies to *all* emotional episodes and so does not draw a clear-cut division between basic and nonbasic emotions: according to it, all emotions come in complex organismic patterns subject to both evolutionary and developmental pressures. In this sense, this view can thus be seen as entailing a version of the unity thesis, although importantly not a building-block one. According to it, in fact, emotional episodes are whole organismic patterns and as such do not contain other emotional episodes as parts. Thus, for example, an episode of jealousy comes as a whole (open and flexible) organismic form and does not contain within itself a different emotional episode, such as anger. An episode of jealousy may *lead* to one of anger, and vice versa, and overlap partially with it in the sense that some of the neural, autonomic, and expressive processes constituting an episode of jealousy may also be recruited in the same organism during an episode of anger. Yet the overall form of an episode of jealousy will entrain the organism in a different pattern from an episode of anger and will thus not be reducible to an episode of anger (or some other emotion) "plus" something else. From the present dynamical perspective, it is thus possible for two or more emotions to blend and form mixtures of various kinds, but only by being integrated into a new form that is not a linear sum of different emotion forms.

Rejecting the building-block approach does not imply that looking for cross-cultural and culture-specific emotional manifestations is not a valid research enterprise. Quite the contrary, from a dynamical systems perspective, it is interesting to investigate whether certain configurations remain stable or robust across cultures, including when and in which contexts they appear in development, and the range of variations they exhibit (if they do), including whether recurrent variations depend on specific control parameters. Importantly, however, this investigation would not have to be restricted to a small number of emotions. Rather, it would be part of a broad research program aiming to explore the facial and bodily expression of a large number of emotions across cultures, with no prejudice that only some emotions will be found to be manifested in similar ways across cultures. At the same time, from a dynamical systems perspective, it would also be interesting to look for culture-specific or even individual differences in emotion expression, with the specific intent of identifying the relevant patterns, their context and developmental trajectory, and the extent to which they can be seen as either culture-specific modifications of the pan-cultural expressions or entirely novel configurations. This research program (which is very much like the one Darwin began almost a century and a half ago) could also be accompanied by an investigation into the functions of specific emotional manifestations and their components, keeping in mind, however, the capacity of context to influence and even modify these functions.

This account is to some extent consistent with Jason Clark's (2010) recent proposal to view the "higher cognitive emotions" as *homologous* with the basic ones. Clark takes issue with Griffiths's (1997) disunity thesis, according to which, as we saw, affect programs and higher cognitive emotions belong to two distinct natural kinds, evolved separately, with different functions and recruiting different structures. Clark, rather, proposes that higher cognitive emotions are united with basic emotions in a pattern of ancestry and descent (i.e., the same way in which human arms are united with other vertebrate limbs, including bats' wings and seals' flippers). He also proposes seeing higher cognitive emotions as modifications of basic mechanisms to adapt to increasingly complex environments: "As environments (especially social environments) become more complex and variable through evolution and development, emotions must keep pace. Simply possessing a set of stereotyped responses to a limited range of stimuli (while still essential in some situations) is no longer a feasible option" (J. Clark 2010, 89).

He illustrates this point with the detailed discussion of one emotion, shame. He argues first against the widespread view that shame, as a "pure" higher cognitive emotion, has no characteristic physiology and expression and is present only in humans. Rather, he maintains that human shame in its present form has emerged from a rank-related emotion in nonhuman mammals, whose primary function was to signal subordinance to a dominant other so as to appease him (see also, e.g., Fessler 2007; Gilbert 2007). Importantly, evidence indicates that this emotion has characteristic expressive and behavioral features such as shrinking posture, gaze aversion, avoiding social contact, and hiding (e.g., Fessler 2007), as well as characteristic patterned physiological (Gruenewald, Dickerson, and Kemeny 2007) and neural (e.g., J. Beer 2007) activity. Second, Clark points out that this form of shame (basic shame, as he calls it) appears to be retained in humans; in particular, autonomic activity seems to be largely the same (e.g., Dickerson, Gruenewald, and Kemeny 2004). However, its functional breadth is wider. For one, in contemporary societies characterized by "prestige hierarchies," shame is associated with loss of prestige (rather than of physical dominance) in competitions for positive social attention and socially valued traits and possessions. Also, it has acquired the function of facilitating cooperation by signaling awareness of the violation of norms and the desire to adhere to them. Clark ultimately suggests that we view the basic form of shame as a precursor of human shame, where human shame has retained many of the traits of basic shame but has also acquired different (yet related) functions, in virtue of the increasing sociocognitive complexities of humans. Human shame is thus not an entirely new and different emotion from its basic form but is continuous with it. Precisely what kind of homology exists between the two forms of shame, Clark specifies, is not possible to say in light of existing evidence. One possibility is that human shame is a more complex version of basic shame that has entirely replaced the earlier form and thus become the only form of shame present in humans (single-trait homology). Another possibility is that basic and more complex forms of shame coexist in humans; in particular, basic shame is retained within modular structures, whereas more complex shame recruits cognitive resources (serial homology).

Clark's general suggestion that complex emotions are homologous with basic ones is largely consistent with the dynamical conceptualization proposed here, because it posits unity among emotions without adopting a building-block view and acknowledges the plasticity of basic emotions (though it retains the construct), as well as the power of the environment to mold these basic emotions into different ones that retain basic features while also adapting to new contexts and developing new functions. The two views differ, however, in that the dynamical perspective predicts that human emotional episodes will manifest a broader spectrum of variability than the one Clark seems willing to acknowledge (based on existing evidence). If it is the case, as Clark himself suggests, that as the environment becomes more complex, the emotions must keep pace, then the dynamical prediction is that they will become more complex not just in *function* but in appearance, so to speak, namely, in their neural, behavioral, and bodily manifestations. Thus one is likely to find forms of shame in humans that not only have broader functionality than homologous states in other mammals but also show larger variability in terms of facial expressions, neural concomitants, autonomic changes, and so on—as well as a sensitivity toward a wider and more complex range of stimuli. The extent to which shame comes in different forms in humans, and the extent to which one can find homologies across mammals, cross-cultural similarities, and culture-specific differences in manifestations of shame, are all empirical questions that still need to be addressed.

3.5   Discreteness and Boundaries

The dynamical characterization of emotional episodes proposed earlier has implications also for the notion of *discrete* emotions. This label is widely used in affective science but is not clearly defined. Basic emotions are often characterized as discrete (indeed, the phrase "discrete emotion theory" is often used interchangeably with "basic emotion theory") to emphasize that basic emotions are "distinct" or "separate" from one another.[11] What exactly this means, however, is not clear. Discrete emotion accounts are sometimes contrasted with dimensional accounts, according to which all the emotions have something in common; namely, they all vary along the same dimensions, such as valence and arousal (as in Russell's and Barrett's models; see chap. 2). However, this contrast is misleading, because BET does not deny that basic emotions vary in valence and arousal; recall, for example, that Tomkins (1962) divided his affect programs into positive and negative ones and acknowledged that each of them varies in intensity. On the other hand, dimensional theorists do not deny that emotions differ from one another; recall, for example, that Russell (2003) listed other components of emotion besides core affect.[12] In addition, a closer look at BET reveals that its basic emotions are not discrete in the sense of being entirely separate from one another. Only the affect programs appear to be nonoverlapping (if we think of them as sets of internal rules for the generation of patterned responses). Yet the *outputs* of such programs are shared between different basic emotions. For example, in the case of facial expressions, in BET activation of action unit 4 (the brow lowerer) is considered part of the prototypical expressions of anger, sadness, and fear; similarly, the activation of action unit 5 (the upper lid raiser) is considered part of the prototypical expressions of both fear and anger (Ekman and Friesen 1978). Although it is true that, as Scherer and Ellgring (2007) emphasize, BET predicts that some facial expressions will come in "tight packages" with minimal overlap, BET does not predict *total* separateness. This is even more apparent in the case of autonomic activity, where basic emotion theorists look for specific directions and magnitudes of the *same* dimensions of autonomic arousal, such as skin conductance, skin temperature, heart rate, and so on (see, e.g., Matsumoto and Ekman 2009, 71: "Anger, for instance, produces vasodilation, pupil constriction, foaming, and piloerection. ... Fear, however, produces vasoconstriction, pupil dilation, and bulging eyes"; see also Levenson 2003). In other words, they look at the autonomic system as a *whole* complex system and are interested in whether or not, as such a whole, it behaves differently for each affect program. Finally, neuroscientists sympathetic to BET do not see the neural circuits of basic emotions as nonoverlapping, either. Notably, according to Panksepp (e.g., 1998a, 2005, 2007), basic emotional systems are associated with distinctive complex patterns of neural and chemical activity; these neurochemical patterns, as Panksepp (2007, 288) claims, are "distinct," though "neural diversities do not mean that many brain emotional action systems do not share some common arousal functions. Clearly, brain norepinephrine and serotonin systems influence every emotion." Panksepp (2005, 33) also reports a table representing global neurochemical dynamics that, he claims, characterize *all* basic emotional systems.

From a dynamical systems perspective, every emotional episode is a mode of self-organization of the whole organism (an emotion form, as defined earlier). Some recur more often and robustly than others and exhibit a small range of variations; other forms recur reliably only in some cultures or even individuals; still other forms emerge only on a few occasions. So in the sense that emotional episodes differ from one another, they can be seen as "discrete." But otherwise there is no expectation that all emotional episodes are classifiable as instances of more or less universally or culturally recognized categories; some are, but some may well not be— rather, some will be idiosyncratic, messy-looking patterns with their own irreducible form, at times reminiscent of more familiar configurations, at other times definitely strange.

What about the *boundaries* of emotional episodes? As mentioned in chapter 2, affect programs in BET are initiated by automatic appraisals that mark the beginning of an emotional episode, which is typically short-lived and lasts as long as the various processes making it up occur. Emotional episodes thus have a clear beginning and end. From the present dynamical systems perspective, it is also possible to identify with relative precision when a certain emotional episode begins or ends: specific events may induce rapid shifts in the state space, with a quick entrainment of the organism into an emotion form; likewise, emotion forms may be rapidly undone. Other episodes, however, may involve a slower process, with emotion forms emerging and dissolving gradually (think of irritation that builds up during the day, or of anger that lingers on even after its cause has been modified or removed).

If we return to the broader framework of enactivism, we can add that, from an enactive perspective, emotional episodes as dynamical patterns should not be seen as forming against an otherwise nonaffective background (as seemingly implied by BET). The proposal, rather, is to view emotional episodes as coherent patterns of an organism that is always already affective in virtue of its being a sense-making system, as discussed in chapter 1. Emotional episodes as characterized here are instantiations of such sense-making activity, where the organism self-organizes into this or that emotion form. To the extent that these emotion forms can be identified and distinguished from one another, we can consider them "discrete." Yet between them, so to speak, the organism remains affectively engaged.

3.6 Moods

The question of the boundaries of emotional episodes is also related to the question of the relationship between emotions and moods. We saw in chapter 1 that affective scientists do not draw a clear or sharp distinction between the two; they conceive of moods generally as less intense and longer lasting than emotions. We can now consider this claim more closely. Intensity is not, I think, particularly useful for distinguishing between emotions and moods. Emotional episodes vary considerably in intensity, ranging from the mild to the overpowering, across and within emotion categories; likewise for moods. Certainly not all emotional episodes are intense, and not all moods are mild; one can be moderately amused or annoyed at something, as well as overwhelmingly anxious for a long time. Duration strikes me as a comparatively better marker of the difference between emotions and moods. In particular, it seems important to distinguish between short-lived episodes that involve rapid changes in a variety of brain and bodily processes, and more persistent conditions. What we call moods tend to refer to longer-lasting conditions rather than comparatively short-lived episodes; true, emotional episodes can vary in duration (compare a short-lived episode of disgust at the sight or smell of vomit with an episode of anger during a quarrel), but we do not usually say that one has the blues or is depressed only for just a minute or so.

The relationship between emotions and moods is not completely captured in terms of a difference in duration, however. What is also important is that moods appear to facilitate some emotional episodes more than others, and conversely that the recurrence of certain emotional episodes appears to induce shifts in mood. When one is cranky, for example, one is more likely to burst out at others with anger; or when one is anxious, one is more likely to be frightened by events that would not normally have this effect. On the other hand, reiterated episodes of fear can increase one's wariness and lead to sustained anxiety.

A dynamical systems approach has the conceptual resources to make sense of these interdependencies. As discussed so far, we can think of emotional episodes as rapidly forming emergent patterns of the organism that last for a few seconds or minutes. Changes from one emotional episode to another can be seen as shifts of the organism from one attractor to another. Moods can also be seen as emergent organismic patterns, but as more persistent ones, lasting for hours, days, or even weeks. Note that like emotional episodes, moods appear to exhibit distinctive organismic features. Some of them are familiar and observable in everyday attitudes; someone in a cheerful mood, for example, usually smiles and laughs more than someone in a grumpy mood, whereas someone in a grumpy mood tends to frown and pout more. In addition, empirical evidence indicates that different moods come with different neural and autonomic patterns of activity (Thayer 1989); we know from the rapidly developing field of psychopharmacology that mood disorders such as depression and anxiety are characterized by neurochemical activity that can be modified by specific drugs (e.g., Nemeroff 1998).[13] The suggestion is to think of moods as relatively persistent organismic patterns—*mood forms*, as we may call them—that affect not just the state of the organism at a given time but the kinds of emotional episodes it is likely to enact. Dynamically speaking, we can say that moods make some emotional episodes more likely than others by affecting the topology of the organism's state space. Changes in moods shift the landscape of attractors and repellors, pulling or "enslaving" brain and bodily processes more toward certain emotion forms than others. Conversely, the reiteration of certain emotion forms can carve a topology that leads to the relative stabilization of certain mood forms.[14] It is useful to think of the relationship between moods and emotional episodes as analogous to that between climate zones and weather. A climate zone (e.g., tropical, humid continental, Mediterranean) is a complex system characterized by distinctive conditions (such as average temperature, rainfall, humidity) that remain stable over time. Different climate zones are characterized by different weather, namely, short-lived manifestations of specific conditions. Climate zones are longer lived and set up the conditions for different weather patterns; in particular, some weather phenomena are possible only within certain climate zones and impossible in others (e.g., tropical cyclones develop in tropical regions and not in deserts). On the other hand, the reiteration of certain weather patterns may induce shifts in the climate zone, especially when in conjunction with changes taking place outside the climate zone itself (e.g., recurrent higher rainfalls may change a dry zone into a humid one). Likewise, we can conceive of moods as setting up the conditions for different emotion forms; some emotional episodes typically take place in the context of certain moods rather than others (e.g., a bout of enthusiasm typically takes place in a cheerful rather than grumpy mood). On the other hand, the reiteration of certain emotional episodes may lead to a different mood, especially when in conjunction with changes in the organism's environment; for example, repeated episodes of sadness and disappointment may lead to a depressive mood, especially in conjunction with an unsupportive environment. The analogy can be taken only so far, of course, and we should not stipulate a priori that certain moods make certain emotional episodes impossible, or that a certain emotional episode cannot ever occur unless one is in a certain mood. However, I think the analogy is useful to illustrate the dynamical reciprocities among phenomena affecting the same system but occurring at different timescales.[15]

Another way of drawing the distinction between emotions and moods that is more common in philosophy refers to their intentionality, namely, their capacity to intend, refer to, or be about objects or events in the world. According to some philosophers, the main difference between emotions and moods is that only emotions are intentional states, whereas moods are not about anything. Anger, for example, is typically directed at a specific object (e.g., a colleague's offensive remark), but one does not feel cranky or low about anything (see, e.g., De Sousa 1987). Other philosophers do not deny that moods are intentional, but they take their objects to be general or nonspecific—such as "everything," "one's whole life," or "the world" (see Solomon 2007; Goldie 2000; Ben-Ze'ev 2010). For Solomon (2007, 42), for example, depression involves "a global attitude to the world," in which one "is depressed, not just about something but about everything."

I think it is true that emotions and moods differ in their intentional character, and emotions in particular are about specific objects.[16] However, I do not think that moods are adequately described as being either nonintentional or about general objects. To say that they are not about anything seems to reduce them to a sort of self-enclosed, isolated subjective condition detached from the world. Yet when I am cheerful, for example, I am not in a "free-floating" feeling state, oblivious to the world. Rather, my cheerfulness seems better characterized as involving a specific mode of experiencing various events. We may say that in cheerfulness, aspects of the world appear in a cheerful light, or that I *bathe* in cheerful happenings, so to speak, such that my cheerfulness and their cheerfulness are not distinguished in experience (likewise for the warmth of my skin and the warmth of the water when I am immersed in a bath). Similarly for "darker" moods, such as gloom or grief, where it may be more tempting to claim that the experience is isolated or self-enclosed. Clinically depressed people notably report feeling alienated, isolated, and cut off from the world; this experience is often accompanied by an exaggerated attention toward one's bodily sensations (Fuchs 2005). Yet arguably even in these cases the world keeps looming. The depressive's exaggerated attention to and concern for her body do not appear to involve an absolute lack of world directedness. Rather, such a focus appears to come with an alteration in the ordinary way of experiencing the world. In particular, the world, including other people, is not experienced as affording possibilities for action and affective connectedness with others anymore; it is experienced as further removed from oneself, unreachable and alien. Depressed people also often complain of a sense of suffocation, of being cut off from the world, while at the same time they retain a sense that other people are not affected in the same way (for more details, see Ratcliffe 2008, 61–63; 2009).

Should we say, then, that moods are about general rather than specific objects? I find it hard to make sense of the notion of a general intentional object. How can an experience be *about* "everything" or "the world"? It does not seem possible for an experience to refer at once to all objects or events in the world. The source of the difficulty, it seems to me, is the assumption that to be intentional, an experience has to be *object* directed. Given this assumption, if one wants to deny that moods are about specific objects without denying that they are intentional, the only option is to say that moods are about nonspecific, that is, general, objects.

A way around this is to say that moods are intentional not in the narrow sense that they target objects but in the broader sense that they are "open" to the world. This broader sense of intentionality does not usually feature in analytic philosophical accounts but has been recognized and elaborated in phenomenology. Husserl notably identified a non-object-oriented form of intentionality, which he called "operative intentionality" (*fungierende Intentionalität*) and characterized as a broad "openness" toward otherness (see Thompson and Zahavi 2007). This concept was taken up by Merleau-Ponty ([1945] 1962), who in the preface to his *Phenomenology of Perception* portrayed it as an "enlarged notion" of intentionality, at work in our desires, evaluations, and "landscape" of consciousness *before* intentional acts are directed toward specific objects. Moods can be seen as intentional in this "operative" way, as conscious states that do not intend objects but are open to the world before any object-directed intentional act.

Interestingly, Husserl himself discussed the intentionality of moods in unpublished manuscripts, where he portrayed moods as having an "unclear intentionality" and yet as playing a decisive role in the constitution of objects in experience, by disclosing or "illuminating" the world in the first place (see N. Lee 1998, 114–118). This work may well have influenced Heidegger's ([1926] 1996) account of mood, according to which, as we saw, moods are fundamental modes of existence that disclose one's embeddedness in the world, indeed, that make it possible in the first place to direct oneself toward anything in particular. Heidegger's view has been taken up more recently by Ratcliffe (2008) in his account of what he calls *existential feelings*, namely, "background feelings" that present the lived world to the experiencing subject in one way or the other—as familiar, inhospitable, empty of possibilities, uncanny, and so on. Like Heideggerian moods, existential feelings are not object directed (Ratcliffe calls them "pre-intentional") but rather backdrop experiences against which specific intentional states such as emotions take place, and which make emotions possible in the first place. As Ratcliffe (2010) also puts it, existential feelings, as background conditions of possibility for specific object-directed emotions, are "deeper" than the specific emotions.

I see the present suggestion to conceptualize moods as topologies that make some emotional episodes more likely than others as complementing these phenomenological considerations. In particular, however, this suggestion needs to be placed back in the broader context of the enactive approach and the notion of sense making introduced in chapter 1. From an enactive perspective, even deeper than moods and existential feelings is the sense-making activity of the organism, its primordial affectivity in virtue of its being an adaptive autonomous system. As we saw, this deep level of meaning generation is not a prerogative of human beings only; it belongs to all living systems. We can think of human beings as able to manifest a variety of moods and emotions in virtue of their being first of all living organisms. The capacity for sense making grounds or makes possible the human capacity for more complex cognitive-affective states, in a progressive differentiation and refinement of forms, from Heidegger's moods or existential feelings, to more ordinary moods, to emotional episodes.

3.7 Conclusion

To recapitulate, drawing on various strands of empirical evidence, as well as more theoretical proposals in dynamical affective science, in this chapter I have argued that emotions, or better emotional episodes, are best conceptualized as dynamical patterns, namely, as self-organizing configurations of the organism or "emotion forms." These patterns are flexible and loosely assembled, can be culture specific and even individual specific, but may also recur reliably across cultures. Affective science should investigate the occurrence and frequency of these patterns, and whether and how they come in variations of the same "themes." Importantly, this investigation should occur without prejudice as to which episodes are expressed pan-culturally and which are not. In place of the view that some emotions are more fundamental than others, in the sense of being building blocks of other emotions (see previous chapter), I claimed that each emotional episode should be seen as a complex dynamical pattern that has been shaped over evolutionary and developmental time. I also discussed moods, proposing to conceptualize them as dynamical patterns of the organism as well (as "mood forms," in this case). Compared to emotional episodes, moods are usually longer lived and are not about objects, although they remain "open to the world." I suggested that an important difference between emotion forms and mood forms is their timescale. In particular, a dynamical systems perspective can naturally account for the fact that the mood one is in influences one's emotions, and conversely that recurrent emotional episodes of a certain kind can induce changes in moods.

4 Reappraising Appraisal

4.1 Introduction

I now leave the debate around basic emotions and turn to the so-called *cognitive* approach in affective science and its central notion, *appraisal*. In particular, in this chapter I focus on the relationship between this notion and what are usually seen as the bodily aspects or components of emotion (e.g., autonomic arousal, expression, action tendencies). As we shall see, in psychology, appraisal has typically been characterized as a factor or component of emotion neatly *distinct* from these bodily aspects. In other words, appraisal has been characterized as a *disembodied* cognitive phenomenon. At the same time, the bodily aspects of emotion have been relegated to the role of noncognitive "responses," extrinsic to the process of appraising.

The enactive approach entails a very different conceptualization of appraisal. As we saw in chapter 1, the enactive approach characterizes cognition at its most basic level as a process of sense making enacted by the situated organism as it brings forth its own world of meaning. In this chapter, we shall see that this notion of cognition has implications for the notion of appraisal and its relationship to the body; specifically it implies that appraisal is not neatly distinct from the bodily aspects of emotion but in fact embodied.

Before outlining this idea, I trace the history of the notion of appraisal in psychology, showing how the cognitive approach to emotion became progressively uninterested in the body in the 1960s and 1970s. At the time, the body was seen, at best, as contributing to emotion merely in the form of an undifferentiated pattern of physiological arousal that needed to be interpreted by cognition to give rise to specific emotions. Experimental research was primarily interested in the effects on emotion of manipulating cognition, with little or no interest in the body (for instance, in its possible autonomic differentiation or in its possible influence on appraisal itself). This attitude changed in the 1980s, and cognitive emotion theorists today see the body as an important and differentiated component of emotion. In addition, they acknowledge that the body can affect appraisal. Even so, however, they still view appraisal as clearly distinct from the body. Even in complex interactive frameworks such as the component process model discussed earlier, appraisal remains a disembodied, "wholly heady" cognitive phenomenon whose function is to evaluate objects and events and steer the body accordingly.

Next I point out that some recent neuroscientific accounts have started to challenge this framework, arguing that cognition and emotion overlap widely at the brain level. These arguments undermine the view that appraisal can be neatly separated from the rest of emotion as its cognitive component (or from emotion altogether, when it is seen as its cognitive antecedent). Finally, I turn to the enactive approach, to its notion of cognition as sense making, and what it implies for the notion of appraisal. After showing in which sense, from an enactive perspective, appraisal is not disembodied but enacted by the living organism, I turn to the phenomenology of appraising (rarely discussed in affective science) and argue that, at the level of lived experience, it is not appropriate either to separate appraisal from the rest of emotion, including its bodily feelings.

4.2 Beginnings

The notion of appraisal was introduced in modern psychology by Magda Arnold (1960a), largely as a reaction against the most influential emotion theories of the time. These theories, Arnold remarked, were interested only in the bodily and behavioral aspects of emotion, with no concern for how emotions are elicited in the first place. Notably both James (1884) and Lange ([1885] 1922) had identified emotions with perceptions of bodily changes; behaviorism had reduced emotions to "pattern-reactions" in the body (e.g., J. Watson 1919); and activation theories had identified emotions with different degrees of "activation" or "energy" of the organism (e.g., Duffy 1941). Arnold complained that these accounts could not explain why, for example, the same stimulus can induce different emotional responses in different individuals; or why at different times the same individual can react differently to the same stimulus. She then argued that these differences depend on the fact that individuals respond not to stimuli per se but to *appraised* stimuli. In particular, stimuli elicit emotions when they affect an individual "personally," in relation to her or his aims: "To arouse an emotion, the object must be appraised as affecting me in some way, affecting me personally as an individual with my particular experience and my particular aims" (Arnold 1960a, 171).

For Arnold, the process of appraisal was first and foremost what she called a *sense judgment*; namely, it was "direct, immediate, nonreflective, nonintellectual, automatic, 'instinctive,' intuitive" (175). Deliberate, conscious appraisals (which she called *reflective judgments* or *secondary evaluations*), in her view, were rare and in any case always dependent on intuitive appraisals. Importantly, Arnold considered appraisal to be just one component of emotion. Emotion, in her view, also included changes in autonomic nervous system (ANS) activity, motor tendencies, actual approach and withdrawal behavior, and feeling. In particular, like James and Lange, she held that different emotions involve different patterns of ANS activity. Summing up her approach, she defined emotion as "the felt tendency toward anything intuitively appraised as good (beneficial), or away from anything intuitively appraised as bad (harmful). This attraction or aversion is accompanied by a pattern of physiological changes organized toward approach or withdrawal. The patterns differ for different emotions" (Arnold 1960a, 182).

Arnold's concept of appraisal was further elaborated by Richard Lazarus (1966), who distinguished between the continuous process of monitoring whether what is happening is *relevant* to one's goals and values (what he called the *primary* appraisal), and the assessment of how one can *cope* with events that are appraised as relevant, for example, as threats or opportunities (the *secondary* appraisal). For example, evaluating failing a university exam as an obstacle to the goal of graduating is a primary appraisal; considering the reasons for the result, blaming oneself or others for it, deciding to study more, and so on, are all secondary appraisals.

Lazarus later also introduced the notion of *core relational themes*, which refers to the fundamental "topics" around which the various appraisal processes that elicit an emotional episode are organized. The idea is that each emotional episode is elicited by a set of separate appraisals that evaluate different aspects of an event (this event is relevant for my goal, it prevents me from attaining my goal, I can do something about it, etc.). Individually, these appraisals provide only "partial meanings"; yet in an emotional episode they are combined into "a terse synthesis," namely, a larger, "holistic" meaning, which is the core relational theme of the emotion in question (Lazarus 2001, 64). Each emotion has its own core relational theme. For example, the core theme of sadness is "having experienced an irrevocable loss," the theme of anger is "a demeaning offense against me and mine," the theme of guilt is "having transgressed a moral imperative," and the theme of envy is "wanting to have what someone else does" (Lazarus 2001, 64, lists core relational themes for seventeen emotions). Core relational themes and appraisals thus represent different levels of abstraction, with the themes being more abstract than the appraisals, that is, "idealized statements" expressing the core meaning of individual emotions. Another way to characterize the difference is to say that core relational meanings capture the paradigmatic topic or object of each emotion, whereas individual appraisals are specific evaluations of aspects of a situation that are not distinctive of any emotion but can be shared among them.

Experimental work also began in the 1960s to show how emotional responses are affected and modulated by appraisals. In an influential study, Speisman et al. (1964) showed subjects a distressing anthropological documentary portraying crude genital operations conducted among Australian aborigines on adolescent boys undergoing a rite of passage into adulthood (the rite involved cutting the underside of the penis with a sharpened piece of flint). In the "silent" condition, subjects simply watched a silent version of the film. In the "traumatic" condition, they listened at the same time to a sound track that emphasized the harmful character of the events, such as the pain and the danger of the operation. In the "denial" condition, a different sound track explained that the operation was safe and painless, and the boys looked forward to it as part of the process of becoming adults. In the fourth condition, the sound track intellectualized the events by providing a scientific description from the perspective of a detached anthropologist. Measures of skin conductance responses showed that subjects in the traumatic condition were most distressed, followed by those who watched the silent version. Subjects in the denial and intellectualization condition were less disturbed than subjects watching the silent film. This study confirmed the hypothesis that the same visual stimulus can induce a different emotional response (a stress response, in this case) depending on how subjects appraise it. In a follow-up study, Lazarus and Alfert (1964) focused on the denial condition and set out to establish whether providing information minimizing the risks of the operation *before* rather than during the film can also influence the subjects' response. They found that providing denial information before the film reduced physiological stress even more than providing the same information during the film. This finding provided further support for the claim that cognition can influence the emotional response; in particular, it showed that emotional responses to the same stimulus can be influenced by manipulating cognition even before the stimulus is presented.

4.3   Downplaying the Body in the 1960s and 1970s

These were the first of a large number of studies conducted in the 1960s and 1970s on the effects of cognition on stress and emotion more generally. For present purposes, it is notable that in these years the cognitive approach to emotion distanced itself from Arnold's views; in particular, it came to markedly *downplay* the role of the body in emotion, in various respects.

4.3.1   The Assumption of Physiological Uniformity

For one, it oversimplified the contribution of the body to emotion by reducing it to an undifferentiated pattern of physiological (i.e., autonomic) arousal. Arnold, as we saw, believed that emotions are physiologically differentiated. Indeed, previous evidence, which she reviewed systematically, had indicated that at least some emotions involve distinct patterns of ANS activity. Ax (1953), for example, had found that fear and anger differed along seven physiological dimensions, including respiration, muscle tension, blood pressure, heart rate, and skin conductance; similar results had been obtained for anger by Funkenstein, King, and Drolette 1954 (see also Mittelmann and Wolff 1943; and further references in Arnold 1960b). Yet in the 1960s and 1970s cognitive emotion theorists embraced the half-a-century-older view of physiological arousal as largely *undifferentiated*, and thus insufficient to discriminate among emotions. This view went back to Cannon (1914), who had developed it as part of his critique of the thesis, advanced by James (1884) and Lange ([1885] 1922), that different emotions involve different patterns of bodily changes. Cannon (1914) maintained that the visceral processes occurring in fear, anger, and pain resemble those occurring in intense joy, sorrow, and disgust. In his later, more detailed critique, he reiterated, among other things, that visceral activity is too uniform to differentiate between emotional episodes, and between emotional and nonemotional episodes: "The sympathetic system goes into action as a unity. ... The responses in the viscera seem too uniform to offer a satisfactory means of distinguishing emotions which are very different in subjective quality" (Cannon 1927, 110).

In spite of later contrary evidence, this view influenced theories and experiments widely from the 1960s to the early 1980s. Notably, it played a major role in the elaboration of Schachter and Singer's (1962) *two-factor theory* of emotion. Schachter and Singer characterized physiological arousal as "a general pattern of excitation of the sympathetic nervous system" (379) and maintained that it is *cognition* that distinguishes between different emotional episodes; physiological arousal contributes only to their felt intensity. Specifically, for Schachter and Singer, an emotional episode necessarily involves a state of physiological arousal, and a process of *labeling* this state on the basis of situational cues. Thus, for example, an episode of anger corresponds to a state of physiological arousal labeled "anger" by the subject on the basis of the detection of some event as offensive. Note the stark appraisal/body dualism entailed by this view, where appraisal is taken to do all the "smart" interpretive work, and the contribution of the body is relegated to one of mere excitation that by itself remains meaningless. The body in the two-factor theory is by itself "naked," so to speak, and it needs to be cognitively "dressed" to give rise to emotion.

Schachter and Singer (1962) conducted a famous study in the attempt to provide evidence for the two-factor theory. This study has been extensively discussed and criticized (e.g., Maslach 1979; Reisenzein 1983), but it is worth presenting once more in some detail, to illustrate how the assumption of a uniform physiological arousal influenced experimental practice in these years.

Schachter and Singer recruited subjects by telling them that they were interested in the effects on vision of a vitamin supplement called "Suproxin." They first divided the subjects randomly into two groups and injected one group not with Suproxin but with epinephrine (adrenaline), which induces sympathetic arousal; they injected the subjects in the other group with a saline solution without side effects. Then they reassigned all subjects to one of three conditions that differed in terms of the information provided about the possible side effects of the injection:

(1) "Epinephrine ignorant" subjects were not told anything; after the injection, the experimenter simply left.

(2) "Epinephrine informed" subjects were told that Suproxin can have some side effects such as palpitations, trembling, and flushes (these are indeed typical side effects of epinephrine).

(3) "Epinephrine misinformed" subjects were told that Suproxin can have some side effects such as itches and headaches (these are not typical effects of epinephrine).

Finally, all subjects were led to a waiting room to let the injection take effect. In the room, another subject was waiting, who in reality was a confederate in the experiment. Subjects were assigned to two conditions intended to manipulate their emotional state. In the *euphoria* condition, the confederate behaved in a happy and funny way, including making paper planes and playing with a hula hoop. In the *anger* condition, subjects had to fill out a questionnaire that contained indiscreet questions about their sexual habits and those of their mothers; the confederate was grumpy, became increasingly angry at the questions, and eventually ripped up the questionnaire. The experimenters observed the subjects through a one-way mirror and measured their emotional state via self-reports immediately after the manipulation; they also measured the subjects' pulse rate before and after it.

As one would expect with such a complicated experimental design, the results were mixed and difficult to interpret. Schachter and Singer (1962) nevertheless identified results that, in their view, clearly supported three theoretical points. First, subjects injected with epinephrine in the "epinephrine ignorant" condition gave behavioral and self-report indications that they had been manipulated into either euphoria or anger, supporting the point that "given a state of physiological arousal for which an individual has no immediate explanation, he will label this state and describe his feelings in terms of the cognitions available to him" (398), that is, in terms of how he appraises the situation in which he is. Second, subjects injected with epinephrine in the "epinephrine informed" condition were immune to the manipulation, supporting the point that "given a state of physiological arousal for which an individual has a completely appropriate explanation, no evaluative needs will arise and the individual is unlikely to label his feelings in terms of the alternative cognitions available" (398). Third, subjects injected with the saline solution in the "epinephrine ignorant" condition could not be manipulated into either euphoria or anger, hence: "Given the same cognitive circumstances, the individual will react emotionally or describe his feelings as emotions only to the extent that he experiences a state of physiological arousal" (398).

Note the minimal consideration shown to the body in this study. The experimenters took only a crude measure of physiological arousal, namely, the pulse rate. This measure indicated that epinephrine did in fact induce a stronger physiological arousal than the saline solution. However, no other physiological dimension was measured. Thus it is not possible to know whether physiological arousal became differentiated in the euphoria and anger conditions, and therefore whether differences in physiological arousal may have contributed to the subject's different behavioral and self-reports in these conditions (on this point, see also the early critique in Plutchik and Ax 1967).

Similar considerations apply to many other studies conducted in the 1960s and 1970s, which were influenced by the two-factor theory. So-called *misattribution* and *arousal transfer* studies were particularly interested in showing that physiological arousal can induce different emotions depending on how it is interpreted. In a classic study, Zillmann and Bryant (1974) had some subjects ride an exercise bicycle vigorously to increase their arousal, and others perform a nonarousing task (disc threading); some subjects in either condition were then insulted by a confederate. When given the opportunity to retaliate after a short delay, subjects in the state of heightened arousal displayed more aggressiveness toward the confederate. Subjects in the high arousal condition who were not insulted, however, did not display high levels of aggressiveness. This result was interpreted as supporting the view that physiological arousal needs to be labeled or attributed to an emotional source to induce an emotion. In another much-cited study, Dutton and Aron (1974) told subjects that they were interested in the influence of landscape on creativity. They asked some male subjects to narrate a story to an attractive female confederate while standing in the middle of the swaying Capilano Bridge in Vancouver, hanging 230 feet over shallow rapids; other subjects had to do the same, but on a solid cedar bridge with high handrails built 10 feet over a small rivulet. Subjects in the first condition turned out to use more sexual imagery in their story, and relatively more subjects in this condition also ended up calling the confederate after the experiment to learn more about it (she had given them her phone number as part of the study). The experimenters explained the result by claiming that the physiological arousal induced by being on the swaying bridge was "transferred" and induced attraction toward the confederate.

Note that in both studies, physiological arousal was simply *assumed* to be uniform throughout the experiment. As in Schachter and Singer's study, no attention was given to the possibility that different experimental conditions could have induced physiological differentiation that was itself (rather than some process of cognitive attribution) responsible for the observed different emotional responses. Being insulted and being in the presence of an attractive person could indeed well have induced specific patterns of physiological arousal that might have influenced the subject's emotion and behavior.

Perhaps the most extreme illustration of this downplaying attitude toward the body can be seen in Valins's (1966) study, intended to show that *believing* that one is physiologically aroused is sufficient to elicit emotion (some kind of labeling or causal attribution is still necessary). In his experiment, male subjects were shown pictures from *Playboy* while they listened to what they thought was the sound of their own heartbeat. In fact, the pictures were paired with prerecorded sound tracks that provided "bogus internal feedback," inducing the subjects to believe they were aroused. Results showed that the pictures paired with faster heartbeats were judged to be more attractive. However, Valins did not pay any attention to *actual* physiological arousal. As he acknowledges only briefly, physiological arousal could have been influenced by the sound tracks. In addition, he never considered the possibility that, irrespective of bogus bodily feedback, different pictures could have induced different patterns of physiological arousal, which could have contributed differently to the subjects' preferences.

In sum, the hypothesis that arousal is uniform largely influenced the cognitive approach to emotion in these years. Experiments focused on manipulating cognition, understood as a psychological faculty separate from bodily arousal; when physiological arousal was measured, it was only to assess whether a certain manipulation had managed to "heighten" it. Experimenters paid no attention to the possibility that physiological arousal may be different in different experimental conditions, and that this could explain differences in subjects' behavior and self-reports. Also, no attention was paid to the possibility that a subject's actual physiological state may constrain the range of cognitions available to her and influence how she interprets a certain situation.

4.3.2   Phenomenological Implausibility

Another manifestation of the body-downplaying attitude characteristic of the cognitive approach of these years is its *phenomenological implausibility*. The two-factor account is strangely at odds with lived experience. It reduces arousal to a uniform condition of the organism that, without a label or a cognitive interpretation, is felt merely as a generic state of excitation that contributes only to the felt intensity of emotion experience. Thus without the mediating intervention of a cognitive evaluation, arousal remains unintelligible and meaningless for the subject—a raw pattern of excitation that comes "naked," without any specific affective clothing or quality.

Yet from the perspective of lived experience, this account is clearly implausible.[1] There seem to be many occasions in which one experiences one's body in specific affective ways, irrespective of the fact that one appraises one's context as irritating, conducive to one's goals, funny, and so on. Some mornings I wake up feeling edgy and irritable, before I can even wonder why; often in the early afternoon, irrespective of the situation, I feel distracted and unmotivated, including a sense of heaviness and slowness; taking a brisk walk can change my feelings of bodily arousal, and accordingly my affective state, and actually help me better deal with whatever situation I am in (e.g., irritating colleagues, pending deadlines).

Indeed, earlier attempts to replicate Schachter and Singer's (1962) results found that unexplained arousal was not experientially neutral but, in these experiments, distinctly negatively toned. Maslach (1979) used hypnosis to induce states of unexplained arousal in her subjects, which they experienced as distressing. Marshall and Zimbardo (1979) found that subjects injected with epinephrine could not be manipulated into feeling euphoria; the confederate's behavior had only a mild effect on them and could not override the negative feeling induced by the injection. As the authors concluded, "There are definite limitations to the power of cognitive control" (982). More recent evidence supports this point. Bejjani et al. (1999) report the case of a woman who displayed facial expressions of sadness and cried and sobbed as soon as an electrode stimulated a specific part of her brain stem. Once the electrode contact was removed, the sobbing stopped, together with the feeling of sadness, and the subject reported that she did not know why she had felt so awful (see also Damasio 2003, 67–73). Another interesting case is the one of subjects with a condition called "pathological laughter and crying," who suffer from sudden attacks of uncontrollable laughing or crying, or alternations of the two, often in inappropriate circumstances (they laugh at bad news and cry at funny jokes). Parvizi et al. (2001) studied a subject with this condition, whose social behavior was otherwise appropriate. Although he was aware of the inappropriateness of his behavior, he reported that he would eventually feel happy or sad after episodes of prolonged laughter or crying, respectively. "A feeling was in fact being produced, consonant with the emotional expression, and in the absence of an appropriate stimulus for that emotional expression" (Parvizi et al. 2001, 1711). Finally, we know that drugs can change experience in specific ways by altering metabolism; for example, selective serotonin reuptake inhibitors (like Prozac) work as antidepressants, whereas drugs that block GABA receptor sites have anti-anxiety effects.

A related phenomenologically problematic claim of the two-factor view is the one implied by Schachter and Singer's (1962) second conclusion, according to which when one is in a state of physiological arousal for which one has "a completely appropriate explanation," no necessity to interpret or evaluate one's arousal ensues; accordingly, physiological arousal is not accompanied by an emotion experience. This account is also at odds with lived experience. If I drink a bit too much at a party and as a consequence feel "physiologically aroused," I usually know that my arousal is induced or facilitated by the alcohol; this knowledge, however, does not prevent me from, for example, enjoying myself and feeling euphoric. Similarly, knowing that my exhilaration is due to physical exercise does not make it go away; likewise with knowing that my irritability is due to hormonal changes before my period, and so on. Indeed, further studies have been conducted that do not support Schachter and Singer's point. Reisenzein (1983, 249–250) already mentioned several pre-Schachterian experiments showing that injections of epinephrine can induce genuine anxiety even when the subjects are informed about the cause of their arousal, and that misattribution manipulations can fail for subjects particularly prone to certain emotions.

In sum, then, the body-downplaying attitude that dominated the cognitive approach to emotion in the 1960s and 1970s can also be characterized by its neglect for lived experience, in particular in its assumption that bodily arousal always needs to be cognitively attributed or explained to be experienced as an emotion.

4.4 Appraisal Theory Today: The Body as a Mere Interactant

The cognitive approach to emotion has gradually abandoned the two-factor view and the related assumption of physiological arousal as uniform. Until recently some affective scientists still claimed that only a few emotions have distinctive physiological profiles, and that cognition provides further differentiation (e.g., Cacioppo et al. 2000). Yet in the last decade, much progress has been made in the development of devices that can measure a variety of dimensions of physiological arousal in a noninvasive way. Affective scientists now often measure finger temperature, respiration rate, and systolic and diastolic blood pressure (just to mention some of the more popular measures), in addition to skin conductance and heart rate. These developments are revealing that several dimensions of physiological arousal vary from emotion to emotion. As already mentioned in chapter 2, in a groundbreaking meta-analysis of 134 studies, Kreibig (2010) showed autonomic differentiation not just for BET's alleged basic emotions but for fourteen emotions including anxiety, embarrassment, and a number of "positive" emotions such as affection, relief, amusement, contentment, and pride.

In this context, the cognitive approach is not at odds anymore with an emphasis on physiological and, more generally, bodily differentiation. An influential idea today is that cognition, in the form of a complex structure of appraisal processes, explains and predicts the variety of bodily changes observed in emotion, and not just autonomic ones. For example, in Scherer's component process model (CPM), as we saw in chapter 2, differences in appraisal processes and stimulus evaluation checks (SECs) explain why different emotions come with different autonomic, expressive, and motor manifestations. Recall that according to the CPM, emotion is a system composed of five components, of which appraisal is one. The appraisal component is in turn composed of four appraisal subprocesses that evaluate, respectively, the relevance of an event for the agent, its implications for the agent's goals, the agent's coping potential, and the normative significance of the event. Each appraisal subprocess is itself in turn composed of a number of SECs. Thus, for example, the appraisal subprocess of "relevance" consists of a SEC for novelty, one for intrinsic pleasantness, and one for goal conduciveness; the appraisal subprocess of "implications" involves SECs for causality, outcome probability, discrepancy from expectation, conduciveness, and urgency; and so on. The hypothesis is that different SECs cause distinctive changes in all other emotion components, and empirical work is aimed at identifying precisely which SECs cause which changes (see Scherer 2009).

In addition, the CPM acknowledges that changes in the body can themselves influence appraisal, at least indirectly. Specifically, according to the CPM, changes in the various emotion components other than appraisal influence one another, and although they do not directly affect individual SECs in turn, they can influence other cognitive processes outside the emotion system (notably attention, memory, motivation, reasoning, and self-representation), which in turn can influence the various appraisal subprocesses (see also Scherer 2009, 1315, fig. 2; the black arrows from autonomic physiology, action tendencies, motor expression, and subjective feeling do not reach all the way up to the appraisal component; however, as shown by the red arrows, they exert influence on it by affecting cognitive processes outside the emotion system).[2]

This acknowledgment is important, for by now evidence from various sources demonstrates that the state of one's body influences appraisal, as well as emotion experience more generally. Influential studies have shown that manipulating in particular one's facial expression changes how one responds to the same stimulus. In a famous study, Strack, Martin, and Stepper (1988) asked subjects to hold a pen horizontally between their teeth without letting it touch their lips, thus manipulating their expression into a smile. Then they asked subjects to rate the funniness of some cartoons while holding the pen in this way. Self-reports indicated that these subjects evaluated the cartoons as being funnier than did the subjects who held the pen in their mouth like a straw (i.e., with rounded lips). Berkowitz and Troccoli (1990) asked some subjects to keep a pen horizontally between their teeth (to induce a smile) and other subjects to bite into a towel (to induce a frown) while listening to the description of a fictitious person. They found that subjects who held the pen in their mouth rated the person more positively than did subjects who bit into the towel. In a similar study by Larsen, Kasimatis, and Frey (1992), subjects asked to draw their eyebrows together (which induced a frown) judged pictures as being sadder than did control subjects. An analogous effect was found by manipulating bodily posture; Stepper and Strack (1993) showed that success at achieving a task led to greater feelings of pride if the outcome was received when subjects where in an upright position rather than in a slumped one (see also Gibbs 2006, chap. 8; Niedenthal 2007; see also chap. 7 for further references).

This is not to say, however, that current appraisal theory has entirely shed the assumptions of the preceding cognitive approach. Although the CPM attributes a more important role to the body than the two-factor theory and related cognitive approaches, this role is still relatively limited. First and most apparently, the CPM emphasizes that appraisal is the *driving* component, and research within this framework remains primarily aimed at revealing the cognitive structure of emotion, considered to be what explains and predicts the rest of emotion and its unfolding; aside from granting, at the level of theory, that bodily components of emotion influence appraisal, little attention (if any at all) is paid in experimental research to how the body influences appraisal. I think it is fair to say that attention to this direction of influence is still viewed as outside the scope of appraisal theory (see Roseman and Smith 2001; Scherer and Ellsworth 2009).

Second, today's appraisal theory still characterizes appraisal as a disembodied aspect or component of emotion, clearly distinct from the arousal component and, more generally, from other bodily aspects of emotion (such as expression, behavior more generally, action tendencies). The CPM, in this respect, remains a "good old-fashioned" cognitive model. Its various appraisal processes are clearly distinct from the bodily changes they supposedly bring about; as such, they are themselves not bodily. Although not an immaterial Cartesian thinking thing (for it is presumably implemented somewhere in the brain), and although distributed across several appraisal checks, the cognitive component of emotion in the CPM remains in the head, separate from the body. A correlate of this assumption is that the nonappraising components of the emotion system remain extrinsic to the appraising process: they merely *interact* with it. Borrowing Hurley's (1998) terminology, we can say that the body in the CPM is at best merely *instrumentally related* to the appraising process; namely, it is, at best, a *means* to the appraising process, not a *part* of it.

To clarify this point, it is helpful to compare the notion of cognition assumed by the CPM with the one advanced by dynamical cognitive science, briefly introduced at the beginning of the previous chapter. Scherer likes to think of the CPM as a dynamical model and to contrast it with "modular" accounts. Scherer (2000), for example, characterizes his own approach as "componential-dynamic," in opposition to the "structural-modular" one according to which cognition, emotion, and motivation are separate and independent (as in Zajonc 1980). Scherer's model differs from the structural-modular one, he argues, because according to it, emotion consists of "continuously changing configurations of component states including cognitive and motivational processes" (Scherer 2000, 71). Yet from the perspective of dynamical cognitive science, this is not enough to make Scherer's model dynamical. In fact, from this perspective, the CPM is itself modular, in the sense that it posits cognition (appraisal) as a separate component inside the emotion system, which merely interacts with other components. Supporters of the dynamical systems approach in cognitive science, however, typically argue that cognition is not *within* a dedicated structure (such as a collection of symbols, a neural network, the brain, or a part of it) but *emerges* in time from the mutual influences of several processes.

As an illustration of this stance, take, for example, Thelen et al.'s (2001) field theory of infant perseverative reaching. This theory addresses what is known in developmental psychology as "the A-not-B error." This error is usually made by seven- to twelve-month-olds when they are asked to reach for an object that has first been hidden in a certain location A and then removed and hidden, in full view, in another location B; seven- to twelve-month-olds typically keep reaching for location A. According to Thelen et al., this behavior is not the output of a specific stage of cognitive development but a complex phenomenon that, like others, depends on (emerges from) the mutual influences of processes spanning brain, body, and world. In support of this claim, Thelen et al. show that relatively small changes in experimental design (e.g., in the attractiveness of the hidden object, in the distance between A and B, in the time delay before the infant is allowed to reach) can modify the infant's behavior and prevent the error. This finding suggests not only that the error emerges from a specific configuration of organismic and environmental processes but that "normal" behavior also does—versus the idea that it is driven or controlled by some internal cognitive mechanism. Or take R. D. Beer's (2003) dynamical model of the development of the capacity for categorical perception (the capacity to divide the world into objects with distinctive properties) in a simulated embodied agent with no preprogrammed instructions coding for stimulus features. This agent, Beer shows, is able to come to discriminate diamond-shaped and circular objects through its continuous interactions with them. Its capacity to discriminate shapes in this model is not preprogrammed into the system but shown to emerge over time from agent-environment interactions.[3]

Although the CPM emphasizes the interactivity of the various emotion components and the temporal nature of emotion, compared to these dynamical models, it clearly holds a view of cognition that is still very much modular and disembodied. As the CPM characterizes it, appraisal is a separate component that merely interacts with the rest of the organism. Unlike the dynamical approaches just mentioned, the CPM does not consider bodily events part of the complex network of processes from which cognition self-organizes; rather, in the CPM, the capacity to appraise is from the beginning attributed to the appraisal system, and the body merely responds to it and influences it in return (and, even so, primarily indirectly). In this respect, the CPM still relies on a head–body dualism: the smart, evaluative aspect of emotion is all in the head, and the rest of the organism has no evaluative function.

4.5   Eroding the Neural Boundaries between Cognition and Emotion

In the next section, I explain in which sense from an enactive perspective the body does not just interact with the cognitive process of appraisal. Before turning to this point, however, let us note that recent neuroscientific accounts have started to question the view that cognition and emotion are distinct psychological faculties implemented in separate neural areas. These accounts are relevant here because if they are right, they raise difficulties for the CPM and other models that conceptualize appraisal as a cognitive process neatly distinct from emotion, or from the rest of emotion (as is the case in the CPM, where appraisal is modeled as a cognitive component "inside" the emotion system).

One such account has been provided by Pessoa (2008). On the basis of an extensive review of neuroscientific data indicating that brain regions traditionally viewed as emotional are also involved in cognition, and vice versa, he concludes that "parceling the brain into cognitive and affective regions is inherently problematic, and ultimately untenable" (148). The amygdala, for example, seen by some as a "fear module" (Öhman and Mineka 2001) and generally considered central to fear responses (including preparation for action) and fear recognition, turns out to be critical also for functions usually linked to cognition, such as attention and associative learning, as well as value representation and decision making (see also Pessoa 2010). Conversely, Pessoa (2008) mentions the increasing segmentation of the prefrontal cortex (traditionally seen as implementing primarily cognitive functions) into territories now known to be important for emotion, as well—such as the anterior cingulate and the orbitofrontal and ventromedial prefrontal cortices. Moreover, he points out that even the lateral prefrontal cortex, traditionally associated solely with cognition, has been shown to be sensitive to the emotional character of stimuli, in particular in working-memory tasks. Ultimately Pessoa proposes to view emotion and cognition as interdependent dimensions of behavior resulting from the activity of a variety of brain areas, none of which is intrinsically either emotional or cognitive, but all of which contribute to behavior differently depending on the broader neural context in which they happen to participate.

Similar considerations can be found in Lewis (2005), who specifically addresses the relationship between appraisal and emotion. Again on the basis of an overview of various strands of neuroscientific evidence, he concludes that appraisal and emotion as broad psychological categories do not appear to map neatly onto dedicated brain systems. Rather, "Many systems mediate functions that can be assigned either to emotion or to appraisal. Or, to put it differently, many neural systems that become activated in appraisal also take part in emotional functions, and systems that generate emotional responses may also serve appraisal functions" (182). These systems turn out to span the entire neuroaxis, from the brain stem to the cortex. They include, for example, the amygdala (again), which is involved in evaluation, as well as memory, action tendencies, arousal, and attentional orientation; and the anterior cingulate cortex, which is involved in planning and attentional orientation, as well as emotional feelings; they also include neural systems in the brain stem and hypothalamus, which mediate autonomic and endocrine activity to maintain the organism's internal equilibrium or homeostasis, contribute to emotional feelings, enhance attention, and prepare for action.

Lewis (2005) also distinguishes various psychological components of both appraisal and emotion. For appraisal he lists perception, evaluation, attention, memory, and higher-order executive functions (such as planning and reflection); for emotion he lists arousal, action tendencies, attentional orientation, and affective feelings. He then emphasizes that each of these components is itself a complex neural system, spanning brain areas that are shared among components. As Don Tucker (2005, 219) aptly recapitulates in his commentary on Lewis's article:

Apparently, psychological function and physiological function are not aligned in any simple harmony, at least not in the way we approach them in psychological theory. The conclusion, then, must be unsettling for psychologists. Whereas the separation of emotion and cognition seems to be obvious to a functional analysis, the complexity of interactions among multiple systems, for arousal, for specific action tendencies, or for more general attentional and memory biases, leads to great difficulty in saying what is cognition and how it differs from emotion.

We can read Lewis's and Pessoa's overviews as providing an argument against the separation of cognition and emotion that is logically equivalent to Hurley's (1998) critique of the separation of perception and action. Hurley argues that perception and action depend on overlapping and recursive subpersonal processes; output from motor systems influences perception even if input to sensory systems remains constant, and vice versa. The complex, dynamical reciprocal relations that characterize the subpersonal level prevent any neat one-to-one mapping between the personal or psychological level, and the subpersonal or neurophysiological one. As she also puts it, perception and action are not *vertical modules*; namely, they do not reduce to separate neural systems that interact in a linear way but are best characterized as *constitutively interdependent* or *co-constitutive*. Likewise, Lewis's and Pessoa's arguments can be interpreted as making the point that cognition and emotion are not vertical modules, because the subpersonal processes underpinning them are too complexly entangled; cognition and emotion do not correspond or map in a one-to-one way to dedicated neural systems but are "constitutively interdependent."

If this is the appropriate way to conceptualize the cognition-emotion relationship, then to characterize appraisal as a separate cognitive process not overlapping with (other) emotional components (as the CPM, for one, does) is misleading, because it does not do justice to the real complexities of the neural level. Note also that this neuroscientific picture has implications for existing accounts of the distinction between basic and nonbasic emotions discussed in chapter 2. We saw there that some accounts characterize this distinction as one between noncognitive emotions, and cognitive or highly cognitive ones. The latter, in particular, are taken to include cognitive, non-emotional brain areas (typically cortical ones), whereas the former depend entirely on noncognitive, emotional brain areas (such as the limbic system). Yet if it is not true that no part of the brain is either strictly cognitive or strictly emotional, then it is not possible to draw the distinction in this way.

4.6   Enacting Appraisal

Let us go back to the assumption that appraisal is "all in the head," and the body merely interacts with it. The enactive approach, as we are about to see, entails a different view.

Recall that the enactive approach characterizes cognition at its most basic level as organismic sense making, namely, as the bringing forth of a world of significance (an Umwelt) on the part of the living organism, in virtue of its adaptive autonomy in precarious conditions (see chap. 1). Importantly, cognition thus characterized does not reduce to neural activity in the brain; in fact, it does not even *require* a brain or a nervous system. Extremely simple living organisms lacking a nervous system still count as cognitive systems. In their case, adaptive autonomy is realized entirely non-neurally, by biochemical processes of metabolism.

This view of cognition has direct consequences for how to conceptualize the phenomenon of appraisal. We saw that appraisal in affective science refers to the process of evaluating an object or event as "personally meaningful," namely, as relevant or salient in relation to one's own goals, coping capacities, needs, and so on. The enactive notion of sense making refers to just such a process: organisms, according to the enactive approach, continually evaluate the world in relation to their needs and purposes. In other words, from an enactive perspective, cognition in its simplest forms is already a form of appraisal. Importantly, however, this evaluating activity is not executed by some dedicated part of the organism that monitors the environment and passes motor instructions on to other parts; rather, it is realized entirely *immanently*, in virtue of the organism's autonomous organization. Thus *as* the organism maintains itself via self-organization and self-regulation, it enacts a specific world of significance (an Umwelt). Otherwise put, normativity is intrinsic to the organization of living systems. This view also implies that the activity or behavior of the organism is constitutive of the activity of appraising (in the sense that it enacts or performs it) and does not merely "interact" with it as an extrinsic phenomenon (see also Di Paolo, Rohde, and De Jaegher 2010).

This point pertains to all living organisms, including those with a nervous system. The presence of a nervous system inside the organism does not make sense making suddenly "shrink" to it (and, correlatively, it does not relegate the rest of the organism to a mere interactant that provides inputs to the nervous system and receives outputs from it). Rather, from an enactive perspective, it augments and diversifies the sense-making capacity of the organism, enabling new modalities of interacting with the world, as well as new modalities of self-maintenance and self-regulation.

Importantly, even if enactivism regards the nervous system as an autonomous system,[4] it also underscores its deep interconnectedness with the rest of the organism at multiple levels. As Thompson and Cosmelli (forthcoming) point out, the brain and the body continuously regulate each other and are best seen as coupled systems (see also Cosmelli and Thompson 2010). Their strategy is to address the philosophical thought experiment of the "brain in a vat," in which the brain is imagined to be separated from the rest of the organism, kept alive in a vat filled with a nourishing liquid, and hooked up to a computer that simulates inputs to the brain so that the brain keeps having normal experiences. Thompson and Cosmelli call attention to what it would take to realize this scenario, reviewing the many complex ways in which the real brain and body relate to each other. First, the body keeps the brain "alive and up and running." The brain, and more broadly the nervous system, floats in cerebrospinal fluid, which provides a protective shield and continually removes waste products of neural metabolism. These products are recycled via the circulatory system, which also delivers adequate blood supplies that are crucial to brain functioning, as well as substances such as oxygen, glucose, soluble ions, proteins, and other biomolecules that regulate and nourish the cerebrospinal fluid. This supply is made possible by a pumping system that satisfies the brain's demands but also keeps the concentration of circulating molecules and ions within a physiological range.

Second, it is not just that the body regulates the brain "from the outside," so to speak. The brain also generates what is known as "intrinsic activity," which influences the body and to which the body responds locally, moment by moment.

The brain isn't a reflex machine whose activity is externally controllable through input instructions. Rather, it's a highly nonlinear and self-organizing dynamical system. ... Inputs perturb such complex systems but don't specify particular outcomes.

Furthermore, most inputs arise as a consequence of the system's own intrinsic activity. Hence to get the body-type inputs to match the normal inputs precisely would require getting them to match the bodily inputs to the brain that arise from the brain's nonlinear and unpredictable intrinsic activity. (Thompson and Cosmelli, forthcoming)

Given this complex relationship, it is more appropriate to say that the whole organism regulates itself via a close coupling of brain and body, in which each responds to the other in the service of the organism's continuation. The organism is most aptly seen as a "dynamic singularity," or a tangle or knot of recurrent and reentrant processes (as Thompson 2007, 243, puts it, drawing on Hurley 1998).[5]

In the context of this tangle, from an enactive perspective, choosing to describe one of its component systems as under the control of another, receiving inputs from it and sending outputs back to it, amounts to taking a *heteronomy* or "other-governed" perspective (Varela 1979; Thompson 2007, 49–51). This perspective is characteristic of more traditional accounts of cognition, and we can see it at play also in the view that appraisal is a distinct input–output mechanism inside the organism (as in the component process model). Of course, one can choose to look at things this way, and often with good reason. As Thompson adds, however, "This stance does not illuminate—and indeed can obscure—certain observable patterns of behavior; namely, patterns arising from the system's internal dynamics rather than external parameters" (2007, 50).

Take, for example, the suggestion that the amygdala functions as a *relevance detector* that appraises objects and events in relation to the subject's goals (Sander, Grafman, and Zalla 2003). This suggestion draws on empirical evidence showing that the amygdala is significantly active not just in the recognition and experience of fear but also in the recognition of anger, sadness, and disgust, as well as in the processing of positive events such as happy faces, positive pictures, pleasant tastes, amusing films, and more (Sergerie, Chocol, and Armony 2008; Sander 2009). The enactive approach does not deny that brain areas can exhibit specific functions (by analogy, consider that from an enactive perspective, it still makes sense to identify the different functions played by the different parts of a living cell). Yet from an enactive perspective, it is important not to lose sight of the broader dynamic patterns in which individual brain areas operate. It is possible to describe the amygdala as "detecting" some stimuli as relevant and communicating this information to other areas of the brain and the body. However, to do so obscures the context (or better, contexts) in which the amygdala operates, namely, the broader dynamic patterns of neuronal activity in which it is situated, and the even broader self-organizing and self-regulating activity of the nervous system, itself embedded in the rest of the organism.

An account that is more in line with the enactive approach here is the one advanced by Freeman (1999, 2000; see also Thompson 2007, 366–370). As we saw in the previous chapter, Freeman advances an "activist-prag-matist" view, according to which the organism does not simply move in response to sensory information (this is the "passivist-cognitivist" view). Rather, the organism is endogenously driven to explore the world, and during its exploratory activity it continuously anticipates sensory inputs and prepares for further action. Freeman (1999, 2000) describes activity at the brain level in terms of three interrelated circular causal loops centered on the limbic system—a space-time loop, a control loop, and a reafference loop.[6] The space-time loop refers to reciprocal influences at the level of the limbic system between the entorhinal cortex, which is connected to all the primary sensory areas of the cortex, and the hippocampus, involved in memory and the orientation of behavior. This reciprocal activity induces a large-scale coherent oscillatory pattern that is transmitted to the motor system (the control loop),[7] mobilizing viscera and muscles, and to the sensory systems (the reafference loop), preparing them for the consequences of motor activity. The activity of these three loops is modulated by two further loops traveling outside the brain, into the body and environment respectively: the proprioceptive loop, consisting of pathways from muscles and joints to the spinal cord, cerebellum, thalamus, and somatosensory cortex; and the motor loop, involving motor actions in the environment and sensory stimulation resulting from such actions.

In this model, the amygdala influences how the organism orients itself and acts in the world in accordance with its intentions. It also influences its sensory expectations. In particular, together with other areas of the limbic system, it contributes to shaping the large-scale oscillatory patterns that, in the model, emerge in the sensory cortex following sensory stimulation. Depending on the organism's intentional orientation, the same stimulus will thus lead to different oscillatory activity in the sensory cortex, reflect-ing a different meaning of that stimulus for the organism. So the amygdala in this model *is* involved in determining what counts as relevant for the organism, not in the simple sense that it "detects" relevance but in the sense that it continually modulates how sensory stimuli impinge on the organism relative to its intentions. Relevance here is thus *enacted* as the intentional (purposive) organism explores the world.[8]

A similar view is also entailed by a recent hypothesis advanced by Barrett and Bar (2009). According to it, visual perception is imbued with affectivity throughout, including the earliest stages at which the brain has not yet formed a detailed visual representation of objects. Work on "the proactive brain" (Bar 2007) indicates that the brain continuously makes predictions about the nature of percepts on the basis of previous associations. After an initial "rough guess" about the nature of the perceived object, the brain then constructs a more refined representation (see also, e.g., Friston 2009). Barrett and Bar argue that the initial sketch already recruits brain areas known to be involved in emotion; in particular, it recruits sensorimotor patterns, where "sensory" refers to exteroception as well as interoception. They indicate the orbitofrontal cortex (OFC) as the brain area critical for the integration of stimuli about the world and about the body, and specifically the medial OFC as the area activated very early by gist-level visual information that initiates bodily changes needed to guide subsequent actions, and "modif[ies] the perceiver's bodily state to re-create the affective context in which the object was experienced in the past" (Barrett and Bar 2009, 1329). The lateral OFC, on the other hand, is supposed to receive information about these bodily changes and to integrate it with later, more refined visual information, such that the complete representation of the object will include a representation of the affective value of the object in the form of a bodily pattern. Support for this hypothesis, Barrett and Bar argue, comes from evidence about anatomical connectivity, and from data about the reaction times of different parts of the OFC during visual perception.

Visual perception, in this account, is a multilevel process of gradual construction that recruits affective bodily processes from the beginning. If Barrett and Bar are right, visual percepts are not affect free, and in particular bodily arousal is not just a "response" that occurs only *after* an object has been perceived. Rather, the body participates in the construction of affect-laden visual percepts. As they put it, "Sensations from the body are a dimension of knowledge—they help us identify what the object is when we encounter it, based, in part, on past reactions. If this is correct, then affective responses signaling an object's salience, relevance or value do not occur as a separate step after the object is identified—affective responses assist in seeing an object as what it is from the very moment that visual stimulation begins" (Barrett and Bar 2009, 1326–1327). With respect to appraisal, this view implies that visual stimuli already "come appraised," as it were, and that the body is not extrinsic to the process of appraisal but itself a vehicle of significance or salience.[9]

In sum, then, an enactive approach to appraisal characterizes it as an organismic phenomenon rather than merely a "brainy" one. In complex organisms with a nervous system, appraisal remains an organismic phenomenon and does not shrink to the skull. Although it is plausible to see certain parts of the organism, such as the brain or some parts of it, as having specific roles in the appraising process, these specific roles need to be understood in the broader context of the autonomy and immanent normativity of the organism—not as themselves *doing* the evaluations or *detecting* values but as contributing, in their own distinctive way, to the construction of certain events as having specific values for the organisms. The body, in this framework, is not just a provider of input and an executor of outputs but an integral part of this construction process.

4.7 Phenomenological Connections

I shall now complement these structural considerations with an exploration of the relationship between appraisal, emotion, and the body at the *experiential* level. Appraisal theorists rarely address the phenomenology of appraising. As we saw, appraisal is characterized primarily as an automatic or nonconscious process. In fact, this feature is often emphasized in response to the worry that appraisal theory overintellectualizes emotion, allegedly by making it too reliant on some kind of conscious intellectual judgment. This does not mean that appraisal is necessarily nonconscious, and sometimes appraisal theorists point out that appraisals can also be conscious, effortful, or deliberate (see, e.g., Roseman and Smith 2001, 7). Aside from relatively quick considerations of this kind, however, little more is usually found about "the feel" of appraising something.

As we are about to see, a closer look at this feel reveals that the experience of appraisal is not clearly distinct from the experience of the emotion it is said to elicit. Also, the bodily feelings experienced in emotion are not mere "responses" deprived of an evaluative tone but part of the experience of appraising. Appraisal is not just structurally but also phenomenologically entangled with emotion and the body.

Let us consider first the case of conscious appraisals. We certainly often consciously evaluate our situation (e.g., as difficult to cope with, at odds with our moral values, incongruent with our motives, detrimental for our future) and experience related emotions. How do these conscious evaluations relate to emotion experience, however? It seems to me that it is not possible to clearly distinguish appraisal and emotion in experience, and in particular it is misleading to suggest that a separate appraisal can produce or elicit an emotion in a "linear" way, as it were—that is, to suggest that one *first* (consciously) evaluates something as being a loss, for example, and *then* feels sadness. When I appraise something as being a loss and experience sadness accordingly, my appraisal is already, I submit, imbued with sadness; there are not two clearly separate and successive moments in my experience, one evaluative and the other emotional.

Suppose, for example, that, in a meeting with my supervisor, I am told that I am inefficient and not sufficiently productive; I evaluate this judgment as unfair and get angry (I am taking this example from Roseman and Smith [2001, 15], who advance it as an illustration of how appraisal can be the cause of an emotion). Phenomenologically, it seems to me that my supervisor's negative judgment, as soon as it is consciously appraised as unfair, is the object of my anger; the appraisal and the emotion are inextricably entangled in experience. (This is so, I think, also for cases in which the object of the emotion is remembered, imagined, and even inferred. As I remember hiking in the Alps, I do not first appraise the memory as pleasant and then feel happy; rather, the memory is given as a "happy memory" from the start; the Alps and my hike are recalled in memory *as* pleasant events. As I imagine undergoing surgery, I do not first appraise it as risky and then feel worried; rather, the surgery as I imagine it worries me; it is imagined as worrisome. Analogously, as I realize that I will earn a substantial interest on my savings, I do not first evaluate this outcome as positive and then feel satisfied or perhaps relieved; rather, the amount is given in experience as satisfying or relieving as soon as it is reached in my calculations.)

Dewey (1895) was thus right, I think, when he claimed that it is only "in reflection" that we discriminate between appraising a stimulus in a specific way and having an emotion; appraising something as dangerous, for example, and feeling fear are otherwise not distinct in experience: "The frightful object and the emotion of fear are two names for the same experience. ... The 'bear,' considered as one experience, and the 'fright,' considered as another, are distinctions introduced in reflection upon this experience, not separate experience" (Dewey 1895, 21).[10] Dewey was criticizing in particular the idea that emotion experience follows from a "purely intellectual" act of perceiving an object as having a certain value. Yet his considerations continue to hold, I believe, even if we grant that the experience of appraisal is not "purely intellectual" but in some sense already broadly "affective," for example, that it is an experience of personal relevance or salience. Still, I maintain, to segment the experience into two distinct phases or moments would be phenomenologically inaccurate.

Moreover, I think that it would also be phenomenologically inaccurate to separate the experience of appraisal from the bodily feelings that often occur in emotion experience in the form of either visceral sensations (feeling one's heart racing or one's stomach contracting) or "action readiness" (felt urges to move toward or away from something, as well as to perform more specific actions such as running, punching, jumping, or slouching; see Frijda 1986 and also the next chapter). It seems to me that when these bodily feelings occur, they are not experienced as mere "responses" to the appraisal. To take up my previous example, suppose that as I appraise my supervisor's negative judgment of my performance as unfair, I also feel my fists clenching and an urge to shout at him. These bodily feelings, I want to suggest, are not felt as "mere bodily sensations" lacking evaluative character; rather, they are part of my experience of assessing my supervisor's judgment as unfair (as I discuss in more detail in the next chapter, bodily feelings in emotion experience can also be that *through which* I experience something as scary, offensive, enjoyable, etc.).

I grant that there may be a felt temporal delay between my (conscious) evaluation of my supervisor's claims as unfair and the experience of my body tensing up in a certain way. Sometimes I may be so engrossed in what he is saying ("I can't believe he thinks I don't work enough!") that I "forget" my body, so to speak (see the next chapter for a discussion of phenomenological bodily inconspicuousness and even absence). Other times, however, after the initial appraisal, as the emotion experience unfolds, I may experience my body "welling up" and organizing itself into a certain configuration. Thus in the example, my anger, as it unfolds, may include a sense of my body rapidly organizing itself into an offensive attitude, with fists clenched, heart pounding, jaws tightened, brows furrowed, and so on. The relevant point is that in this process, my bodily feelings, once they appear, are experienced not as mere "responses" to my evaluation of the supervisor as unfair but as part of it (and as part of my anger).

What about cases in which emotion experiences are elicited extremely rapidly by "automatic appraisals"? Take, for example, my feeling of fear as a car coming in the opposite direction suddenly appears in the middle of the road from behind a curve. Although in this case it seems correct to say that no conscious evaluation of the other car as dangerous (or more specifically as relevant for my survival, unpleasant, too fast) preceded my experience of fear, again it would not be correct to characterize my experience of fear as just a "response," somehow disconnected from the world and without any evaluative character. Rather, I am aware of the relevance and dangerousness of the car as soon as I spot it (and feel fear). Phenomenologically, we can say that my fear comes *as* such a conscious evaluation; the conscious evaluation is not an "add-on" to my experience of fear—I do not feel scared and, as a separate experience, evaluate the car as dangerous. The experience of fear *is* at the same time an experience of danger, which is world oriented and evaluative.[11] Also, again, the bodily feelings that may occur in this experience do not feel like "mere" responses lacking world orientation; rather, I want to suggest, they are felt as part of the experience of appraising the situation in a certain way.

In sum, it looks as if phenomenological considerations rejoin the structural ones, in the sense that, at the level of lived experience as well, appraisal appears to be intimately connected to the rest of emotion, including its bodily components.

4.8 A (Brief) Comparison with Prinz's "Embodied Appraisal"

Before concluding, I shall say something about how the outlined enactive approach to appraisal relates to another "embodied" account that also departs in some respects from more mainstream conceptions, namely, the one developed by Jesse Prinz. Prinz (2004a, 58) writes that "in developing a theory of emotion, we should not feel compelled to supplement embodied states with meaningful thoughts: we should instead put meaning into our

bodies and let perceptions of the heart reveal our situation in the world."
The enactive approach is certainly sympathetic to this recommendation,
but it otherwise differs from Prinz's account substantially in several respects.
A detailed comparison and discussion are outside the scope of this chapter,
so I will only briefly highlight a few differences.[12]

Prinz puts meaning into the body by characterizing emotions (basic as
well as nonbasic ones; see chap. 2) as *embodied appraisals*. Embodied appraisals are noncognitive states (in the sense, here, that they do not include
any judgment). Rather, they are perceptions of bodily changes that, in perceiving the body, simultaneously also *represent* properties relevant to the
survival and well-being of the organism—such as danger, loss, offense, infi-
delity, and so on (Prinz refers here specifically to Lazarus's core relational
themes; see sec. 4.2). Prinz in particular borrows Dretske's (1981) theory of
mental representation, according to which something represents X if it is
reliably caused by X and has developed or evolved to detect X; "a mental
representation is a mental state that has been set up to be set off by something" (Prinz 2004b, 54). Thus an emotion such as fear is the perception of
bodily changes "set up to be set off" by danger; sadness is the perception of
bodily changes set up to be set off by loss, and so on.

This representational framework goes together, in Prinz, with the view
that things like danger, loss, offense, and so on, are objective properties
that exist independently from their being represented by the organism.
Prinz (2004b, 63) acknowledges (somewhat in passing) that core relational
themes refer to "relational" properties or "organism-environment relations," but he then goes on to argue that they are not "response-depen-
dent." So, for instance, something such as the death of my favorite pet
turtle "would be a loss even if I didn't represent it as a loss. It is a loss before
I make the discovery that my turtle is dead" (63).

From an enactive perspective, on the other hand, danger, loss, and
other core relational themes (offense, existential threat, progress toward
the realization of a goal, and so on; see Lazarus 2001) are not represented
or detected but enacted, namely, brought forth in the world-organism
encounter—in other words, they *are* response dependent. As Di Paolo,
Rohde, and De Jaegher (2010, 47) also put it in their discussion of "values"
from an enactive perspective, "The organism is an ontological center that
imbues interactions with the environment with significance they do not
have in its absence, and this significance is not arbitrary. It is dynamically

constructed, and that is the essence of the idea of sense-making." Objects
or events need not be consciously appraised as dangers or losses to count as
such; they are such, however, relative to their effects on the organism and
to its goals and needs. The organism, striving to maintain itself (chap. 1),
meets the world "on its own terms," and the world acquires various meanings in relation to the organism's purposes.

Another difference is that, according to Prinz, emotions (embodied
appraisals) can sometimes be elicited by "disembodied judgments" (Prinz
2004b, 74–77, 98–100). This causal mechanism is parasitic on perceptually
triggered emotions and is set up in development as subjects acquire "a host
of disembodied concepts" (76) associated with emotional situations. Eventually entertaining such concepts becomes sufficient to set off an emotion:

> At first, the thought "I am in danger" is an effect of fear. It is an assessment of the
> situation that triggered an emotional response. But through associate learning, that
> thought becomes a trigger for fear as well. Eventually, the explicit thought "I am
> in danger" becomes capable of initiating fear responses in situations that lack the
> physical features that are predisposed to upset us as a function of biology. ... In this
> way, disembodied judgments about core relational themes can become inner causes
> of our emotions. (76)

For Prinz, disembodied judgments are not immaterial, but they supervene
on the brain (only). Although it comes in a different terminology, this view
is precisely the one that this chapter has questioned. Prinz's disembodied judgments correspond to disembodied (i.e., brainy) appraisals distinct
from the bodily changes they bring about. For Prinz, perceptions of bodily
changes are "embodied appraisals"; however, there is clearly room in his
framework for disembodied appraisals as well.

4.9   Conclusion

To conclude, then, it is undoubtedly important to recognize that organisms
do not merely "get aroused" in emotional episodes but also evaluate the
world and their relationship to it. Indeed, all our affective life is bound up
with these evaluations. Yet acknowledging this point need not lead to the
further claim that appraisal exists as a separate process or mechanism that
triggers emotional responses. Indeed, as we saw, neuroscientific considerations as well as phenomenological ones suggest otherwise and indicate
rather that evaluating the world and responding emotionally to it are not

distinct processes. From an enactive perspective, the process of appraising is best characterized as an organismic activity, not separate from but overlapping with what are usually seen as noncognitive, bodily components of emotion. Phenomenological considerations complement this view, as the experience of appraisal does not seem adequately characterized as separate from other aspects of emotion experience, including bodily feelings.

In the next chapter, I continue the exploration of the nature of emotion experience, this time in more detail and specifically in relation to the place of bodily feelings in it. I aim to distinguish between different ways in which we can be aware of our body in emotion experience. The discussion will also further contribute to characterizing the nonseparate nature of appraisal, particularly how bodily feelings can be part of the experience of making sense of the world.

5 How the Body Feels in Emotion Experience

5.1 Introduction

A long-standing question in affective science concerns the bodily character of emotion experience. Do we always experience our body when we experience an emotion? William James famously thought so; indeed, he argued that it is necessary to experience "bodily symptoms" to feel an emotion:

If we fancy some strong emotion, and then try to abstract from our consciousness of it all the feelings of its characteristic bodily symptoms, we find we have nothing left behind, no "mind-stuff" out of which the emotion can be constituted. ... What kind of emotion of fear would be left, if the feelings neither of quickened heart-beats nor of shallow breathing, neither of trembling lips nor weakened limbs, neither of goose-flesh nor of visceral stirrings, were present, is quite impossible to think. (James 1884, 193–194)

According to the philosopher Peter Goldie, on the other hand, "It surely seems correct to say that there are certain sorts of emotion which might have associated feelings, but which do not have associated *bodily* feelings" (2000, 52; italics in original).[1]

I have to admit that, like James, I find it "quite impossible" to think of an emotion experience abstracted from bodily symptoms. However, I shall not push this point here and maintain that bodily feelings are necessary for emotion experience. Rather, what I will do is argue that for a feeling to be a *bodily* feeling, it need not be *about* the body, namely, it need not take the body as an intentional object—as when one notices one's trembling legs or one's tight shoulders. As we shall see, the body can also enter awareness as *that through which* one experiences something else. I think that many instances of emotion experience are bodily in the latter sense;

even when they appear to be all about an object or event in the world, they remain bodily in that the lived or feeling body contributes to the quality of the emotion experience as that through which the object or event is experienced. This idea also relates to the discussion of the experience of appraisal in the previous chapter, and its relationship to bodily feeling. In an emotion experience, I claimed, the experience of appraising is not clearly distinct from bodily feelings. As we shall see more precisely here, bodily feelings can be that through which one experiences a situation in a certain way.

This move intends to enrich (rather than settle) the debate around the bodily nature of emotion experience by pointing out that there are various ways to experience one's body in it, some of which are quite subtle. James (1884, 192) himself wrote that the body can be "acutely or obscurely" felt in emotion. He did not elaborate on this distinction, however, and what he meant by an "obscurely felt" body remains unclear. As I interpret this claim, the idea is that the felt body is not always prominent in emotion experience but can also enter it inconspicuously, and my goal in this chapter is to clarify how this can be. If my analysis is correct, then many of the feelings that do not prima facie have "associated bodily feelings" (as Goldie puts it) will turn out to be also bodily feelings, after all.

More specifically, in what follows I begin by providing a taxonomy of bodily feelings that applies generally to self-consciousness, not just specifically to individual emotion experiences. I first introduce a distinction between the body as an *intentional object* of experience and the body as a *medium through which* something else is experienced, and compare it with existing phenomenological constructs such as *Leib* and *Körper* (already briefly introduced in chap. 1) and *reflective* and *prereflective bodily self-awareness*. I then apply this taxonomy to the case of emotion experience to specify the various ways in which the body can be more or less conspicuous in it. Finally I turn to the experience of "being absorbed" in an activity and argue that, far from involving a totally transparent or absent body, being absorbed is characterized by a complex dynamics of conspicuous and inconspicuous bodily feelings. Although absorption itself is not ordinarily considered an emotion, it is an affective state that can come with different emotion experiences, and its bodily phenomenology is quite complex; as such, I believe, it is best characterized with reference to the distinctions drawn here.[2]

Importantly, in this chapter I am concerned only with the *phenomenological* question of the bodily character of emotion experience: how do bodily feelings enter emotion experience? This question should be distinguished from the *structural* question concerning how actual bodily processes (ANS activity, somatic activity, etc.) relate to emotion experience. I discuss this relationship in the next chapter. Here I am interested in how emotions feel, in particular how experiences of the body can be part of the experience of emotion, irrespective of what happens in the actual living body.

5.2 A Taxonomy of Bodily Feeling

Let us begin by distinguishing cases of bodily feeling in which the body (or a part of it) is the *intentional object* of experience from cases in which the body is felt as that *through which* something else is experienced.

When I touch my arm to feel the strength of my biceps, for example, my arm is an intentional object of experience. Likewise for parts of my body to which I attend proprioceptively, such as my legs stretched under the desk as I am typing these words. In particular, the body can be an intentional object at the center of attention (as in the first example) or at the margin of attention—for example, as I focus on typing these words, I am also aware of a tension in my left shoulder that, however, remains at the margin or periphery of my attention, very much like the various objects scattered on my desk around my laptop.

We should also distinguish between two ways in which the body can be an intentional object of experience. Recall here the distinction, briefly introduced in chapter 1, between two senses of the term "body": the lived, experienced body (or *Leib* in German), and the body qua physical thing, as it appears when examined like any other extended object (the *Körper*).[3] When I attend proprioceptively to my legs stretched under the desk, this part of my body is an intentional object, but it is not *objectified*, namely, experienced as a mere thing. In other words, in this case it is the *Leib* and not the *Körper* that is an object of experience. The intended body here is taken for granted as a locus of experiencing, a lived body; I do not intend my legs as just a physical object.[4] However, *Körper* can also be an intentional object of experience. Examples include measuring one's waistline, looking at the shape of one's legs in the mirror, and touching one's lips to check whether they are chapped. Here the objects of experience present themselves as physical, "thinglike" features of the body, rather than as lived, feeling bodily parts.

The whole body or just some parts of it can become intentional objects of experience. Also, when the intentional object is the lived body, it can come with different hedonic and affective qualities—as pleasant, annoying, tickling, painful, and so on. Finally, the lived body or parts of it can become objects of experience spontaneously or involuntarily, by "popping out" into awareness (think of a cramp in the foot suddenly grabbing your attention), or by way of a voluntary act of paying attention to the body—as when one chooses to sequentially scan various parts of one's body proprioceptively from head to toe. This distinction corresponds to one drawn by Seigel (2005) between *reflexivity* and *reflectivity*. The two terms are often used interchangeably, but in Seigel's characterization they indicate almost opposite phenomena: reflexivity refers to reflexlike, that is, passive and involuntary experiences, whereas reflectivity refers to a voluntary, distanced, second-order stance toward first-order experience.

In feeling *through* the body, on the other hand, the body is not taken as an intentional object but is felt as the medium through which something else is experienced. Take the case of exploratory touch with the hand. When I run my hand along, say, a piece of velvet to feel its smoothness, the intentional object of my feeling is the textured surface of the fabric. My touching hand is not absent from my experience, however, but neither does it linger on as a peripheral object of experience. Rather, it is experienced in a different way, as an organ of perception, as that through which the velvet is felt (see also Ratcliffe 2008, chap. 3, for a discussion of the phenomenology of touch illustrating how something can be a bodily feeling and, at the same time, a feeling of something else). Note, though, that the "felt-through body" can become an intentional object of experience; for example if, while exploring the texture of the velvet, I turn my attention to my touching hand and focus on the proprioceptive sensations in it, the touching hand becomes the intentional object of my awareness.

The distinction between the body as an intentional object of awareness and the body as the medium through which something else is experienced partly overlaps with the one between *reflective* and *prereflective* (sometimes also called "tacit") self-awareness, and specifically between reflective and prereflective *bodily* self-awareness. As Zahavi (2005) discusses in detail, most phenomenologists agree that one can be aware of oneself in a reflective, as well as a prereflective or tacit, way (Sartre is perhaps the best-known defender of a phenomenological theory of self-awareness, but relevant discussions can also be found in Husserl, Heidegger, Henry, and others; see also Zahavi 1999). In reflective self-awareness, one's self is taken as an intentional object—as, for example, when one reflects on one's own intentions or actions to assess whether they are appropriate to a certain situation. Likewise one can reflect on one's bodily experiences, making them into an intentional object. In prereflective self-awareness, on the other hand, one's self is experienced or lived through as the *subject* of awareness. Arguably *all* my conscious experiences include a minimal form of prereflective self-awareness, in that they are all tacitly experienced as *mine* (see Zahavi 2005, 124–132). Prereflective *bodily* self-awareness has been characterized specifically as the nonobservational or nonthematic experience of one's own body as the subject of experience—as when, in writing these words, my attention is focused on them, but I am also aware that I am writing through my typing hands, or that I occupy a specific position in relation to the computer screen, and so on. My body here is not an intentional object, but neither is it completely invisible or absent from my experience. As Legrand (2007) summarizes it, reflective bodily self-awareness is a thematic, observational consciousness of one's own body, whereas prereflective bodily self-awareness is an unmediated, nonthematic way of being aware of one's bodily self as the subject of one's experiences.

Following this characterization, we can then say that when the body is an intentional object, consciousness of one's body is reflective (it is a thematic, observational consciousness of one's body), whereas in bodily feeling-through, consciousness of one's body is prereflective (it is a specific way of experiencing one's body as a subject, through which something else is experienced).

Not all instances of prereflective bodily self-awareness, however, are instances of bodily feeling-through. Legrand (2007) importantly distinguishes two forms of prereflective bodily self-awareness: the *transparent* and the *performative* body. Bodily feeling-through corresponds to the transparent body (the transparent body is that through which the world is experienced), but not to the performative body. The performative body is neither transparent nor an intentional object of awareness; it is the body as experienced during the skillful performance of a specific activity, when one need not attend to one's body but is nevertheless very much aware of its presence and activity. Legrand illustrates this phenomenon with the example of the professional dancer, who need not attend to her body to control her moves, but for whom the body is not entirely out of awareness and out of control, either; rather, in a professional dancer's own words, she "moves from a sharp and very present physical state" (Legrand 2007, 501). The performative body is mainly constituted by prereflective proprioceptive and kinesthetic sensations, namely, sensations of bodily position and movement that are not attended. Gallagher (2005) also talks of a form of "pre-reflective pragmatic self-awareness" (46) that does not take the body as an intentional object and can be characterized as "performative awareness" (74). In his words, performative awareness "provides a sense that one is moving or doing something, not in terms that are explicitly about body parts, but in terms closer to the goal of the action" (73). Legrand sums up the distinction between the performative and transparent body as follows: "Dancers mostly experience their *body* pre-reflectively, whereas normal people in normal circumstances mostly experience the world in a *bodily* way" (Legrand 2007, 506; italics in original). This qualification is important, because prereflective bodily self-awareness is often characterized in terms of a body that is so transparent as to become invisible or "absent" (e.g., as in Leder 1990; see sec. 5.4).

5.3   Conspicuous Bodily Feelings in Emotion Experience

With these distinctions in place, we can now turn to emotion experience specifically and provide an account of the various ways in which the body enters into it, either conspicuously or inconspicuously ("acutely" or "obscurely," to put it as James did). In this section, I focus on conspicuous bodily feelings, and in the next section I address the more obscure ones.

I can easily think of several emotion experiences that come with acute bodily feelings. Sometimes before giving a lecture I am nervous, and my nervousness comes with distinct tingling "butterfly" sensations in my stomach; when I walk by a patch of vomit on the pavement, I feel my stomach and throat contracting in disgust; when I am embarrassed, I often feel my face becoming very hot.

In these examples, the bodily feelings in question are *localized* bodily sensations. Bodily feelings in emotion experience can also be more *diffuse*—that is, they may involve the whole body, or most of it (see also, for example, Ryle 1949, 84). For example, one may feel energized and upbeat in one's whole body after receiving good news; when embarrassed, one may feel not just the face but a larger part of one's body getting warm; depression often comes with feeling apathetic, heavy, and encaged. Diffuse bodily feelings are often best characterized as experiences of "action readiness" (Frijda 1986), namely, awareness of action tendencies or urges to act, in which one's body is felt as wanting to move. In joy, I may feel the urge to run, jump, and throw my arms up in the air; in anger, I can feel like hitting the desk, grabbing and shaking objects around me, and so on. The diffuse character of bodily feelings in emotion experience shows up also in how people speak—for example, when English speakers say that they feel "empty," "drained," or "buoyant," or when they say, "The speech *stirred* everyone's feelings," "I am all *shook up*," "He was slightly *ruffled* by what he heard" (Kövecses 2000, 80; italics in original). One can also "tremble," "shiver," and "quiver all over" with emotion (81). Some emotions are associated with specific whole-body metaphors. For example, angry people "blow up," "burst out," "blow their stack," "flip their lid," or "hit the ceiling," suggesting that anger often feels like "hot fluid under pressure in the bodily container" (148–149).[5]

These linguistic expressions and metaphors of emotion also reveal the *dynamical* and *kinetic* character of emotion experience. In this sense, research on language converges with and complements the phenomenological account developed by Sheets-Johnstone (e.g., 1999, 2009), who particularly emphasizes the close link between emotion experience and experience of movement or kinesthesia.[6] As she discusses, when experiencing an emotion, one often feels urges or tendencies to approach, kick, withdraw, sink, slow down, accelerate, clench, and so on (see also Gibbs 2006, 243–246). Conversely, one's own movements come with distinct emotional or affective qualities—they can feel graceful, clumsy, floppy, expanding, constricting, releasing, tense, and so on. Sheets-Johnstone's point is well illustrated in the visual arts (painting, sculpture, but also theater and dance), which draw heavily on representations of movement to evoke specific feelings. Many of these "kinetic portrayals" evoke subtle affective nuances that are not easily put into words, but whose specific quality is nevertheless directly grasped by the observer. In dance and theater, the same movement, such as a head lift, can have very different qualities, depending, for example, on the speed at which it is executed (paintings and sculptures can also evoke movement by representing, e.g., humans and animals, but also objects, in specific actions and by exploiting light and texture). Arguably, these portrayals can effectively evoke specific emotions because they reproduce bodily movements analogous to those we often experience in our body when we feel the portrayed emotions. Even music, it has been suggested, evokes emotion by reproducing the dynamical-kinetic character of specific emotion experiences (Gabrielsson and Juslin 2003; Johnson 2007, chap. 11); a piece of music that feels "angry" (think heavy metal) arguably feels so because it mimics the kinesthetic character of anger, with its sense of bodily upsurge and frantic impulse to shake and kick.

Localized bodily sensations in emotion experience appear to be mostly interoceptive, whereas more diffuse feelings appear to involve primarily kinesthetic sensations or action urges.[7] Yet in some cases one can have relatively distributed visceral sensations, spanning, for example, the middle of the body from the throat to the lower abdomen (in my experience, the sense of guilt can feel like this); in the case of felt temperature, the sensation can involve the whole body or most of it (as in some cases of embarrassment). In still other cases, relatively localized kinesthetic sensations may be most prominent, as in feeling the urge to clench one's fists and punch in anger. To complicate the picture, not only kinesthetic but visceral sensations have their own dynamical-kinetic character. Think of the heart beating in fear, for example; or in some experiences of disgust, the stomach or even throat can be felt contracting and "pulling back," so to speak. Finally, localized and diffuse bodily feelings are not mutually exclusive. Localized bodily sensations (either visceral or kinesthetic) can take place in a context of specific whole-body feelings: for example, I may feel the desire to throw my arms up in joy in a context of feeling upbeat and energized; or in grief I may sense a painful knot in my upper stomach in a context of a more diffuse feeling of "weighing down."

How do these conspicuous bodily feelings relate to the taxonomy outlined in the previous section? Often they are feelings *of* the body, where the body is an intentional object and is at the center of attention—as when I notice my short and constricted breath in anxiety, my heart beating fast in fear, or my diffuse upset bodily state in fury. In some cases the upset state of my body or bodily parts will involuntarily grab my attention, whereas in others they will become conspicuous following a voluntary act of shifting attention. Also, in these bodily feelings, ordinarily the intentional object is the *Leib*. But note that in some psychiatric disorders, it is the body as a physical object that predominates in awareness, and this awkward experience gives rise to peculiar distortions of emotion experience. In depersonalization, for example, patients report feeling as if they were observing themselves from the outside, or even feeling like "robots" or "automatons." At the same time, they often report a general emotional dampening, with the exception of fear and anxiety (Simeon and Abugel 2006). Similarly in schizophrenia, patients report a heightened awareness of their body as a thinglike object, while "flat affect" is a classic negative symptom of the syndrome (Sass 2004; Stanghellini 2004; Fuchs 2005).[8]

In addition, I want to suggest that the body in emotion experience can be conspicuous *without being an intentional object of awareness*. This phenomenon is closely related to that of performative prereflective bodily self-awareness introduced earlier. Recall that the latter refers to awareness of one's body as a subject of experience during the skilled performance of a specific activity, where the body is not an intentional object but is nevertheless very much present in experience, mainly via prereflective proprioceptive and kinesthetic sensations. As Legrand (2007, 505) puts it, compared to the transparent body, the performative body is very much "at the front" of awareness, namely, conspicuous, clearly present in experience. It seems to me that the body in emotion experience is often analogously "at the front" or, as I shall put it, in the *foreground* of awareness without being an intentional object of experience (see also Colombetti 2011). We can elaborate this thought further by appealing to the metaphor of the "self-luminosity" of consciousness, and suggest that the prereflective, subjectively lived body can come in different *degrees* of self-luminosity. The metaphor of self-luminosity appears for example in Zahavi (2005, 61), to emphasize that "experiential states do present themselves, but not as objects." The idea here is that experiential states glow from within, so to speak, without having to be made visible by an extrinsic source of illumination, such as a second-order act of consciousness (as Zahavi also puts it, experiential states are "self-intimating" or "self-presenting" [61]). Drawing on this metaphor, my suggestion then is that in emotion experience one's own body can be conspicuous without being an intentional object (neither in the center nor at the margin of attention), but rather by being present in the foreground of experience as a subjectively lived body with a relatively *high degree* of self-luminosity. Even when we do not pay attention to our body in emotion experience (perhaps because we are focusing instead on some aspects of the world), it makes itself present via proprioception, kinesthesia, and even interoception. When we are absorbed in an activity with manifest emotional overtones, the body can move to the front of awareness without being taken as intentional object. Feelings of sexual intimacy and connection perhaps provide the best illustration of this phenomenon. In this context, the body may be highly present, even when one does not pay attention to it and is rather immersed in the situation (I discuss further cases of bodily absorption in sec. 5.5).

5.4 The "Obscurely Felt" Body

Let us turn now to the inconspicuous or "obscurely felt" body. As mentioned, James (1884) did not explain what he meant by this expression. It seems to me that the body can be inconspicuous in emotion experience in two ways. First, it can be a marginal or peripheral object of experience. While engaged in an uncomfortable conversation at a party, for example, I may every now and then notice, proprioceptively, that I am tightly clutching my glass of wine; my hand, however, remains otherwise peripheral in my attention, very much like the objects scattered on my desk in the vicinity of my laptop as I am typing these words.

Second, the body can be obscurely felt in emotion experience in what I have called *background* bodily feelings (Colombetti 2011). Take, for example, a situation in which I am sitting in a delayed train, proceeding very slowly, just before a flight. My attention is focused on worldly objects rather than my body (the time indicated by my watch, the speed of the train, the conductor's announcements), and yet my body is not completely transparent or absent. Rather, it contributes to my feelings of anxiety, and specifically to my experience of the situation as tight and confining; in particular, it is *through* my tense and constrained body that I experience the situation as such. While on the train, I am too concerned with external events to pay attention to my body (although once I finally relax in my plane's seat, I may notice the tension that has built up in my neck and shoulders, in which case my body is again an intentional object). Similar considerations apply to, say, my fear of a dog that chases after me as I cycle along the river. Although my attention is directed toward the dog, I also sense my bodily vulnerability and agitation—I have a nonattended sense of my body as rigid and ready to be attacked, through which I attend to the dog.

To borrow another useful metaphor, if one way to characterize the body as a medium of experience is as a transparent window out of which one looks at the world (see, e.g., the discussion in Legrand 2005), my suggestion here is that background bodily feelings in emotion experience are like colored window glasses: one may be mainly oriented toward the world and nevertheless experience it as affectively toned (colored) depending on how one's body is felt-through in the background (depending on the color of the glass); different emotions affect the body (color the glass) in different ways, and the affective quality of the experienced world (the perceived color of the world beyond the glass) changes accordingly.[9]

The notion of a bodily background of experience is not new; different characterizations have been proposed in various contexts, some of which come closer than others to what I mean by background bodily feelings in emotion experience. Among the scientists, Damasio (e.g., 1994, 149–151) distinguishes three varieties of feeling: feelings of basic emotions (happiness, fear, anger, etc.), subtle variations of those (ecstasy and euphoria, panic and shyness, etc.), and *background feelings*. According to Damasio, background feelings are the "images" or conscious representations of what, as we saw in chapter 1, he calls "background emotions," namely, bodily changes that occur all the time in the organism as part of its self-regulatory activity. A background feeling "is not the Verdi of grand emotion, nor the Stravinsky of intellectualized emotion, but rather a minimalist in tone and beat, the feeling of life itself, the sense of being. … [It] is our image of the body landscape when it is not shaken by emotion" (Damasio 1994, 150–151). Damasio's background feelings are typically unattended, but they can easily be reported if attention is turned to them: "We are only subtly aware of a background feeling, but aware enough to be able to report instantly on its quality" (150). As bodily, unattended, and nevertheless "subtly felt," Damasio's background feelings resemble my background bodily feelings. A main difference, however, is that Damasio characterizes background feelings as present only between emotion experiences: "A background feeling corresponds … to the body state prevailing *between* emotions" (150; italics in original); it contributes mainly to our sense of well- or ill-being, coloring our awareness when we are not in the grip of specific emotions.

I think that whereas it is important to point to a pervasive background "affective" bodily experience—as I would rather call it—we should not overlook the fact that background bodily feelings play a role also in specific emotion experiences (as shown by the examples of the anxiety in the train and the fear of the dog). Another important difference is that bodily feelings for Damasio are always feelings *of* one's body undergoing some changes; they are "images" of the body, as he often puts it. Thus his account has no room for bodily feelings in which the body is not an intentional object of experience.

A different account of background bodily awareness is given by Leder (1990), who distinguishes various modes of "disappearance" of the body, or the various ways in which we do *not* pay attention to our body and our body is therefore "absent." Leder (1990, 24) discusses the example of a person who starts listening to music while driving. As her attention shifts to the music, the bodily movements she performs to drive disappear from her awareness: they are relegated to the background of a bodily "I can" from which they can reappear if needed. Leder's term for this mode of disappearance of the body is *background disappearance*. Note, however, that what I call background bodily feelings are not supposed to disappear in this way. In Leder's example, the body, once disappeared, does not influence the experience of what is central in the subject's awareness at the moment (the music, in the example). Background bodily feelings, on the other hand, do contribute to the quality of one's current emotion experience.

Leder (1990, chap. 2) also talks of deep, recessive visceral processes that we never feel, and yet they support our organism and its conscious life. This form of background is even farther removed from the one I am trying to point out, because here the background cannot be brought to attention; in other words, Leder's "recessive body" is not transparent in any sense but rather entirely "invisible" (to borrow a term from Legrand 2007). Leder's discussion comes closest to my notion of background bodily feelings when it acknowledges that the absent body can be felt via a change in how the world is experienced. In hunger, for instance, Leder (1990, 51–52) notes that the whole corporeal field can be affected, and importantly, "since my corporeal field is always in relation to a world, the visceral saturates my environment as well. ... The world itself shifts with a shift of the visceral."

Aron Gurwitsch (1964, 1985) gives another account of background bodily awareness. Gurwitsch maintains that "feelings of central adjustment as well as other bodily feelings may accompany mental activities and ... some awareness or other of our corporeity is actually there at every moment of conscious life" (1985, 28). He also comments that this pervasive bodily awareness can be particularly "dim and indistinct" (31). Hence although he does not discuss emotion, his account seems to leave room for the possibility that a kind of dim and indistinct bodily awareness (akin to background bodily feelings) may characterize some emotion experiences. Crucially, however, for Gurwitsch bodily awareness, even if pervasive, is always *irrelevant* to what is going on centrally or focally in the subject's attention. More precisely, Gurwitsch distinguishes three "domains" or "dimensions" of consciousness that are supposed to be simultaneous and unified within each conscious act:

First, the *theme*: that with which the subject is dealing, which at the given moment occupies the "focus" of his attention, engrosses his mind, and upon which his mental activity concentrates. Secondly, the *thematic field* which we define as the totality of facts, co-present with the theme, which are experienced as having material relevancy or pertinence to the theme. In the third place, the *margin* comprises facts which are merely copresent with the theme, but have no material relevancy to it.[10] (Gurwitsch 1964, 55–56; italics in original)

For example, the sentence that I am writing right now is the theme, the thoughts and chains of inferences that are relevant to what I am writing now make up the thematic field, and my legs stretched under the desk belong to the margin.

Now, Gurwitsch is clear that he takes the body to be always in the margin (unless, of course, the body is itself the theme, as when I examine the wrinkles of my hand). As such, the body can be copresent with the theme (as we saw, for Gurwitsch bodily awareness is pervasive), but it can never influence it. The theme is completely indifferent to, and disconnected from, the margin; the margin does not in any way concern the *contents* of the theme and can only "interfere" with it by becoming itself thematic (Gurwitsch 1985, xliv).

Background bodily feelings in emotion experience do not involve a marginal body in Gurwitsch's sense, however; namely, the body in background bodily feeling is not irrelevant or unrelated to what "engrosses one's mind" at a given time. Take again the example of my fear of the dog running after me while I am cycling. If we apply Gurwitsch's tripartition (but note that he does not address the case of emotion experience), the theme is the dog, or rather the noises it makes behind me; the thematic field comprises my thoughts that it may bite me, and that I could bleed or fall from the bicycle; the margin is made up by an indefinite number of copresent yet unrelated conscious thoughts, perceptions, bodily feelings, and so on, including an awareness of my body as rigid and ready to be attacked. The body here is thus contingent and irrelevant to the theme and cannot influence its contents; at most, the body can enter the focus of attention and become itself thematic, thus interfering with the initial theme.

This account overlooks, however, that the theme, in the example, is not just the noises made by the dog but the *danger* they signify for me. I am afraid, and in fear what I am focusing on is the danger. In this sense, what engrosses my mind is *not* indifferent to how I feel my body in the background. Were I to feel my body as being immune to dog bites or strong enough to kick the dog away if it attacked me (and assuming that I am not cynophobic), my experience of the affective quality of the situation would be different. I might not experience it as dangerous anymore; or I might still experience it as dangerous, I may still have a sense that my body is vulnerable and the dog could bite me (perhaps because it happened in the past), but at the same time the awareness that I could repel the dog would, I think, give my fear a different quality. In sum, Gurwitsch acknowledges the existence of an unattended, dimly felt, and indistinct bodily awareness that resembles my background bodily feelings. Yet he relegates the body to a marginal background that, even if pervasive and always copresent with the theme, does not in any way affect the theme. The body in background bodily feeling as I understand it, however, is not marginal in this sense. In being able to contribute to the affective quality of a situation, it can affect the theme.

With some caution, some examples from Sartre can help further characterize my notion of background bodily feelings. As Sartre discusses in a much-cited passage of *Being and Nothingness* ([1943] 1958, 331–339), one experiences physical pain "*implicitly*" (332; italics in original), by experiencing the world in an altered way. In Sartre's example, he is sitting late at night trying to finish reading a philosophy book, and "at the very moment that I am reading *my eyes hurt*. Let us note first that this pain can be *indicated* by the world; *i.e.*, by the book which I read. It is with more difficulty that the words are detached from the undifferentiated ground which they constitute; they may tremble, quiver; their meaning may be derived only with effort, the sentence which I have just read twice, three times may be given as 'not understood,' as 'to be re-read'" (132; italics in original).

We can take this example as illustrating a background bodily pain that is not attended but nevertheless influences the experience of the world. The caveat, however, is that arguably Sartre's own conception of consciousness does not allow him to say that the body in this example can experience itself as painful (see the discussions in Fell 1965; Wider 1997; Svenaeus 2009). Consciousness for Sartre is necessarily "vacuous" and ecstatic, i.e., directed toward something other than itself; as he famously put it, consciousness is "nothing," and becomes "something" only when attended by the other's regard (or by the subject looking at itself from the perspective of the other). Thus a painful consciousness cannot properly inhabit my body, i.e., my body cannot feel painful "on its own," so to speak. My pain is either indicated by how the world is given to me (in which case my body is entirely "passed over"), or made known to me as an object by the other's regard.[11]

Likewise for Sartre's ([1939] 1962) discussion of the emotions. Here he claims that "during emotion, it is the body which, directed by the consciousness, changes its relationship with the world so that the world should change its qualities" (65). Specifically, the world acquires for the subject "magical qualities" of dangerousness, sadness, and so on. Importantly, this takes place via a transformation of the whole body: the body, by undergoing changes distinctive of specific emotions and by being directed by consciousness, leads to an experience of the world as having a specific affective quality. Again, however, because of his own account of consciousness, Sartre cannot say that the body that is upset in emotion, and through which consciousness transforms the world, experiences itself as upset (see also Fell 1965, 202–203). In emotion the body is used by consciousness to change the world; consciousness even "degrades itself" in this process, but the body never experiences itself: "consciousness has no thetic consciousness of [itself] as abasing itself [= *comme se dégradant*] to escape the pressures of the world: it has only a positional consciousness of the degradation of the world, which has passed over to the magical plane" (79).

In background bodily feelings, on the other hand, the world comes to be experienced as having specific affective qualities via a body that is "self-luminous," "self-presenting," or "self-intimating," in the sense specified earlier. It is not an object of awareness but is nevertheless experienced as a feeling body—though it remains quite "dim" or recessive. We can keep Sartre's central idea that the affective quality of the world is experienced through the body by specifying, however, that the body is not merely directed and "passed over" by consciousness but is and remains inhabited by it. As Patočka ([1995] 1998) might have put it, in background bodily feelings the body is felt as that on which the world impinges "physiog-nomically" (see discussion in chap. 1, sec. 1.4).

Finally, a notion of background bodily feelings that comes very close to the present one plays a role in Ratcliffe's characterization of his "existential feelings." Very much like Heidegger's moods (chap. 1), existential feelings are "background orientations through which experience as a whole is structured" (Ratcliffe 2008, 2); they affect the way reality is experienced holistically by the subject and include, for example, feelings of the surreal, the unfamiliar, the uncanny, feelings of comfort, feeling at home, and so on. Ratcliffe also calls them "feelings of being," or feelings of how one finds oneself in the world. At the same time, existential feelings are *bodily* feelings *through* which things are experienced (36). The feeling body in existential feelings is explicitly the medium through which one experiences and makes sense of the world. Importantly, however, it does not completely disappear from awareness. Rather, it remains felt as that which does the feeling (106). One way in which Ratcliffe illustrates this point is via the analysis of the experience of various psychiatric conditions. He shows that these conditions often involve an altered sense of reality that goes together with altered bodily feelings. The latter are not necessarily attended, but even so their altered nature contributes to alterations in one's sense of world-belongingness.

5.5 Feeling Absorbed

I shall now use the distinctions drawn so far to characterize the experience of *being absorbed* in an activity in a way that, I want to suggest, does more justice to its phenomenology than existing accounts. Absorption is not traditionally seen as an emotion, but we can have little doubt that it is a highly motivated and interested state that comes with different affective tonalities, including specific emotion experiences; for example, it can be characterized by more or less engagement, interest, frustration, and so on. Its bodily phenomenology is complex, and as I hope to show, the distinctions drawn so far can help to do it justice.

There is a widespread tendency to view absorption in an activity as primarily world oriented and, correlatively, as involving a hidden and even nonconscious body. Leder (1990, 71), for example, discusses the case of a tennis player who suddenly feels an acute pain in his chest. Before the appearance of the pain, the player is characterized as totally absorbed in the game; his body is absent, or more precisely *ecstatic*—projected outward toward the world and away from itself (18, 21–22). The other side of this view is that noticing one's own body leads to a *disruption* of the state of absorption. In Polanyi's words: "If a pianist shifts his attention from the piece he is playing to the observation of what he is doing with his fingers while playing it, he gets confused and may have to stop" (Polanyi 1958, 56; quoted in Leder 1990, 85). Ratcliffe (2008) also observes that often when one's body becomes conspicuous, one's experience of the world loses fluidity and seems to be impeded: "The conspicuous body is ... often a retreat from a significant project in which one was previously immersed, a loss of practical possibilities that the world previously offered" (125). He gives the example of realizing, while giving a lecture, that one's audience is getting bored (114). Before this realization, the body is inconspicuous, and the lecture proceeds smoothly; as soon as the realization dawns, the body becomes gradually more conspicuous, and the fluidity of one's gestures and speech breaks down.

It is certainly the case that taking a reflective stance toward one's body while being absorbed in an activity can disrupt one's absorption and performance. But how are we to understand the experience of absorption itself? Does it really involve an invisible or absent body? I think that this account is inappropriate, and absorption is better characterized as involving alternations of conspicuous and inconspicuous bodily feelings.

Let us take a closer look at the example of being absorbed in playing the piano. In my experience, this state does not go together with an invisible body. Rather, it is best described as involving a complex variety of conspicuous and inconspicuous bodily feelings. During this activity, my posture, my facial expressions, and the way my fingers touch the keys often come to the foreground of my experience, without, however, being attended—rather, with high degrees of self-luminosity or self-intimation. Yet I also feel my body more "dimly" or "obscurely," in the background, as that through which I experience the music as having certain dynamic and affective qualities. Sometimes I also explicitly attend to specific parts of my body—the way my right hand jumps over several keys in more acrobatic passages, for example, or just the way my fingers feel when they articulate a particular phrase. Importantly, these bodily feelings do not cease to occur when I play a piece I know well, although arguably in this case they are more smoothly integrated with other forms of bodily self-awareness. More generally conspicuous bodily feelings (where the body is either an intentional object, or in the foreground) are not disruptive; on the contrary, they are part and parcel of the excitement, as well as of the enjoyment of the situation. They do not disturb the overall experience but enrich it by adding texture to it.

Sudnow's (1978) first-person account of his experience of learning how to improvise jazz on the piano supports this description. It is clear from his report that at the beginning of his training, he took an observational and highly reflective stance toward his hands and technique. For example, he knew *that* high- and low-pitched passages should alternate in relatively quick succession, and he put this knowledge into practice by deliberately moving his hands from right to left regions of the keyboard; he also looked at his hands and fingers most of the time. As he improved, however, he shifted to a more embodied and nonreflective knowing *how* and began to be guided more by touch and proprioceptive sensations: "Looking workload progressively lightens. ... As I reached for chords ... I was gaining a sense of their location by going to them, experiencing a rate of movement and distance required at varying tempos, and developing, thereby, an embodied way of accomplishing distances" (12).

This more absorbed way of playing did not lead Sudnow to eventually forget his body and was clearly never aimed at achieving an automatic performance deprived of bodily presence. Rather, Sudnow's report indicates that, with practice, he learned to "submit" to the increasing skills of his hands (interestingly, in the narrative "the hand" gradually replaces the "I" as the improvising agent) and eventually learned to "sing with his fingers"— as he often likes to put it in the book. This expression aptly evokes a state of immersion in one's body in which the body is, however, still experienced as a source of feeling, affect, agency, and expressivity. Sudnow's account also shows a progressive expansion of bodily self-awareness, from the hands to the rest of the body. Here is a passage from the final part of the book, which describes his experience as a now-accomplished jazz improviser:

The articulational course could now take up in downbeat synchrony with the foot; now in upbeat synchrony with the left hand's rise toward a next chord; now in top-of-the-turnaround synchrony within the one-shoulder-sway-per-four-foot bounces; now jumping in on the upbeat phase of a chordal reaching arc and taking a soundful traverse through thus and so many places to a foot downbeat, one that was "located within" the course of the broader reaching arc of the chordal stretch. (Sudnow 1978, 140)

Not only the fingers but the whole body is here experienced as involved in the performance. Even if this description is post hoc, it is hard to imagine that it could have been produced in the absence of any form of bodily feeling. It is more plausible to grant that Sudnow is here tapping a dimension of bodily self-awareness that clearly reveals not a forgetting of the body but a dynamic of bodily feelings, in which some parts of the body stand out and are more conspicuous (both as foreground bodily feelings and as feelings *of* the body intended as a *Leib*), and others shift to the margin and background.

Csikszentmihalyi (1992, 5), in his popular book on happiness, discusses many real-life instances of what he calls the experience of *flow*, "the state in which people are so involved in an activity that nothing else seems to matter." One context in which flow experiences come about, he argues, is when people perceive their body skillfully performing a specific activity, such as playing an instrument, dancing, hiking, climbing, practicing yoga and martial arts, and so on (see his chap. 5, titled "The Body in Flow"). Csikszentmihalyi is primarily interested in identifying the various activities in which the body is "in flow," and does not really provide a detailed characterization of how this state is experienced. What he says, however, is inconsistent with the view that during bodily flow the body is forgotten or absent—or so I want to suggest. On the one hand, Csikszentmihalyi insists that a high level of expertise is required to experience bodily flow; expertise is necessary for the activity to proceed smoothly, without breakdowns and frustrations. Yet on the other hand, he also repeatedly emphasizes the importance of feeling *challenged* during the activity, as well as feeling that one can *cope* with the challenge. The experience of bodily flow, then, must involve a delicate equilibrium of mastery and effort, such that the experience of being challenged and the experience of dealing with the challenge unfold seamlessly, in a state of uninterrupted absorption. How could such an equilibrium be achieved and experienced without any kind of bodily feeling? One ought to be able to feel one's body as it is being challenged, and to feel when the challenge is being overcome. Bodily flow, I maintain, involves not an invisible body but a dynamical interplay of prereflective bodily feelings with their different degrees of self-luminosity, interspersed with occasional feelings of the body where the body is intended (as either a marginal or peripheral object). The body is not forgotten but experienced as actively immersed in a demanding but not overpowering pursuit.

Similar considerations apply to a variety of sensual experiences, most obviously erotic experiences, but also listening to music, enjoying a walk, exercising, and so on. They do not apply to pleasant experiences only, however. As I am calling a relative to communicate some bad news, I may feel overwhelmed by an impulse to cry that comes to the foreground, and from which more specific feelings (a knot in my throat) may also pop out involuntarily and grab my attention; I push them into the background, from which they keep shaping my experience, giving it a character of tightness and effort. Or I may be absorbed in a boring activity, like entering dozens and dozens of grades into the dedicated form; it is drizzling outside, and the whole experience is suffused with sleepiness; my face feels long, my jaws lazy and my eyelids heavy. These bodily feelings become conspicuous every now and then and otherwise remain "obscure," giving the experience of boredom its character of heaviness and slowness.

5.6   Conclusion

This chapter has illustrated various ways in which the body can enter emotion experience, as well as the experience of being absorbed in an activity. As we have seen, the body can be more or less conspicuously felt in emotion experience. Conspicuous feelings include instances of feelings of the body where the body is an intentional object of experience, in particular where the body is in the center of attention. They can also include "highly self-luminous" *foreground* bodily feelings, namely, bodily feelings where the body is not an intentional object of experience but is nevertheless very much at the front of awareness. Inconspicuous bodily feelings include feelings of the body where the body is an intentional object at the periphery of attention and, more interestingly perhaps, what I call *background* bodily feelings, where the body is unheeded but nevertheless enters emotion experience as that through which the world is experienced. In particular, differences in how the body feels in the background accompany different experiences in how the world is evaluated or appraised.

These distinctions have been motivated in the first place by the consideration that the debate on the bodily nature of emotion experience cannot progress without a phenomenological account of bodily feelings that does justice to their complexity. Without such an account, some emotion experiences may be mistaken as "nonbodily" because they do not involve feelings *of* the body. Yet as we have just seen, the body need not be an intentional object to enter emotion experience and make it "bodily."

As anticipated at the beginning of this chapter, I turn now to the relationship between the lived experience of emotion, and the subpersonal brain and bodily processes underpinning it. Importantly, figuring out whether and how these two levels of description relate to each other is an empirical question. As we shall see, it is not enough to feel one's stomach contracting in disgust to establish that one's stomach is in fact contracting. The relationship between the lived and the living body is a complex one that needs to be investigated with a variety of tools. In the next chapter, I show how the enactive approach can help specify these tools, in particular how it can help integrate current affective neuroscience with the study of lived emotion experience, including bodily feelings.

6 Ideas for an Affective "Neuro-physio-phenomenology"

6.1 Introduction

According to the enactive approach, phenomenological analyses are useful not just to clarify the nature of lived experience per se but also to make sense of patterns of brain and bodily activity as measured in the laboratory. Varela (1996) proposed the term *neurophenomenology* to refer to a research program aimed at integrating the "third-person methods" of neuroscience (brain imaging, but also bio-behavioral measurements) with "first-person methods" for the study of consciousness (such as self-observation and self-reports), and some explicitly neurophenomenological studies have been conducted since then.

In this chapter I first illustrate the neurophenomenological method and clarify its place in consciousness studies. Then I indicate how it could be used to augment the current neuroscientific approach to emotion—or more precisely, how it could be applied to the study of the relationship between emotion experience and physical (brain and bodily) activity. I think that this augmentation would benefit both research fields. On the one hand, as we shall see, affective neuroscience has not paid much attention to the lived or phenomenological features of emotion, focusing instead on the search for distinctive patterns of neural and physiological activity for different emotions. On the other hand, no explicitly neurophenomenological study has so far addressed emotion experience; moreover, existing studies have been limited to an investigation of lived experience and brain activity, with no consideration for bodily activity. In addition, the integration of neurophenomenology and affective neuroscience could help to make progress on some long-standing questions in affective science, as well as, more generally, to clarify the relationship between lived experience and the living organism.

6.2   Neurophenomenology in Theory and Practice

In Varela's (1996) original characterization, neurophenomenology is a method for the integration of third-person and first-person data, where the former refer to data about brain and bodily activity, and the latter to data about consciousness or lived experience. Varela, Thompson, and Rosch (1991) had already emphasized the need to develop appropriate methods for the study of consciousness, including the cultivation of first-person practices for the collection of first-person data. Varela (1996) continued this project, adding that "meaningful bridges" need to be created between first- and third-person data, and also that first- and third-person data need to "constrain" one another. More precisely, first-person data should be collected to shed light on, or interpret, physical activity, whereas third-person data should in turn be used to guide experiential reports and to help subjects discover and report on previously unnoted aspects of their experience.

Varela's initial suggestions have been taken up by his colleagues and students, and a few explicitly neurophenomenological experiments have been conducted so far (Lutz et al. 2002, 2008; Cosmelli et al. 2004; Petitmengin, Navarro, and Le Van Quyen 2007; Christoff et al. 2009). To illustrate the approach, we can look at Lutz et al.'s (2002) pilot study on the perception of autostereograms, also known more informally as "magic-eye pictures." These are two-dimensional dot distributions that, when fixated for some time, can induce the illusory perception of three-dimensional images. In the study by Lutz et al. (2002), four subjects initially fixated a random dot pattern (a dot pattern that was not a magic-eye picture). After seven seconds, the initial random pattern changed to a magic-eye picture. When subjects became able to see the three-dimensional image, they pressed a button and gave a brief description of their experience. Subjects' brain activity was measured with EEG throughout the experiment, from the presentation of the random-dot image to the button pressing.[1]

One distinctively neuro-*phenomenological* feature of this experiment is that subjects described their experience using terms identified during a previous training session. In this session, subjects repeatedly practiced the task to improve their perceptual discrimination and to pay attention to and identify changes in their awareness. Lutz et al. mention that the experimenters used "open questions" to direct subjects' attention to their state of awareness; for example, they initially asked subjects what they felt before and after the image appeared, and then guided them toward a more specific characterization (the use of open questions can be seen as a *second*-person method for the generation of first-person data; I will come back to this idea later).[2] This training session led to the identification of three categories of "phenomenal invariants" describing how *ready* subjects felt before the perception of the three-dimensional image, and how *well* they perceived the image once it had emerged. These categories were labeled, respectively, *steady readiness* (subjects were "'ready,' 'present,' 'here,' or 'well-prepared'"), *fragmented readiness* (subjects were less sharp and less focused and made a voluntary effort to see the image; the emergence of the image was accompanied by a sense of surprise), and *unreadiness* (subjects were not prepared; they saw the image only because of the correct position of their eyes; the appearance of the image was experienced as surprising and interrupted other thoughts) (Lutz et al. 2002, 1588).

These categories were subsequently used to divide the experimental trials, including patterns of EEG-measured brain activity, into corresponding "phenomenological clusters." Results showed that different phenomenological clusters were characterized by different and yet distinctive patterns of brain activity across subjects (important individual differences in brain activity within the same cluster were also found). Notably, the condition of "steady readiness" turned out to be characterized by frontal phase synchrony that emerged early between frontal electrodes and was maintained on average throughout the trial. In the condition of "unreadiness," no stable phase synchrony could be identified on average in the first seven seconds, but when the dot pattern changed, a complex pattern of weak synchronization and desynchronization or phase scattering between frontal and posterior electrodes occurred; subsequent frontal synchrony slowly appeared while the phase scattering remained present for some time.

Lutz et al. (2002) call these patterns of neural activity the *dynamical neural signatures* of first-person experience. They emphasize that it is thanks to the identification of phenomenal invariants during the training session that they could make sense of neural activity. Without this identification, the observed patterns of synchronization and desynchronization would have appeared as mere noise and would have been disregarded accordingly.

This study has strengths and weaknesses. Its major strength is that it illustrates how first-person data can be used in neuroscience to organize, analyze, and interpret third-person data; as Gallagher (2003, 86) puts it, first-person data here "contribut[e] to an organizing analytic principle" (see also Bayne 2004). Second, it is important that salient qualitative features were identified via a process of open questions enabling subjects freely to describe their experience; in this way, subjects were not constrained by the experimenter's own assumptions. Third, the study looked at both neural activity and experience as they unfolded over time, rather than reducing them to static events; in this respect, the study is relatively ecologically appropriate. Fourth, distinctive dynamical neural signatures were discovered for specific experiential states—or, in more philosophical jargon, a type-type correspondence was found between neural signatures and conscious states.[3] More specifically, the results even suggest that changes in lived experience go together with changes in global brain dynamics as measured by EEG; for example, in the "unreadiness" cluster, the subjective experience of unpreparedness may correspond to lack of frontal synchrony and then phase scattering.

As for the weaknesses, note that the correspondence just mentioned is only suggested because, as Lutz et al. (2002) themselves acknowledge, data about experience were not obtained "on the fly," in real time, while subjects were performing the task and their brain activity was being recorded. Another limitation, at least from a neurophenomenological standpoint, is that the study did not explore in any way how third-person data can guide first-person ones. More generally, to my knowledge, this possibility has never been addressed concretely by any purportedly neurophenomenological study. At best, we have some suggestions for how to go about it. For example, Le Van Quyen and Petitmengin (2002, 176) suggest that EEG data could be used as *biofeedback* to help epileptic subjects become more sensitive to the onset of their seizures (epileptic seizures are usually preceded by changes in awareness, and subjects can be trained to perceive these changes; this increased awareness is particularly useful for therapeutic purposes, because if subjects catch the preictal moment in time, they can then engage in various mental exercises to prevent the onset of the seizure). Biofeedback as a technique involves continuously measuring some dimension of a subject's biological activity and showing the measurement to the subject in real time, as it is taking place. Indeed, EEG biofeedback has already been used to treat epilepsy (see, e.g., Sterman 1993), as well as a variety of other conditions (see Birbaumer and Kimmell 1979), and could be used in further neurophenomenological studies of emotion experience (more in sec. 6.5).

In spite of these weaknesses, I believe that neurophenomenology has much to recommend to the current neuroscientific approach to emotion. Before explaining why and how, however, I want to say something more about the place of neurophenomenology in consciousness studies.

6.3   Neurophenomenology and the Study of Consciousness

From a philosophical standpoint, neurophenomenology can be seen as a method for "naturalizing phenomenology," in the general sense of making experience amenable to natural scientific inquiry. Yet importantly neuro-phenomenology does not call for the *reduction* of the experiential level to the physical one; it does not attempt, for example, to *translate* first-person data into third-person data (for this approach, see Roy et al. 1999). Quite the opposite, its main tenet is the proposal to include first-person methods and first-person data *as such* in the natural-scientific enterprise of understanding how the organism enacts consciousness. In other words, neurophe-nomenology can be seen as wanting to "phenomenologize" naturalism.[4]

Neurophenomenology should be distinguished from *heterophenomenol-ogy*. The latter is a "third-person" method proposed by Dennett (1991), which invites the experimenter to use first-person reports in scientific investigations of consciousness as third-person data, together with third-person data from other sources. In a recent commentary on Thompson 2007, Dennett (2011, 32) claims that heterophenomenology is a way of "taking first-person data seriously within the third-person domain of cognitive science," and as such it is not at odds with neurophenomenology. Yet neurophenomenology does not only claim that first-person data should be taken seriously; unlike heterophenomenology, it also emphasizes that consciousness needs to be studied from the first-person perspective, with *first-person methods* that include various forms of mental training (see Thompson 2007, 303–311; 2011b, 191).

To be sure, not all phenomenologists are happy with the proposal to marry phenomenology and natural science. This is because phenomenology since Husserl has been conceived of, at least in part, as a "transcendental" enterprise. A common objection raised to the project of naturalizing phenomenology is that the transcendental subject is not the same as the psychological and neurobiological subject. The latter is part of the natural world, whereas the former is what allows the natural world to be known.

As Murray (2002, 30–31) puts it: "In seeking to lay bare the fundamental structures of experience, phenomenology is also seeking to establish the foundations of any possible knowledge. … The difference between phenomenology and neurobiology is not just a difference with respect to the objects of their investigations, but a fundamental difference in their theoretical orientation" (quoted in Zahavi 2004, 338).

The extent to which phenomenology can be naturalized, however, is an ongoing debate; Husserl himself held different views on the issue, which differ further from those of other phenomenologists (see Zahavi 2004). For present purposes, it suffices to point out that phenomenology need not be at odds with natural science, and in fact, several voices within phenomenology have proposed and even implemented ways of reconciling the two approaches. As Husserl sometimes recognized, a careful and precise investigation of the structures of consciousness that respects its features and distinctive characteristics (what he occasionally called *phenomenological psychology*) can well be a "way into" transcendental phenomenology (Zahavi 2004). More concretely, a careful investigation of how consciousness is embodied, for example, can participate in the enterprise of revealing how subjectivity is constituted and how the world is disclosed to it in experience. The later Husserl and the early Merleau-Ponty were certainly sympathetic to this stance. The idea behind neurophenomenology and the enactive approach more generally is that the empirical subject and the transcendental subject are not two different subjects but two ways of looking at the same subject, which are not at odds but complementary (Thompson 2007).

A related issue involves the relationship between phenomenology and introspection. Phenomenologists emphasize that phenomenology is *not* mere introspection. Yet others fail to see a substantive difference. According to Bayne (2004), for example, Varela and colleagues' appeal to careful, disciplined, and systematic observation of one's own experience amounts to an appeal to introspection—to careful, disciplined, and systematic introspection as opposed to sloppy introspection, but to introspection nevertheless. Although I am not particularly bothered by the word "introspection," and I am quite happy to use it to refer broadly to the observation of lived experience from a first-person perspective, it is useful to remember that the term carries connotations that phenomenologists explicitly reject. Notably it suggests that the observation of lived experience amounts to gazing "inward" (to introspect literally means to "look inside") as opposed to "outward," arguably implying that the world as it is given in experience is not part of the phenomenological inquiry. Phenomenologists, however, adamantly deny that their interest is the investigation of inner or private objects of experience. Rather, their aim is to reveal the structures of subjectivity through which the world is disclosed in experience—such as the various ways in which different conscious acts intend objects, or the structure of time consciousness (see Gallagher and Zahavi 2008; Zahavi 2007, 2011b).

It is also important to appreciate that neurophenomenology does not aim to explain how physical processes *cause* consciousness; more generally, it does not aim to *close* the "explanatory gap" between experience and physical processes and thus to *solve* what Chalmers (1996) famously dubbed the "hard problem of consciousness," namely, the problem of understanding how consciousness is possible at all in the physical world. Admittedly, Varela (1996, 340) did propose neurophenomenology as "a natural solution that can allow us to go beyond the hard problem in the study of consciousness." However, he also emphasized that this solution is entirely *methodological*: it is a *pragmatic* way to deal with the explanatory gap. "Going beyond the hard problem" means here going beyond the methodological impasse that emerges when consciousness is taken to be irredeemably subjective and first-personal and therefore not describable by the third-personal language of science. As Thompson (2007, x) puts it at the beginning of his book, "To make real progress on the explanatory gap, we need richer phenomenological accounts of the structure of experience, and we need scientific accounts of mind and life informed by these phenomenological accounts. Phenomenology in turn needs to be informed by psychology, neuroscience, and biology." Neurophenomenology as an experimental method aims at making progress precisely in this sense.

Neurophenomenology is also importantly related to enactivism's thesis of the deep continuity of mind and life. Recall (see the introduction and chap. 1) that according to this thesis, mind shares the organizational properties of life. As Thompson (2007, 128) also puts it: "Mind is life-like and life is mind-like." Neurophenomenology can be seen as an experimental method to explore this thesis, namely, the extent to which mind reflects the organizational properties of the living organism (at the neural level, but not only).

A question that is sometimes asked about neurophenomenology is how exactly it differs from the search for the neural correlates of consciousness (NCC) that characterizes more mainstream cognitive neuroscience, namely, the search for the set of neural events minimally sufficient for consciousness (see Chalmers 2000). First, as we have seen, neurophenomenology does not only search for correlations between experience and neural activity. It proposes, on the one hand, to generate first-person data that can be used in interpreting physical activity and, on the other hand, to use third-person data to refine first-person data (this is the idea of "mutual constraints" between first- and third-person data). The proposal, in other words, is that first-person data should guide the organization and interpretation of third-person data, and also that first-person data should be revised in light of third-person data, in a process of codetermination and covalidation.[5]

Second, neurophenomenology does not interpret the "dynamical neural signatures" of conscious experiences (see earlier) as "minimally sufficient" for consciousness. This point is easy to overlook; after all, neurophenomenology has so far investigated correlations between experience and *brain* processes only, and the term "neurophenomenology" itself may suggest that brain processes are taken to be sufficient for consciousness. Yet neurophenomenology, as an offshoot of the enactive approach, is not committed to this view. According to enactivism, brain activity is only a *part* of the larger biological system (the situated organism) that enacts the mind, including consciousness. Enactivism emphasizes that the brain and the body are densely interconnected and mutually dependent for their survival and functioning (see chap. 4). Thompson and Cosmelli (forthcoming) argue that this dense interconnectivity and reciprocity imply that it is arbitrary to claim that consciousness supervenes only on neural processes in the brain, and that bodily processes are mere background conditions for consciousness. Following Bayne (2007), they point in particular to the phenomenon of *creature consciousness*, namely, the experience of being a specific creature, with its various global, nonmodal experiential states, such as wakefulness and dreaming. Creature consciousness is different from *state consciousness*, or the "what it's like" to have a specific experience with a certain phenomenal character, such as seeing red. State-conscious experiences always take place against the background of creature consciousness—and, crucially, there is no evidence that creature consciousness supervenes only on brain processes. Rather, drawing primarily on Parvizi and Damasio (2001), Thompson and Cosmelli argue that evidence indicates that the biological basis of creature consciousness includes subcortical areas involved in life regulation and homeostasis, which modulate bodily processes "by being densely interconnected to them on multiple cellular and molecular levels." Given this dense interconnectedness, it makes "little biological sense" to draw a line around the brain and stipulate that consciousness supervenes only on processes inside the line: "If the physiological system that supports creature consciousness comprises densely coupled neural, endocrine, and immune processes, and if it comprises sensorimotor loops through the body and the environment, then the biological basis of consciousness isn't brainbound."

From this perspective, observing brain activity provides only a partial glance into the organismic dynamics that enact lived experience (contra the NCC approach). This is also why neurophenomenology, which has so far limited its third-person methods to brain activity, ought to include recordings of bodily activity—thus becoming what I shall call, using a somewhat convoluted term, a *neuro-physio-phenomenology*. As we will see, the neuroscientific study of emotion already includes a variety of methods for recording bodily activity; the integration of these methods would thus provide a natural way of extending neurophenomenology to the rest of the organism.

Now that the place of neurophenomenology in the study of consciousness has hopefully been clarified, we can start to think about the possibility of applying it to the study of emotion experience. As mentioned, neurophenomenology has so far neglected emotion.[6] Affective neuroscience, for its part (as I am about to show in some detail), has focused primarily on the brain and bodily aspects of emotion and has paid relatively much less attention to its lived or conscious dimension, and to the possibility of integrating first-person methods with third-person ones.[7] Yet both approaches could benefit from each other: by incorporating the third-person methods of affective neuroscience, neurophenomenology could easily extend its attention from the brain only to the rest of the organism; on the other hand, by adopting a neurophenomenological approach, affective neuroscience may be able to address and answer some long-standing questions about the nature of emotion that require more careful consideration of how emotion is experienced.

6.4 Affective Neuroscience and Emotion Experience

What do I mean when I say that affective neuroscience has so far neglected emotion experience? In spite of impressive technological progress in neuroimaging and physiological measurements, affective neuroscience still exhibits a general lack of confidence in self-reports. Typically, specific emotions are attributed to (human and animal) subjects on the basis of their behavior and the nature of the stimuli used in the experiment (e.g., scary pictures, elating music), and these attributions guide the interpretation of brain activity (in the case of animal subjects, experimenters also act directly on brain activity via electrical stimulation; see, e.g., Panksepp 2005).

Little attention is paid to self-reports. This does not mean that no self-reports at all are ever collected; in experiments with human subjects, affective neuroscientists often do record first-person data, but reliance on these data is extremely cautious and minimized, in various senses. First, first-person data are typically obtained *at the end* of the experimental manipulation, mainly as a form of control, together with more reliable "objective" third-person measures; first-person data are not really incorporated into the experimental situation, for example, they are not used as an organizing analytic principle to cluster recordings of physical activity (as in Lutz et al. 2002).

Second, first-person data are typically obtained with *questionnaires* that ask subjects to *rate* their emotion experiences or feelings on some numerical scale. No method is usually elaborated or at least suggested for collecting and analyzing qualitative data, and for using these data to shed light on neural and physiological activity. Experience in these studies is thus reported only in a minimal way; no qualitative methods are used that would enable subjects to describe their feelings in a fine-grained way.

Third, the scales in question are usually not produced by the experimenter but borrowed from previous studies and standard questionnaires. These scales thus reflect previous theoretical assumptions about the nature of emotion experience (such as that it varies along the two dimensions of intensity and valence, for example), and subjects are not given the possibility to describe their feelings in their own words. The Differential Emotion Scale (DES) (Izard 1972), for instance, asks subjects to rate on a scale from 1 to 5 (from very slightly or not at all to very strongly) how happy, sad, angry, scared, and so on, they feel. This scale assumes that emotions come in irreducible distinctive qualities and does not allow researchers to explore possible dimensions of affects (i.e., it does not allow one to explore *how* it feels to feel angry, scared, etc.). Another widely used tool is the Positive Affect and Negative Affect Schedule (PANAS) (D. Watson, Clark, and Tellegen 1988), comprising ten words describing positive affects (interested, excited, strong, enthusiastic, proud, alert, inspired, determined, attentive, active) and ten words describing negative affects (distressed, upset, guilty, scared, hostile, irritable, ashamed, nervous, jittery, afraid). Subjects have to rate each item on a 1–5 scale according to how they feel (from very slightly or not at all to extremely). The scale can be used to ask subjects how they are feeling at the present moment, or how they have felt during the day, or in the past few days, weeks, year, or "on the average." As its name indicates, this scale is used to measure how good and bad a subject feels (positive affect and negative affect are here considered independent dimensions); again, however, it does not allow any further exploration of the quality of their experience.

Fourth, experimenters sometimes use standard clinical scales that are not designed to capture dimensions of experience *while* it is lived. For example, the Hamilton Anxiety Scale (Hamilton 1995), used by Critchley, Mathias, and Dolan (2001), consists of fourteen items, each defined by a series of symptoms such as "anxious mood (worries, anticipates worst)," "fears (of the dark, of strangers, of being alone, of animal)," "somatic complaints (muscle aches or pains, bruxism)," "insomnia (difficulty falling asleep or staying asleep, difficulty with nightmares)," "respiratory symptoms (chest pressure, choking sensation, shortness of breath)," and so on. Each of these items is rated by the subject on a five-point scale—from 0 (symptom not present) to 4 (severe). Clearly these items are not intended to capture dimensions of present lived experience, namely, of emotion as experienced *here and now*; at best, they capture how subjects feel "in general." Likewise for the Beck Depression Inventory (Beck and Steer 1993), which consists of twenty-one items, each of which identifies a specific symptom (sadness, pessimism, past failure, loss of pleasure, guilty feelings, crying, loss of energy, irritability, etc.) and asks subjects to rate each of these symptoms on a 0–3 scale.[8] Or consider the "body perception questionnaire" used by Critchley et al. (2004) to measure awareness of bodily and stress responses. The original questionnaire (Porges 1993) has five subtests, one for "awareness," one for "stress response," one for "autonomic nervous system reactivity," one for "stress style," and one for "health history." The questionnaire as a whole has 122 items to be answered on a five-point scoring scale that asks for frequency of sensations. For example, in the "awareness" subtest, subjects are asked to rate how often they are aware of "swallowing frequently," "an urge to urinate," "goose bumps," "stomach and gut pains," and so on. In the "body awareness" subtest, they are asked to rate how frequently they "feel nauseous," "have chest pains," "are constipated," "have indigestion," and so on. Again, this type of questionnaire is not meant to capture dimensions of bodily self-awareness in the here and now; therefore it could not be used in a study looking for correlations between lived experience and physiological activity.[9]

Fifth, affective neuroscience tends to reduce emotion experience to a *static* phenomenon. Take the fascinating study by Blood and Zatorre (2001) of the "chills" that many people often experience while listening to highly pleasurable music. Subjects listened to their favorite music tracks while their regional cerebral blood flow activity was recorded with PET, and bodily activity was also measured along various dimensions (heart rate, facial muscle contraction, respiration depth, skin conductance, skin temperature). After each PET scan, subjects rated their affective response to each stimulus along three analog rating scales—one for "chill intensity" (from 0 to 10), one for "emotional intensity" (from 0 to 10), and one for "unpleasant versus pleasant" feelings (from –5 to +5). The study found that intensity of felt chills was correlated with cerebral blood flow in brain regions involved in reward/ motivation, emotion, and arousal, also known to activate in response to other euphoria-inducing stimuli (sex, food, drugs). So in this study, self-reports were used to interpret brain activity, but only for the goal of localizing areas of the brain significantly responsible for the *intensity* of feeling. No data were obtained about the *temporal* unfolding of the experience of listening to highly pleasurable music, or about the temporal profile of the accompanying brain activity. The methodology employed to collect first-person data instead zoomed in on static features of the experience, somehow distilling and abstracting the phenomenon under observation (this abstraction process is particularly apparent given the temporal nature of the stimulus, i.e., music). As we shall see shortly, the situation is slowly changing, and more studies are looking at the temporal unfolding of experience. However, it remains fair to say that the mainstream approach is still quite static.

The reasons why affective neuroscience has not explored more elaborate methods for collecting first-person data are probably the familiar ones that led the scientific study of the mind more generally to reject the introspectionist methods of early scientific psychology (e.g., Wundt 1907), such as the proliferation of incompatible descriptions of experience from different laboratories. These methods were further undermined by much-quoted authors like Nisbett and Wilson (1977, 233), who famously concluded, after reviewing a variety of empirical evidence, that "the accuracy of subjective reports is so poor as to suggest that any introspective access that may exist is not sufficient to produce generally correct or reliable reports." They mentioned evidence showing, for example, that subjects often cannot correctly identify the stimuli that caused a certain response, cannot correctly recall the opinions they previously held on a certain topic (thus showing lack of awareness that their views have changed), and cannot access the cognitive processes underlying their evaluations, problem solving, and attitudes toward others. Note, however, that these studies do not show that subjects cannot accurately report the *contents* of their experiences. What they show, rather, is that subjects are not good at reporting the causes of their behavior and mental states, and the cognitive processes underlying them—but reporting causes and underlying cognitive processes is not part of the enterprise of describing lived experience in its various dimensions and temporal unfolding (see also Vermersch 1999; Petitmengin and Bitbol 2009). Nisbett and Wilson themselves drew a distinction between "cognitive processes" and "mental contents" and emphasized that it is the former (the causes of, and influences on, our decisions, judgments, etc.), not the latter, that cannot be introspected (see also Hurlburt and Schwitzgebel 2007, 26–27).

Researchers today generally agree that the possibility of developing first-person methods for the observation and study of experience was dismissed too quickly. The last decade has seen a revival of introspection, with a renewed interest in the elaboration of first- as well as second-person methods for the study of experience (e.g., Varela and Shear 1999; Velmans 2000; Jack and Roepstorff 2003, 2004; Petitmengin 2009; Price and Barrell 2012). These methods do not involve asking subjects to introspect the causes (the "why") of their experiences and actions, as well as the cognitive processes producing them. Rather, they aim at enabling subjects to attend to and describe their experiences as they unfold. In particular, as we shall see shortly, they require subjects to focus not only on *what* they experience but also on *how* they experience it. The working assumption of neurophenomenology in particular is that these descriptions, when gathered rigorously with appropriate methods, can be used to interpret and make sense of brain activity.

Affective neuroscience has hardly been influenced by this renewed interest in first- and second-person methods. At the moment, it wavers between recognizing the need to ask subjects how they feel (see the use of questionnaires mentioned earlier), and fearing too much reliance on their reports.

In most cases, the fearful view prevails, and consequently researchers sidestep emotion experience. I think it is fair to say that Davidson et al.'s (2003) chapter in the *Handbook of Affective Sciences* (Davidson, Scherer, and Goldsmith 2003) is still paradigmatic of this attitude. The authors initially acknowledge that it is "tempting and often important to obtain measures of subjects' conscious experience of the contents of their emotional states and traits" (9), but conscious experience quickly disappears from their discussion. The chapter instead reviews how various emotional functions have been attributed to specific brain areas via observation of behavior—namely, "using objective laboratory probes rather than relying exclusively upon self-report data" (9). The authors never discuss why it is "tempting and often important" to measure a subject's experience; they rapidly dismiss the issue by appealing to previous failures of using self-reports.[10]

Yet as Davidson et al. (2003) undoubtedly know, one need not rely *exclusively* on self-reports to study emotion experience; rather, data obtained with self-reports can and should be integrated with data about behavior, expression, brain activity, and so on. The question is how to accomplish this integration, and how to develop methods for the collection of first-person data that can do more justice to the complexity of lived emotion experience than the current "just-take-a-look" attitude.

6.5   Outline of an Affective Neuro-physio-phenomenological Method

From an enactive neurophenomenological perspective, affective neuroscience ought to take experience more seriously. Specifically, it should pay considerably more attention to the elaboration of methods for the exploration of lived experience, for the generation of self-reports, and for the integration of first- and third-person data. It should also consider using third-person data to help subjects refine their reports. Finally, it ought to take a more dynamical approach to both experience and physical processes, without reducing them to static phenomena.

In this section, we will see in more detail how these neurophenomenological recommendations could be applied to the neuroscientific study of emotion experience. In what follows, I distinguish five steps that include first-, second-, and third-person methods and how to integrate them. These could serve as an overarching guide for the scientific study of emotion experience, and as a repository of ideas. My impression is that research in affective neuroscience is gradually moving closer to the method outlined here, but given the complexity of the field, it is useful to lay down the guiding principles in a systematic and reasoned way.

(1) Self-observation (first-person methods)

The experimenter could begin by observing her or his own emotion experience as it takes place. As difficult as this task may be, especially when it comes to the details, emotions are at least relatively frequently available. One may not experience strong feelings daily (strong feelings may be easier to observe at first), but still often enough to sample a variety of observations. Given that when it comes to assessing and sampling others' reports, reliance on one's own experience is inevitable, self-observation should be treated as an important aspect of the method.[11]

Crucially, the kind of self-observation advocated here should rely not on an inquisitive, judgmental, and actively discriminating form of attention but on a *passive-observational* stance toward one's mental life—a "bare attention" or "receptive openness," as Thompson, Lutz, and Cosmelli (2005) call it. This stance is akin to what several Eastern meditative techniques recommend, namely, the cultivation of a mental attitude that merely "takes note" of what the subject feels, thinks, desires, and so on, without judging, rejecting, or praising (Wallace 1999; Depraz, Varela, and Vermersch 2003). These techniques are increasingly being applied in the West in clinical contexts (notably, so-called mindfulness-based cognitive therapy aims to prevent depression, for example, by training subjects merely to take note of their current experiences and thoughts, including in particular the negative feelings and ruminative thoughts that can induce and reinforce depression; see Z. Segal, Williams, and Teasdale 2002) and could be used to train and refine self-observation.

Depraz, Varela, and Vermersch (2003) also provide a detailed description of how to achieve such a receptive and open observational stance. They mention three "interrelated acts" of *suspension, redirection,* and *letting go.* What needs to be suspended is one's naive and immersed attention in the contents or objects of experience (the "what" of experience). Attention needs to be redirected toward the "how" of experience, that is, the act of experiencing itself, in its various dimensions. Thus, for example, when exploring one's fear in a certain situation, the focus should be redirected from the feared object to how one experiences the fear (such as its intensity, its bodily character, its hedonic tone); likewise, when observing an instance of intense joy, one should redirect attention to the way one "lives through" the joy (as a sense of expansion, perhaps, accompanied by the desire to jump or throw one's arms up in the air). Importantly, throughout this process, the subject needs to let her experience "go"—that is, let it arise and unfold "as it is," without interfering by judging, analyzing, or trying to find a cause for it.

Observing one's own experience in this way, and for more than a handful of seconds, does not come naturally. Indeed, Eastern philosophies, and Western appropriations thereof, recommend a variety of practices to develop concentration and the ability to sustain an attitude of "bare noticing" of one's experience for extended periods. *Training* of self-observation is therefore a requirement of this approach. Exactly how much training is needed should be established empirically as the method is applied and developed. As for how to train subjects, researchers could employ techniques that have already been developed in the mindfulness-based approach mentioned earlier (Z. Segal, Williams, and Teasdale 2002). This approach involves, among other things, training oneself to just take note of pleasant and unpleasant experiences when they arise, and to explore how they relate to one's thoughts and bodily sensations. One may object that if one trains this way, one's experiences lose their natural spontaneity and may even become something completely different. I think that this objection can be met, and I will come back to it at the end of the next subsection.

For now I want to move on to the question of what could be observed for the purposes of an affective neurophenomenological study. Perhaps the simplest thing to do would be to start by focusing on felt *intensity* and *hedonic tone* (the extent to which an emotion feels pleasant or unpleasant), which, according to several psychological theories, characterize all emotion experiences (e.g., Russell 2003; Barrett 2006c). It is, however, far from clear what makes an instance of, say, anger more intense than another. It may be a more intense motivational drive, which would itself need to be explored; it may be a heightened perception of one's urges to act or of one's visceral activity. As for hedonic tone, it may be interesting to identify experiences that feel undoubtedly good and bad, as well as experiences with a mixed hedonic tone. Do feelings usually come with mixed hedonic tone, or are they most often clearly either pleasant or unpleasant? In the latter case, what gives a feeling its pleasant or unpleasant hedonic tone? When a feeling is hedonically mixed, how is the mixture experienced? It has been suggested, for example, that nostalgia is a mixed feeling (e.g., Prinz 2004b, 165): it feels bad because one is missing something, but it also involves a memory of how good it was to have that something. Does this mixture involve alternations of pleasant and unpleasant feelings, depending on what the subject is attending to (the loss, or the past possession)? Or is it a more intimate admixture, something more like the taste of a sweet-and-sour dish, which feels sweet and sour at the same time?[12]

Self-observation could also be used to find out whether terms like "sadness," "anger," "pride," "jealousy," and so on, pick out exactly the same experiences in different contexts, or whether there are *experiential variations* of the same emotion category. In spite of considerable progress (as we saw in chap. 2), researchers still disagree on the neural concomitants of emotion, and it has proved difficult to find emotion-specific neural and physiological activity. One source of this difficulty may be that scientists lump together under the same folk psychological labels (e.g., "sadness," "anger") what are in fact different emotional episodes or emotion forms, which could be discriminated via a more detailed and rigorous exploration of emotion experience.[13]

Other ways in which self-observation could be used would be in the exploration of experiences of emotions that are often conflated, such as shame and guilt, shame and embarrassment, disgust and contempt, disgust and fear, jealousy and envy. It may well be that these affects have several experiential features in common, which would be useful to identify with precision. Other possibilities would consist in focusing on less popular dimensions than intensity and hedonic tone, such as sense of intersubjective connectedness, sense of control, self-relevance, and temporal orientation (past, present, or future); or maybe even associations with sensory modalities, such as sense of warmth or coldness, softness or harshness, and impressions of colors and tastes (sweet, acid).

The list could continue, but these examples should suffice. The main point of these considerations is to refocus the study of emotion on lived experience itself and invite affective neuroscientists unashamedly to put emotion experience explicitly on their research agenda. Some of the issues I have listed here, such as the mixed nature of some feelings, or the relationship between shame and guilt, and envy and jealousy, have been addressed already, but rarely if at all with an explicit focus on lived experience.[14] When it comes to it, quick glances at experience are the best one can find. The present approach, on the other hand, calls for a more careful and detailed use of self-observation.

At this stage of the investigation, collection of first-person data would consist primarily of written accounts of one's experiences, describing the situation, but above all the quality of the experience. Subjects could also try to identify stimuli (music, films, literary texts) that reliably induce specific feelings, and to observe and report on these feelings as they unfold in real time (these stimuli may be used later in the laboratory). Real-time descriptions of experience, if difficult to report, could be replaced at this stage by immediate retrospective reports. Subjects could also aim to identify particularly salient moments in their experience and to characterize what makes them salient. Some time should also be spent to find the words or expressions that best describe one's experiences. Words or expressions that recur more frequently in one's experiences could then be highlighted and used to produce a list of relevant experiential factors.

(2) Intersubjective validation (second-person methods)

Self-observation by itself would not take the scientific study of emotion experience very far. To validate its findings, second-person methods should be employed—namely, methods whereby data about experience are corroborated and even generated in the interaction of two or more individuals.

Ideally, second-person methods should include both qualitative and quantitative methods. Qualitative methods such as semistructured interviews with open questions could be used by the experimenters to supplement and refine their self-observations. In semistructured interviews, the interviewer aims at establishing a connection with the interviewee. Although she is guided by a preestablished schedule of questions, she need not follow it strictly and need not ask the same questions in all interviews; rather, she uses questions to probe areas of interest and concern and eventually lets the interview be guided by the interviewee (as opposed to structured interviews, where the same set of questions is asked in the same order to all subjects, and there is no room for digressions; see Smith and Osborn 2008). Whereas closed questions invite a yes or no answer, open questions encourage the interviewee to provide the information that is most relevant for her or him, in a nonconstraining way.

So, for example, after having explored and described their own experiences, two or more experimenters could begin by asking one another, in separate interviews, open questions such as "how do you feel when you experience this emotion?" or "what is it like being in this situation?" Based on their previous self-observations, they could help one another to attend to aspects of their experiences that would otherwise go unnoted. For example, if one person does not report any bodily sensation, the interviewer could ask her or him to attend to this aspect of the experience. Similarly for other dimensions of experience that one may have noted in one's own self-observations.

It is important for this questioning to remain as open as possible; interviewers should invite subjects to attend to their feelings so as to explore them in detail, without, however, imposing their own views, but by adopting a stance of nonjudgmental curiosity, interest, and empathetic understanding.[15] Training would thus need to be an important part of the approach at this stage, as well. Again, mindfulness-based cognitive therapy already provides useful indications about the attitude that interviewers should take when guiding others in the exploration of their experiences. It emphasizes nonjudgmental openness, kindness, and patience, as well as a "beginner's mind" attitude that explores the qualities of the other's experiences with renewed curiosity and acceptance of whatever arises. It stresses that the interviewer should encourage participants to develop trust in their capacity to report their experiences, and to cultivate an attitude of nonstriving and dwelling in the present moment (Crane 2009).[16]

Experimenters could at this point distinguish between dimensions of experience that turn out to be shared (if any), and others that appear more idiosyncratic. (Another way to extrapolate such dimensions would be to have the investigators read each other's self-reports several times and identify recurrent factors, as is done in interpretative phenomenological analysis; see Smith and Osborn 2008.) "Functional analyses" could also be conducted at this point, namely, analyses of whether and how identified dimensions of experience vary as a function of each other (see D. Price, Barrell, and Rainville 2002; Price and Barrell 2012). For example, one could explore whether and how changes in the experience of self-control correlate with changes in hedonic tone, or whether and how changes in the urge to move correlate with changes in felt intensity.

Standard psychometric methods could be introduced to generate more quantitative data. The experimenters could create scales and questionnaires on the basis of their findings and have them rated by "theoretically naive" subjects, namely, subjects unaware of the aim of the inquiry (again, see

Price, Barrell, and Rainville 2002; Price and Barrell 2012). Or these scales could be used by one or more independent judges to rate reports of experience provided by a variety of participants (as suggested in Schredl 2010 for the analysis of dream contents).

Another approach would consist in adopting a variety of quantitative and qualitative methods from the beginning to explore subjects' experiences. Le Van Quyen and Petitmengin (2002) did so to explore, specifically, the experiences of epileptic subjects before a seizure (known as preictal experiences). They used a log form to ask hospitalized epileptic patients to reflect every morning on their state of fatigue, stress, and emotional condition in general, as well as on particular bodily, visual, and auditory sensations. Patients had to fill in another log form with similar questions after each seizure; this form also asked them to focus on the quality of their experience immediately before the seizure, to remember what were they doing then, at which moment they started to feel specific sensations, how long did they last, and more. Similar questions were asked in another log form that patients had to fill in after a "mini-crisis," namely, a preictal episode that did not lead to a full seizure. These forms alternated questions in which subjects had to rate their current condition on a numerical scale, and more open questions in which subjects were asked to report on their condition using their own words.[17]

Le Van Quyen and Petitmengin also carried out interviews with the patients. In the first stage, they asked them to recall a specific preictal experience and to "relive" it by remembering in as much detail as possible the images, sensations, sounds, and so on, associated with it. In the second stage, the interviewers helped the patients "slow down" the recollection of their experience, to thematize or attend to aspects of it that had so far remained implicit or unnoticed. In the third stage, they helped patients put their experience into words. Finally, they produced "a synthetic representation of the dynamical micro-temporal structure of the experience, and also of the dimensions of the experience which are not temporal" (Le Van Quyen and Petitmengin 2002, 176).

A similar method could be applied for the exploration of emotion experience. Experimenters could ask subjects to recall events that reliably evoke specific feelings for them (as done, e.g., in the study by Damasio et al. [2000] mentioned earlier; see also Rainville et al. 2006). Immediately after evoking the experience, subjects could fill in a form with more and less open questions intended to draw attention to several aspects of their experience, such as: Is there anything characteristic or unique to this experience? If you had to label it, what would you call this experience? Is the experience accompanied by bodily feelings? If yes, can you describe them? Is the experience accompanied by tendencies or urges to move? If yes, could you describe them in some detail? Or more specifically: Are the bodily feelings localized? Are urges to act directed toward the world or away from it, expansive or contractive? Is the experience pleasant? Is the experience unpleasant? Do you feel in control of the experience, or is the experience overwhelming? An interview could follow, in which the answers given to these questions are explored in more detail. At this stage the interviewer could help the subject expand on aspects of the experience that have not been thematized or made explicit yet, by asking further questions such as which images, thoughts, or further sensations accompany a specific bodily feeling or moment of displeasure. In this way, further dynamics internal to the experience may be revealed.

A recommendation that has not sufficiently been emphasized, not even in qualitative approaches (but see Schwitzgebel 2007), is that before engaging in these kinds of intersubjective methods, it would be important to clarify how participants should understand key terms likely to appear in the inquiry—terms such as "feelings," "awareness," "experience," "attention," "emotion," "consciousness," "bodily sensations," "thoughts," and so on. These terms are typically used in different ways by different people (including philosophers), and it would be essential to find as much agreement as possible from the beginning on how they will be used by all participants.

Interlude: But don't first- and second-person methods distort the experience one wants to investigate?

An objection, or at least a perplexity, that is almost invariably raised at this point about the first- and second-person methods outlined so far is that they *distort* the observed experience. Note, however, that this objection is typically formulated from the armchair, with no particularly compelling evidence. Rather, it is a generic skeptical point. One can choose to adopt a skeptical stance and reject the possibility of phenomenological reflection a priori, but in my view this choice would amount to prematurely closing up potentially valuable research avenues. Pragmatically, it seems to me that we *lose less* if we take a more moderate "middle course" and acknowledge that self-observation "involves a gain and a loss" (Gallagher and Zahavi 2008, 63): it brings clarity and detail, it "discloses, disentangles, explicates, and articulates ... components and structures which were contained implicitly in the lived experience" (63), and in doing so, it changes the immersed and tacit attitude of prereflective experience into something explicit, and therefore different (see also Zahavi 2005, chap. 4). Also, we can acknowledge that subjects' reports need not always be taken at face value, without thereby rejecting the possibility of self-observation altogether, and the suggestion (a working hypothesis) that some conditions and methods of reflection favor the generation of better first-person data than others. The psychologists Lambie and Marcel (2002) make a related point. They distinguish between first-order tacit experience (which they call "phenomenology") and second-order reflective or attentive "awareness," and they argue that even if it is the case that attending to first-order experience changes it, it is implausible to assume that it creates or brings into being all its aspects. Their view is rather that tacit experience depends specifically on the mode of attention one pays to it; specifically, the more analytic the mode of attention, the more abstracted and decontextualized the experience (235), whereas "We can be veridically aware of first-order phenomenology to the extent that we attend highly synthetically at the time. Paradoxical though it seems, we are sometimes in states of both detached awareness and immersion, in which we are aware of our concurrently immersed phenomenology" (237). This is also why, as we saw, neurophenomenology insists on training subjects to adopt a form of nonjudgmental "bare attention" or "receptive openness." This attitude is considered less likely to fragment and distort the observed experience (see also Price, Barrell, and Rainville 2002; Petitmengin and Bitbol 2009; Price and Barrell 2012).

A related perplexity sometimes raised about the first- and second-person methods recommended here concerns the requirement that subjects be *trained*. After all—the worry goes—lived experience is naturally untrained and spontaneous; because neurophenomenology focuses on trained subjects, it is not a study of natural, untrained consciousness.

The reason why training, including guidance by an interviewer, is recommended in neurophenomenology is that it is not easy to switch from our everyday "natural attitude" of immersion in the world to considering and observing the experience itself. Untrained subjects, when asked to do so, find it difficult. Russell Hurlburt, who as part of his "experience sampling" method "beeps" subjects randomly at various moments of the day and asks them to report what they are experiencing at that moment, notes that subjects at the beginning of the process do not know how to describe an experience (indeed, they are not even sure what an experience is), are reluctant to do so, do not distinguish between "apprehension and theorizing" (i.e., between observing the experience and commenting on what the experience should be, what could have caused it, how it fits with one's self-image, etc.), cannot bracket their presuppositions, and do not observe their experience skillfully (Hurlburt 2009). Thus the aim of training is to overcome these difficulties and to provide subjects with observational skills that can generate better first-person data. In addition, training of the kind advocated in neurophenomenology aims to improve concentration; to enable subjects to observe specific aspects of their experience without being too distracted by interfering mental activity, including passing thoughts, sensations, and evaluations; and to distinguish between aspects of the experience and comments or judgments about it. In the absence of training, self-observation is likely to generate inconsistent reports and thus unreliable data.

Now, if the worry is that the reports of subjects trained in this manner provide exceptional data and thus are not representative of "normal" experience, I would first simply reiterate the previous point that there do not seem to be good reasons to adopt such an overly sceptical stance, and assume that training will make subjects' experience into something completely unrelated to untrained experience. Rather, it seems more productive to hypothesize that training can be used to enable subjects to articulate dimensions of experience previously unnoted. Second, neurophenomenology, as we saw, was originally proposed as a method to explore the relationship between consciousness and physical processes. From this perspective, it is not a problem that first-person data are obtained from trained subjects; priority is given to obtaining first-person data that are stable and consistent, and these are difficult, if not impossible, to gather from untrained subjects. To the extent that training helps generate such data, it provides an advantage rather than an obstacle. True, that makes neurophenomenology the study of trained experience, but for the purposes of investigating the relationship between experience and neurophysiological processes, this is not damning. (Note also that nothing prevents a neurophenomenological experiment from obtaining reports from both trained and untrained subjects and comparing how their reports correlate with third-person data. The working assumption of neurophenomenology is that in the case of trained subjects, more robust and reliable correlations will be found between aspects of what they report and third-person data.)

In sum, ultimately my view is that, at the current stage, it is premature and excessively skeptical to dismiss the possibility that subjects can be trained to report on their experiences, and that their self-reports may provide data that will help us to interpret neural activity. At the least, practicing observation of one's experience will enhance sensitivity to its various dimensions and fluctuations (which, incidentally, is likely to enhance well-being as a side effect of increased awareness; see Philippot and Segal 2009). This outcome seems desirable for the purposes of studying emotion experience in its various dimensions and changes over time, in a context like the current one in which no training whatsoever is used in neuroscientific studies of emotion experience, and subjects are merely asked quickly to report how they feel on a numerical scale. It may be that it is precisely because of the lack of a methodology for exploring lived experience that affective neuroscience has so far avoided studying feelings in greater depth and has held, at best, an ambivalent attitude toward first-person data.

(3)   Recording brain and bodily activity (third-person methods)

An important aspect of a neuro-physio-phenomenological approach would involve the collection of third-person data. Affective neuroscience has already developed a variety of methods for recording neural and bodily activity, which could all be used in affective neuro-physio-phenomenological studies.

fMRI and PET are widely used already. Although informative, these techniques, however, overlook the temporal dynamics of emotion and tend to foster the view that different emotions must be localized in specific brain areas (exceptions include temporal fMRI; also, recent studies can combine fMRI with other techniques to improve its temporal resolution). EEG and MEG are less frequently used in emotion research, mainly because they allegedly cannot reach brain activity that is deep enough to detect emotion.[18] However, we saw in chapter 4 that, according to recent neuroscientific accounts, emotion is not buried in the limbic system but largely distributed along the neuroaxis. If this is right, then EEG and MEG *are* relevant for the investigation of emotion. One of their advantages is that they are particularly suited to exploring the temporal unfolding of experience (see, e.g., Rudrauf et al. 2009). It would be interesting to use these techniques to look for *synchronization* of large-scale neural activity during affect (as attempted by Dan Glauser and Scherer 2008; see also the next subsection). In addition, third-person data could be gathered by measuring bodily activity, such as muscular tension and ANS activity. Here in particular it would be interesting to find out whether the temporal profiles of brain and bodily processes correlate. Few of the studies that look at both brain and bodily activities also look at how they vary in relation to one another (see D'Hondt et al. 2010); most often, bodily activity is recorded in brain studies of emotion only as an additional form of control and is not correlated with brain activity.

(4) Correlating first- and third-person data
Investigating whether, for example, emotion experiences carefully discriminated via first- and second-person methods are accompanied by different patterns of brain activity as measured by fMRI or PET would already constitute a step toward a more neurophenomenological approach. Using EEG or MEG would also allow researchers to investigate whether experience and physical processes covary over time. The proposal here, in short, is to look in as much detail as possible at whether—and, if so, how—experience, brain, and bodily activity change together over time.

Some authors have suggested that feelings correspond to phases of functional integration and synchronization of a variety of psychological processes underpinned by neural processes spanning the whole brain (Lewis 2005; Lewis and Todd 2005; Scherer 2009). It would be interesting to investigate whether emotion experience is in fact accompanied by coherent large-scale brain activity (just as Lutz et al. [2002] have done for visual perception), and more specifically whether different feelings are accompanied by different patterns of synchronization. For example, it would be interesting to see whether clearly perceived significant changes in the affective quality of an ongoing emotion experience correspond to, perhaps, momentary desynchronization or phase scattering in brain activity, followed by a new coherent pattern as another experience (re)stabilizes. Lewis (2005) suggests that synchronization in the case of an emotional episode is likely to happen at the level of hippocampal theta waves (waves with a frequency of 4–10 Hz that can be detected with EEG). Although it is not possible to detect brain waves from the deeper layers of the brain in human subjects without using invasive techniques (allowed only in some cases for therapeutic reasons, as in the case of epilepsy), there are so few studies of temporal synchronization in relation to emotion experience that recording cortical waves would already be informative.[19]

Comparatively more studies have explored the relationship between experience and bodily activity—or, as it is sometimes put, the extent to which experiential, behavioral, and physiological responses "cohere" during an emotion. Empirical findings in this field are mixed, with some studies showing some positive correlations between experience and bodily activity (especially facial expressions), but others showing no correlations at all, or even negative ones (for references, see Mauss et al. 2005; see also Grewe et al. 2007; Sze et al. 2010).

One problem with most of these studies, as pointed out by Mauss et al. (2005), is that they rely on retrospective or "aggregated" ratings of experience (i.e., ratings of the experience "overall"), rather than enabling subjects to report on their experiences online, moment by moment. If, however, one is looking for moment-to-moment correlations between experience and bodily activity, one should try to measure experience "on the fly," as it is taking place. For example, subjects could press a button whenever particularly salient feelings appear in the course of the experience—such as perceivable changes in emotional tone, or distinct bodily sensations. Analogical measuring devices could provide more detail about the nuances of the temporal unfolding of the experience. Researchers in the psychology of music have started using such devices to measure experience (perception of emotion conveyed by music, or emotion experience itself) continuously as it unfolds over time. Grewe et al. (2007) and Grewe, Kopiez, and Altenmüller (2009) used the EMuJoy software (Nagel et al. 2007), developed precisely for this purpose: subjects use a joystick while listening to music, moving the cursor in a two-dimensional space (the dimensions are arousal and pleasantness–unpleasantness). Mauss et al. (2005) used a "rating dial" that allows subjects to rate continuously on a 180-degree dial (ranging from 0 to 8) how much fear, anger, amusement, sadness, and so on, they feel at each moment while being exposed to a stimulus. Using this method, Mauss et al. found positive correlations between self-reports of amusement, facial expressions, and bodily activity (cardiovascular activation, skin conductance level, and somatic activity), and between self-reports and facial expressions of sadness. (For an overview of other devices developed for the continuous recording of perceived expression in music, such as tongs, sliders, and foot switches, see Gabrielsson and Juslin 2003; see also Schubert 2001.)

The approach taken in these two studies is more in line with the one favored here; however, notice that the rating dial does not explore dimensions of experience but only asks "how much" of an emotion one is experiencing. Ideally, in an affective neuro-physio-phenomenological experiment, subjects should be able to report on different specific dimensions of their lived experience (preferably in different trials) as it is taking place. Notice also that the two studies do not incorporate or recommend any method for training subjects. It would be interesting to see whether training led to different results. Alternatively, one could select subjects who have already different levels of self-observing skills (e.g., compare music experts, meditators, and nonexperts).

A recent study by Salimpoor et al. (2011) also used a methodology approximating the one outlined here. They investigated how brain, body, and experience correlate over time while subjects listened to their favorite music. First they showed that listening to pleasurable music (measured as a function of the number and intensity of reported "chills"), as opposed to neutral music, correlates positively with ANS activity along all the dimensions they measured, as well as with endogenous release of dopamine in the striatal system. Then they showed that different moments of the experience of listening to pleasurable music—"peak pleasure" and its anticipation, respectively—correlate with dopamine release in different parts of the striatal system. Both this temporal perspective and the use of subjective reports to interpret brain activity are distinctively neurophenomenological features of the experiment. More "mainstream" features include the fact that subjects were asked to press a button only when they experienced chills, and these responses were used post hoc to identify moments of "peak experiences" and of anticipation. Anticipation was identified simply as the experience felt during fifteen seconds before the peak. Hence subjects were not asked to describe their experience as they listened to music, and to identify feelings of anticipation from feelings of pleasure. Also, note that the study did not look for possible different patterns of ANS activity during anticipation and peak experiences. I raise these points not to diminish the relevance of this fascinating study and its impressive technical achievement but to point to what still distinguishes it from a fully neuro-physio-phenomenological approach.

(5)   Use of third-person methods to refine self-observation

Finally, a neuro-physio-phenomenological approach to affect would also try to use third-person data to refine experience and self-awareness. Indeed, when I suggested earlier that disgust may have different experiential subforms, I was partly guided by Kreibig's (2010) recent meta-analysis of 134 studies of ANS activity of emotion; this analysis shows, among many other things, that disgust toward polluting or contaminating stimuli (such as pictures of dirty toilets or cockroaches) is associated with different ANS activity compared with disgust toward stimuli like mutilation, injury, and blood (see also Harrison et al. 2010, discussed in the next section). Kreibig notes that for the purposes of interpreting ANS activity, it is important to clarify the differences between various emotion concepts. Her own work, however, also shows that research on autonomic differences can in turn be used to guide self-observation of emotion experience (and eventually perhaps to refine our emotion categories).

As mentioned, this aspect of Varela's (1996) original proposal has not yet been developed. At present, however, biofeedback techniques are being increasingly used for a variety of purposes, including emotion regulation. Early studies used feedback from the body to train subjects to regulate their bodily activity (see the contributions in Birbaumer and Kimmell 1979), whereas *neuro*feedback is now receiving growing attention. In a recent study, Johnston et al. (2010) showed that it is relatively easy to train subjects to regulate their emotion experience by using "real-time fMRI" (or rtfMRI; see deCharms 2008). The experimenters targeted brain areas known to activate significantly during unpleasant emotions and showed subjects various positive, neutral, and negative pictures (i.e., pictures known to elicit pleasant, indifferent, and unpleasant emotion experiences, respectively). Subjects received feedback about activity in these areas by looking at the picture of a thermometer whose temperature reflected increases in fMRI amplitude signal (feedback was updated every two seconds), and were instructed to regulate activity in the target brain regions by relying on the feedback. Johnston et al. (2010) found that subjects were able to regulate activity in the target areas already from the first run. Interestingly, subjects were not given any specific instructions about how to do so, and most subjects ended up relying on imagery or memory. This study is related to previous findings on the possibility of using rtfMRI to modulate the experience of pain (deCharms et al. 2005). Unlike Johnston et al., deCharms et al. gave subjects strategies for regulating their experience, such as attending toward or away from the painful stimulus or attempting to focus on the "merely physical" aspects of the stimulus.

These studies are primarily aimed at enabling subjects to regulate their brain and body, but the same techniques could just as well be used as self-exploratory tools. In light of recent developments, it would seem to be relatively easy to apply biofeedback techniques to the study of affective experience: subjects could be shown recordings of their neural and autonomic activity while attending to their feelings and specific dimensions of them, which could draw their attention to aspects of the experience that may otherwise go unnoticed.

6.6   Bodily Feelings and Emotion Experience

The place of bodily feelings in emotion experience, and the relationship between bodily feelings and actual bodily arousal, seem perfect topics for a neuro-physio-phenomenological approach. For one, as we saw in the previous chapter, there are divergent opinions regarding the place of bodily feelings in emotion experience. Some, like James (1884), claim that bodily feelings always accompany the experience of emotion; others, like Goldie (2000), claim it is obvious that some emotion experiences are not bodily in this (phenomenological) sense. First- and second-person methods could be used to explore these claims more systematically and in more detail. It may be that, in the interaction with an interviewer, some subjects can become aware of subtle or inconspicuous (see previous chapter) bodily feelings that would otherwise remain unnoted. In fact, it seems that some subjects are just not used to paying attention to their body but with appropriate guidance can become more sensitive to it (see, e.g., Gendlin 1996). Perhaps then, with appropriate guidance, "If the reader has never paid attention to this matter, he will be both interested and astonished to learn how many different local bodily feelings he can detect in himself as characteristic of his various emotional moods" (James 1884, 192). Yet it might also be possible to identify emotion experiences that are, reportedly, not felt as bodily, and to explore their quality in some detail.

Also, first- and second-person methods could be used to address a difficulty noted some time ago by Nieuwenhuyse, Offenberg, and Frijda (1987) regarding empirical studies of the bodily character of emotion experience.

Various studies have shown that subjects report different bodily sensations for different emotions (e.g., Nieuwenhuyse, Offenberg, and Frijda 1987; Scherer and Wallbott 1994; Philippot and Rimé 1997). Yet it may be that participants in this kind of study report not what they actually feel but what they *expect* they should feel on the basis of existing "schemes" or folk psychological assumptions of what count as typical bodily feelings for specific emotions (see also Philippot and Rimé 1997). First- and second-person methods could help here by repeatedly inviting subjects to attend to their bodily sensations. Indeed, it is frequently observed in discussions of second-person methods that subjects initially tend to answer questions about their experience by reporting what they think they should be experiencing, rather than what they actually experience (see, e.g., Gendlin 1996; Petitmengin 2007). The suggestion is that second-person methods could help by redirecting the subjects' attention, to help them stay focused on their actual experience.

It would be interesting also to compare the emotion experiences of subjects with different levels of expertise in bodily awareness, and different training in bodily awareness. Sze et al. (2010) have already conducted one such study. They looked at visceral awareness (measured in terms of awareness of heart rate) in meditators, dancers, and people with no training and found that meditators (who as part of their practice pay attention to breathing and cardiac sensations) reported the highest level of visceral awareness, followed by dancers (taken, in this study, usually to rely more on somatic awareness).[20] It would be interesting to investigate further whether these subjects also differ in terms of the reported bodily character of their emotion experiences. Consider also that different dance styles cultivate different forms of bodily awareness. Whereas traditional ballet dancers use mirrors when training, contemporary dancers rely mainly on proprioception; there are even dance styles, such as the Japanese Butoh, that require the performers to attend also to their interoceptive sensations (Legrand and Ravn 2009). Do these different training styles and practices affect how subjects experience their body in emotion?

Third-person methods could then be used to investigate the relationship between first-person data thus collected and actual bodily activity. How do reported bodily feelings in emotion experience relate to what goes on in the actual body—or, in other words, how does the lived body relate to the living body? In some cases, it is easy to verify whether a specific bodily feeling "tracks" an actual bodily process. For example, when I feel my heart beating fast in fear, I can put a hand on my chest to verify whether what I sense interoceptively corresponds to my actual heartbeat; likewise, when I feel my breathing becoming shallower in anxiety, I can put a hand on my chest or abdomen. That bodily feelings track actual bodily activity in the case of respiration is indicated, for example, by a study by Philippot, Chapelle, and Blairy (2002). In a first experiment, they asked subjects to self-induce feelings of sadness, anger, fear, and happiness by breathing in different ways, and to report on the respiration patterns they used. The reported respiration patterns turned out to correspond to actual respiration patterns previously measured for those emotions (Boiten, Frijda, and Wientjes 1994; see also Rainville et al. 2006 for a more recent study). In a second experiment, they were able to induce feelings of sadness, anger, fear, and happiness by asking (other) subjects to breathe in those specific ways (without asking them to achieve any specific emotional state). Taken together, these results provide evidence that different respiratory patterns not only influence emotion experience in specific ways but also are felt in emotion experience and contribute to its differentiation.

Other cases, however, seem trickier. What is going on in the body when people report "butterflies in the stomach," "chills," or "shivers down the spine" in emotion? Are they reporting actual bodily changes? If so, what kind of changes? And what about feelings of action readiness or urges to act? Or feeling "down" or "up"? As we saw in the previous chapter, there are many ways in which the body enters emotion experience. Not all bodily feelings are feelings of parts of the body that can be obviously identified and measured with third-person methods. Conversely, a multitude of changes occur in the body when subjects experience an emotion, and not all of those changes appear to be tracked as such when subjects report bodily feelings—although they may influence emotion experience nevertheless (as in the case of changes in glucose and hormonal levels). Note that some studies simply assume that bodily concomitants in emotion experience can be studied merely by asking subjects how they feel their body, without carrying out any actual bodily measurement. Scherer and Wallbott (1994), for example, addressed the vexed question of whether at least some emotions exhibit the same patterns of physiological activity across cultures merely by asking subjects from different countries, using various questionnaires, how they felt their body during emotion experience. Likewise, Grewe et al. (2007, 779) studied "physiological responses" to music with question-naires asking subjects to "report their perceived bodily reactions" (see also Sloboda 1991).[21] Most philosophical discussions also assume that bodily feelings in emotion experience register what is in fact happening in the body. Yet how the lived body and the living body relate to each other is an empirical question and needs to be addressed as such.

Addressing this question could also help determine whether differences between emotion experiences that are reported as bodily, and emotion experiences that are not reported as bodily (as established with first- and second-person methods), correlate with differences in actual bodily activity—or whether they depend on differences in bodily self-awareness, such as interoceptive awareness, for instance. Evidence already suggests that some subjects are better than others at perceiving their bodies, as measured (so far) in terms of perception of their own heartbeat (e.g., Craig 2004),[22] and that differences in interoceptive awareness correlate with differences in emotion experience, such as anxiety (Critchley et al. 2004). It may turn out that whereas different emotion experiences involve specific changes in the body, subjects are not equally good at detecting these changes, and therefore some subjects experience emotion as "less bodily" than others. Relatedly, it would be interesting to find out whether subjects can be trained via biofeedback to detect their body more accurately, and whether this training influences their emotion experience in terms of "how bodily" it feels.

Additional relevant first- and third-person data could be gathered from subjects with a variety of bodily impairments, to understand whether and how these affect emotion experience and its bodily character, and how reported bodily feelings (if any) relate to the condition of the body. For example, do subjects with spinal cord injuries experience emotion, and if so, do these emotion experiences include bodily feelings? If they do include bodily feelings, what kinds of feelings are they? Are they visceral sensations? Are they kinesthetic feelings, such as urges to move or even act in specific ways? How and where in the body are these feelings experienced? Existing evidence about the extent to which spinal cord lesions impair emotion experience is mixed (e.g., Hohmann 1966; Chwalisz, Diener, and Gallagher 1988; Montoya and Schandry 1994; Cobos et al. 2002; O'Carroll et al. 2003; Nicotra et al. 2006). Yet the other questions, to the best of my knowledge, have not been explored systematically using the first- and second-person methods mentioned earlier. Even if people who have spinal injuries retain emotion experiences, it may be that these emotions have a different or attenuated bodily character compared to the emotions experienced before the lesion. Further questions could then be raised about the relation between experience and the condition of the body. Spinal cord lesions can impair the capacity to move various muscles, proprioception, the generation of sympathetic and parasympathetic responses, and sensory feedback from the viscera. The type and degree of impairment can vary considerably depending on the location and nature of the injury. A neuro-physio-phenomenological approach might enable us better to understand the relationship between the nature of the lesion and the subjects' experience, and in particular whether and how different aspects of bodily arousal contribute to emotion experience.

A similar approach could be taken toward other conditions, such as pure autonomic failure (which involves a peripheral degeneration of sympathetic and parasympathetic autonomic neurons), Moebius syndrome (which entails a congenital total paralysis of facial muscles), and locked-in syndrome (which involves a paralysis of all voluntary muscles apart from those responsible for vertical movement of the eyes and blinking). We know from autobiographies of locked-in patients (painfully dictated letter by letter through blinking) that they retain bodily sensations, as well as a variety of more or less intense emotion experiences (see Bauby 1997; Chisholm and Gillet 2005). What is the quality of those emotion experiences, however?[23]

Third-person methods could focus not just on the body but on the brain, as well. Which areas of the brain activate significantly when people report bodily emotion experiences? Are they different from the brain areas that activate significantly for reportedly nonbodily emotion experiences? Existing evidence indicates that the anterior insula (also known as the insular cortex), for example, is significantly involved in registering bodily activity and contributing to interoceptive feelings (Craig 2002; Critchley et al. 2004). It would thus be interesting to see whether emotion experiences that reportedly involve bodily feelings correlate with activity in this area more than emotion experiences that reportedly do not involve bodily feelings. Damasio et al. (2000) notably showed that self-induced experiences of happiness, sadness, fear, and anger correlate with activity in brain structures involved in the regulation of the organism, in particular those that receive signals from the internal milieu, viscera, and musculoskeletal system (such as the insula, secondary somatosensory cortex, and cingulate cortex); more-over, they found that the four emotion experiences correlate with differ-ent patterns of neural activity in these areas. Yet we do not know from this study how the subjects experienced those emotions, and in particular whether they felt them as bodily. A more recent study that looked at how experience, body, and brain all correlate with one another is Harrison et al. 2010. This study illustrates well the possibility of correlating first- and third-person data of various kinds in the study of emotion experience and thus comes quite close to the methodology delineated earlier (although more attention could still be paid to first- and second-person methods).

Harrison et al. looked at two forms of disgust: "core ingestive disgust," induced by watching movies of people vomiting when smelling and eating visually repulsive food, and "body-boundary-violation disgust," induced by watching movies of surgical operations. After the presentation of each movie, subjects had to indicate (on an analog scale) how disgusted, light-headed or faint, and nauseated they felt. Harrison et al. found that subjects reported feeling more nauseated in the "core disgust" condition (intensity of disgust and light-headedness were not significantly different). In addi-tion, they found different autonomic patterns (as measured in terms of car-diac and gastric activity) for the two forms of disgust and found that core disgust was accompanied by greater tachygastric responses (i.e., rapid dis-regulated gastric responses). They also found that the two forms of disgust correlated with differential patterns of insula activation. Thus compared to Damasio et al.'s, this study shows that different patterns of activity in insular cortex accompany not just different emotion experiences but also different bodily feelings experienced as part of them; in addition, it shows how these bodily feelings correlate with actual bodily activity.

Finally, neuro-physio-phenomenology could be used to understand the extent to which (if at all) neural activity can "bypass" bodily activity and induce bodily feelings "as if" the body were undergoing specific changes. In a footnote, James (1884, 199) mentioned the possibility of "morbid fear in which objectively the heart is not much perturbed," and pointed out that these cases needed to be better documented and studied: "It is of course possible that the cortical centres normally percipient of dread as a complex of cardiac and other organic sensations due to real bodily change, should become *primarily* excited in brain-disease, and give rise to an hallucination of the changes being there,—an hallucination of dread, consequently, coex-istent with a comparatively calm pulse, &c. I say it is possible, for I am ignorant of observations which might test the fact" (199–200; italics in original). Damasio (1994, 155–160) also discusses this possibility to some extent, calling the brain areas allegedly bypassing the body "'as-if' body loops."

Not only, however, do we have no direct evidence that as-if body loops exist (including how long an as-if body experience could last without registering inputs from the actual body, or how it would feel), but the more we understand the complexity of how brain and body are related, the more suspicious the notion becomes.[24] We have seen already that brain and body continuously influence each other in innumerable ways (Pert 1997; Cosmelli and Thompson 2010; Thompson and Cosmelli, forthcoming). In particular, there are many channels through which the body informs the brain about its status, and no evidence indicates that they can all be "bypassed" and "simulated" by neural activity. Somatic information is conveyed via the spinal nerves and the trigeminal nerve; visceral information is conveyed via the spinal nerves, but also the vagus nerve and the glossopharyngeal nerve (two cranial nerves). Many brain regions also register bodily activity: somatic information is registered in brain stem nuclei, thalamus, and primary and secondary somatic sensory cortex (SI and SII) and parietal areas (Purves et al. 2008, chap. 9). As for visceral information, key areas are the nucleus of the solitary tract, the brain stem reticular formation, and the hypothalamus. The brain stem also contains areas that register circulating humoral signals; these are known as "sensory circumventricular organs" and are situated at the blood-brain interface, such as the area postrema, the organum vasculosum of the lamina terminalis, and the subfornical organ (see Price, Hoyda, and Ferguson 2008; for an overview of the visceral system, see Purves et al. 2008, chap. 21; see Parvizi and Damasio 2001 for a discussion of the many nuclei of the brain stem).

It seems highly unlikely that the brain could bypass and simulate all this activity. As Damasio (1994, 158) originally emphasized, "The brain is not likely to predict how all the commands—neural and chemical, but especially the latter—will play out in the body, because the play-out and the resulting states depend on local biochemical contexts and on numerous variables within the body itself which are not fully represented neurally. What is played out in the body is constructed anew, moment by moment, and is not an exact replica of anything that happened before." In addition, Damasio does not believe that the experience underpinned by as-if body loops feels like one that involves actual bodily loops (see Damasio 1994, 156; 2010, 121).

In sum, then, there are many ways in which we could use a neuro-physio-phenomenological approach specifically to investigate the relationship between emotion experience and the body. First- and second-person methods could be used to investigate the phenomenological or lived bodily character of emotion experience; third-person methods could be added to explore the relationship between reported lived experience and bodily and brain activity, which could help us to understand how reported bodily feelings, as well as reportedly nonbodily emotion experiences, relate to actual neural and bodily processes.

6.7   Conclusion

In this chapter, I have drawn on the enactive approach, and in particular on its neurophenomenological method, to argue that the neuroscientific study of emotion experience could be advanced by integrating a variety of methods: first- and second-person methods for the collection of first-person data, and third-person methods for the collection of third-person data. Current affective neuroscience already employs sophisticated third-person methods for the measurement of brain as well as bodily activity during emotion, but it has not paid much attention to the possibility of developing rigorous methods for the investigation of lived experience, as well. This chapter has indicated various ways in which this imbalance could be redressed.

The development of the suggested affective neuro-physio-phenomenology could, I think, help affective scientists make progress on some longstanding questions, such as the existence of emotion-specific patterns of brain and bodily activity, and the bodily nature of emotion experience. At the same time, it would augment the enactive approach itself by extending neurophenomenology from its focus on brain activity to the rest of the organism—more in line with enactivism's emphasis on the deep continuity of mind and life, particularly the claim that brain processes are not sufficient for consciousness, but rather consciousness is enacted by the living, situated organism.

7 Feeling Others

7.1 Introduction

The discussion so far has centered on the individual. It is now time to rectify this solipsistic trend and turn our focus on our relationship to others. We are social beings and spend much of our existence interacting with other embodied agents, whose presence affects us in various ways, both experientially and physiologically.

A lot has already been written in the philosophy and psychology of social cognition about the mechanisms that may enable us to understand others, in the sense of attributing to them specific mental states that explain and predict their behavior. This debate has been dominated until recently by two approaches, known as the "theory theory" (TT) and the "simulation theory" (ST). Roughly, according to TT, understanding others is achieved via a process of inference to the best explanation; mental states such as beliefs and desires are posited as theoretical entities that, to the best of one's knowledge, explain and predict the other's behavior. According to ST, understanding others involves simulating their mental states: I put myself in the other's situation, decide what I would think or feel in that situation, and eventually ascribe that thought or feeling to the other. This characterization is admittedly coarse and does not do justice to the complexity of the debate. For example, various hybrid accounts exist that combine elements of TT and ST; also, both TT and ST come in different versions (for a more detailed overview and references, see, e.g., Goldman and Sripada 2005; Ratcliffe 2007, chap. 1; Gallagher and Zahavi 2008, chap. 9). Yet as it has been pointed out (e.g., Zahavi 2011a), TT and ST share an important assumption, namely, that the mental states of others are private and hidden, and therefore understanding others requires "getting at" these hidden mental states via an intermediate inferential process (such as a theory or a simulation). This is also known as the assumption that understanding others is essentially a matter of *mind reading* or *mentalizing*.

Philosophers influenced by phenomenology, as well as explicitly enactive accounts of social cognition, have recently called this assumption into question. They have proposed that mentalizing is not the ordinary way in which we understand others, and that to reduce understanding others to mentalizing construes intersubjectivity too narrowly (e.g., Gallagher 2001, 2005; Ratcliffe 2007; De Jaegher and Di Paolo 2007; Thompson 2001, 2007; Gallagher and Zahavi 2008; Zahavi 2008; Di Paolo, Rohde, and De Jaegher 2010). They draw attention in particular to what the developmental psychologist Colwyn Trevarthen (1979) originally dubbed *primary intersubjectivity*, namely, a set of nonconceptual skills present very early in development, or even at birth—such as imitation, a capacity to distinguish between inanimate objects and people, and a responsiveness to others' facial expressions (see also Hobson 2002; Reddy 2008). These skills, it has been proposed, already manifest, or better embody or constitute, a *pragmatic* form of understanding others: "The understanding of the other person is primarily neither theoretical nor based on an internal simulation, but is a form of embodied practice" (Gallagher 2001, 85). Similarly, De Jaegher and Di Paolo (2007) see these skills as constituting a kind of understanding others that they call *participatory sense making*, which is enacted in the concrete interaction between two or more autonomous agents coupled via bodily reciprocity and coordination.

The discussion of this chapter builds on these insights, developing them further to bring into relief and examine in more detail the affective dimension of intersubjectivity, construed as an embodied or jointly enacted practice. As Thompson (2001, 1) points out, "The concrete encounter of self and other fundamentally involves empathy," and importantly empathy is not only a cognitive capacity of "perspective taking" but also an affective phenomenon that involves emotional and feeling responses to the other (see also, e.g., Preston and de Waal 2002; Stueber 2008; Walter 2012). This idea converges with the phenomenological approach to empathy, which emphasizes the *experiential* character of "understanding others" versus a detached, merely "intellectual" form of understanding (more later).

More specifically, in the first half of this chapter, I focus on the various ways in which we experience others when we face them. I distinguish phenomena of what I call basic empathy from impressions, feeling close, feeling intimate, and sympathy. In the second half of the chapter, I turn to empirical evidence of how our bodies respond to the bodily presence of others, in particular to our tendency to "do as others do" when we face them. After discussing and throwing some cold water on the idea that this evidence supports a simulationist account of how we understand others, I turn to an interpretation that has been relatively neglected, namely, that mimicking and more broadly "matching" the other plays an important role in social bonding; I also link this view to some of the phenomenological considerations raised earlier in the chapter.

Before continuing, a qualification. The discussion of this chapter is limited to experiences and bodily changes occurring in face-to-face or "concrete" encounters. These encounters obviously do not exhaust the domain of intersubjectivity, and we certainly "feel others" (and probably respond physiologically to them) in various ways also when they are absent from our immediate perceptual field. How we feel others beyond the concrete encounter—for example, in memory, imagination, planning, virtual reality, use of artifacts—is a fascinating question that I will not address here, as it would require an analysis of its own. In this respect, the theme of this chapter is thus limited. As we are about to see, however, there is already a lot to say about the face-to-face encounter.

7.2   The Experience of the Other as a *Leib*

One dimension of intersubjectivity that is easy to overlook because it is so pervasive, at least in mentally healthy people, is the experience of others as lived bodies, or *Leibe* (rather than mere physical things, or *Körper*), namely, as physical living centers or sources of subjectivity. This way of experiencing others characteristically does not require any explicit process of reasoning or imagination; we usually just *perceive* life and subjectivity in the other's body.

Edith Stein ([1917] 1989), who discusses this phenomenon in detail, emphasizes that my perception of the other as a bearer of experiences is not a judgment (an *Einsicht*, literally a "seeing in") but a feeling (an *Einfühlung*, a "feeling in"). Drawing on her and other phenomenologists' work, we can characterize this mode of experiencing others already as a form of *empathy*, understood, however, precisely not as some kind of detached process of taking the other's point of view but as an *experiential* access to the other's subjectivity. (It helps to remember that the English term "empathy" itself also means "feeling in." The term is a neologism proposed by Edward Titchener [see Wispé 1987], coined from the Greek *en* [in] and *pathos* [emotion, feeling] to translate the German term *Einfühlung*. The latter term started to be used in German only in the second half of the eighteenth century, first in the field of aesthetics, and then to refer to the perception of the other's experience. Since then, the term has been understood and used in different ways, in everyday talk but also among philosophers and scientists. See Stueber 2008 for a helpful overview.)

Stein particularly emphasizes the *sensual* nature of our experience of others as lived bodies. She uses the term *sensual empathy* (*Empfindungseinfühlung*, "the feeling-in of sensations") or *sensing-in* (*Einempfindung*) to refer to the experiential access I have to the other's field of bodily sensations. In her example, when I see a hand resting on a table, I do not see it simply lying there as the book beside it does (i.e., I do not see the hand as a mere thing, a *Körper*). Rather, I see how "it 'presses' against the table more or less strongly" and how "it lies there [limp] or stretched" (Stein [1917] 1989, 58). In other words, when in the presence of another's body, I "sense-in" his bodily sensations, the way his body feels to him.[1] Husserl (Stein's mentor) already touched on this mode of experiencing others:

> In my physical surrounding world I encounter Bodies [*Leibe*], i.e., material things of the same type as the material thing constituted in solipsistic experience, "my Body," and I apprehend them as Bodies, that is, I feel by empathy that in them there is an Ego-subject, along with everything that pertains to it and with the particular content demanded from case to case. Transferred over to the other Bodies thereby is first of all that "localization" I accomplish in various sense-fields (field of touch, warmth, coldness, smell, taste, pain, sensuous pleasure) and sense-regions (sensations of movement). (Husserl [1952] 1989, 172)[2]

Stein importantly points out that in empathy the other's experience is given to me in a specific way, namely, *nonprimordially* (Stein [1917] 1989, 7–11). By this she means that I do not experience the other's bodily sensations, for example, *as my own*. Hence when I see a hand tensely contracted in a fist, I do not experience this tenseness in my own hand, as if my hand were itself tensely contracted in a fist. At the same time, however, I do not just see the other's hand and *judge* that it is tense; rather, I *experience* the tenseness in the other's hand. To clarify the notion of nonprimordial experience of the other, Stein draws a comparison with memory and imagination. When I remember being joyful, for example, the remembering is a primordial experience, but the remembered joy is given to me nonprimordially—that is, I have an experience of it, I "feel" it (I do not just know or judge that I was joyful), but I am not living it through as my joy right now: "Joy is not primordially and bodily there, rather as having once been alive" (Stein [1917] 1989, 8). Likewise when I imagine myself in a certain situation: the experience of imagining is primordial, but the imagined I is not. In the case of empathy, the intentional object of my mental act is not the I anymore, but the primordial/nonprimordial structure of the relationship between self and other remains the same: my experience of the other's subjectivity is primordial (it is my experience as I live it through), but the other's subjectivity is given to me nonprimordially. Thus when I see the other's tense hand, I "live" the other's tenseness, but I do not feel "primordial tenseness" myself.

Another important feature of the empathic experience of the other as a *Leib* is that I do not first perceive the other's behavior and then infer that it is caused by experiences analogous to those that cause a similar behavior in me (e.g., I do not first see a hand touching a fur and then reason that the hand must be experiencing sensations of softness by analogy with the sensations that I usually experience when I touch fur). Rather, I experience the hand "directly" as a locus of bodily subjectivity and sensations.

Emphasis on directedness is what distinguishes more generally the phenomenological approach to empathy and intersubjectivity from TT and ST. The phenomenological approach criticizes both TT and ST for endorsing, more or less implicitly, the Cartesian assumption that one's mind is "internal" and private, and thus opaque or invisible to others (see, e.g., Zahavi 2011a; Ratcliffe 2007). This assumption makes the minds of others never directly experientially accessible; mental states can only be *ascribed* to others via some intermediate inferential process, such as theory or simulation. According to the phenomenological approach, whereas such processes may sometimes be required to make sense of the other's behavior, in the concrete encounter it is more often the case that the other's mental states are picked up "directly" by the observer, namely, without the need to engage in theorizing or pretend states. Thus, for example, the idea is that I "directly" see the other's pain in his convulsions, as opposed to when I "indirectly" infer that he is in pain because I see him taking a painkiller (see Zahavi 2011a).

I shall call the phenomenological notion of directly perceiving the other's subjectivity, including sensing-in, *basic empathy*, to distinguish it from other more elaborate and mediated ways of grasping how others feel—like when I need also to recur to my knowledge of the other and to imagination (I do not deny that sometimes empathy requires these processes, but I shall not discuss them here). Other instances of basic empathy discussed by Stein ([1917] 1989) include experiencing others as centers of orientation of the spatial world, as sources of voluntary movement, and as sources of emotional feelings. These instances all imply the most basic experience of others as lived bodies; also, they all involve taking up the other's experience "nonprimordially."[3]

7.3   Perceiving Emotion in Expression

We do not just generally see the other's *Leiblichkeit* in his body; we also see specific emotions in his countenance. Scheler ([1923] 1954, 260) famously wrote that it is "the simplest of phenomenological considerations" that

we certainly believe ourselves to be directly acquainted with another person's joy in his laughter, with his sorrow and pain in his tears, with his shame in his blushing, with his entreaty in his outstretched hands, with his love in his look of affection, with his rage in the gnashing of his teeth, with his threats in the clenching of his fist, and with the tenor of his thoughts in the sound of his words. If anyone tells me that this is not "perception," for it cannot be so, in view of the fact that a perception is simply a "complex of physical sensations," and that there is certainly no sensation of another person's mind nor any stimulus from such a source, I would beg him to turn aside from such questionable theories and address himself to the phenomenological facts.

In other words, for Scheler it is patently not the case that when I perceive the other, I merely see a *Körper*. Rather, it is a fact about the concrete encounter that I directly perceive the other's lived emotions in his facial, bodily, and vocal expressions. Others have endorsed this point or made it independently (such as Goldie 2000 and Zahavi 2010). Here is also Wittgenstein, quoted approvingly by the psychopathologist Peter Hobson: "'We see emotion.'—As opposed to what?—We do not see facial contortions and make the inference that he is feeling joy, grief, boredom. We describe a face immediately as sad, radiant, bored, even when we are unable to give any other description of the features.—Grief, one would like to say, is personified in the face. This is essential to what we call 'emotion'" (Wittgenstein

1980, vol. 2, sec. 570; quoted in Hobson 2009, 245). Note that one need not be able to *name* the emotion that one empathizes in the expression—even though, arguably, one's emotional vocabulary can affect how one perceives expression; the face, the voice, and the body can be perceived as expressing emotions for which one does not possess specific labels.

Importantly, this view does not imply that one cannot "hide" one's feelings. I can decide to control how my body appears to the other, in such a way that the other does not see it as expressing certain emotions. Thus I may smile even if I am sad, or avoid rolling my eyes to conceal my exasperation. In this way I exploit the expressive power of my body and the natural tendency of others to empathize with it, so that others see feelings in me that are not what I am experiencing. This does not mean that I have hidden feelings that are somehow not embodied, or not embodied in specific ways. If I smile when sad, I am still sad in the rest of my organism (emotional episodes are dynamical patterns of the organism; see chap. 3). I am, however, manipulating some parts of it (the lips) to prevent the other from empathizing my sadness. In addition, it may well be that—perhaps if my sadness is not too intense—if I kept smiling, the smile would recruit other bodily processes and eventually change their configuration, thus modifying my sadness (as we know, empirical evidence suggests that holding specific facial and bodily attitudes influences emotion experience; see chap. 4, and also hereafter). There may also be cases in which the prolonged disguise of my feelings will create bodily tensions due to the effort to control my bodily expressivity. It is interesting that these "bodily tensions" seem to creep up, at least in my experience, in nonvisible or less obviously expressive parts of the body, as in the case of tension in the chest due to prolonged control of anger. Finally, it is actually difficult to disguise one's feelings for a long time, especially from someone who knows us well—namely, someone who is used to our habitual patterns of embodying feelings. Thus it would be difficult to disguise my sadness by smiling at someone who is familiar with my usual way of smiling when my joy is unobstructed and free to inform my body (we also know that observers can distinguish between "enjoyment" and "nonenjoyment" smiles; see, e.g., Frank, Ekman, and Friesen 1993).

The perhaps counterintuitive point that this account of empathy and expression implies is that there may be a mismatch between the feeling that is empathized and the one that the observed person actually experiences.

I do not find this point particularly hard to swallow, however. Most of the time, empathy gives the other's experience in an accurate way. In particular, the other's actions and decisions usually make sense in light of the feelings expressed in his body (cursing, shouting, insulting, and taking revenge usually go together with frowning; caressing and saying loving things go together with smiling and a tender tone of voice, and so on); the other actually often reports feeling the way he looks, and often we see feelings in the other that the other has not noticed yet but recognizes easily once we point them out. It is because empathy is reliable most of the time that we can exploit our (limited) capacity to control our body to manipulate how the other experiences us.

What about the fact that we attribute expressivity also to inanimate objects? If they are inanimate, then we should be unable to empathize with them, and therefore also unable to see them as expressive. But in reality we see expressions everywhere: in dolls, puppets, sculptures, and other artworks, and even in tree bark, cars, clouds, and so on. This happens because these items reproduce features of our bodies that solicit our natural capacity for empathy and thus induce us to interpret them as expressive. We can talk more easily about this phenomenon by introducing the notion of *empathic tendency*, namely, the tendency or the temptation to see feelings in anything that reproduces features similar to those that in humans are expressive of actual experiences. This attribution is irresistible in the case of artifacts that reproduce human facial and vocal attributes. Take, for example, Kismet, the robotic head designed by Cynthia Breazeal at MIT (Breazeal 2002). Kismet can move its neck, eyes, and even eyelids; it can close its eyebrows, and its lips can take various shapes; it also has big animal-like ears that move up and down. It emits noises that sound like spoken sentences with different intonations that imitate human emotional vocal expressions. The way humans who interact with Kismet respond to it clearly shows a tendency to empathize with it, namely, to see emotion in it. For example, if Kismet makes a sad face while it is being scolded by a human, observers of the interaction respond with typical "compassionate" faces and sounds.[4] These observers know well that Kismet is not feeling any sadness or guilt when it is being reproached. Nevertheless they cannot block their tendency to empathize with it when it simulates human features of sadness. Also people usually feel sad when Kismet is switched off (Breazeal 2002).

Watching people interact with Kismet shows well how irresistible certain bodily features are in inviting an empathic response. Even when we know that there is no subjectivity in the other, its human features and lifelike movements demand an acknowledgment of interiority (the other side of this coin, of course, is the difficulty we experience when asked to see subjectivity in a body that appears lifeless). It is thus not surprising that the reproduction of specific bodily features induces empathic experiences. Also, some people empathize strongly with organisms that do not possess a nervous system. To the extent that the these organisms exhibit an "animation" that reminds us of other living beings, we should not find this surprising—for it is the form and movement of life, so to speak, that enable us to connect experientially with other human beings.[5]

7.4   Impressive Others

Basic empathy connects me experientially to the other as soon as he enters into my perceptual field. However, it does not exhaust the way I experience others. Another phenomenon we need to consider is that the other *impresses* me with his presence or, to use Shusterman's (2011) term, his "somatic style," which includes bodily shape, tone of voice, mode of gesturing, and even nonbodily (clothes, accessories, perfume) elements. The other may impress or strike me as handsome, funny, strong, nerdy, weak, mean, fit, smart, dull, mature, youthful, intriguing, kind, and so on. Sometimes the other also strikes me for his resemblance to someone I know. It is indeed remarkable how difficult it is to keep an even-minded attitude when facing someone. We may think we are indifferent or immune to impressions, but if we reflect on our feelings in the encounter, the other rarely (if ever) appears affectively neutral or meaningless. At most, we may say that at the prereflective level some others do not strike us as particularly salient.[6]

Impressions have much in common with the *atmosphere* of a place or situation, to use Schmitz's term (see Schmitz, Müllan, and Slaby 2011).[7] An atmosphere is by nature difficult to define with precision but is not for this reason hidden or marginal. It has been characterized as a spatially diffuse phenomenon, a feeling that is experienced as pervading the situation one finds oneself in. Spaces and events within them (e.g., a meeting, a concert) affect one with their specific atmosphere. Dewey identifies a similar phenomenon when he talks of the *pervasive quality* of a work of art, as well as of entire situations (Dewey [1934] 1980; see also Johnson 2007). Phenomenologically, impressions appear to *exude* from the other, so to speak, and I sense them as I sense the other's smell or heat; likewise atmospheres appear to exude from a place or situation. This does not mean that impressions and atmospheres are "out there" and exist independently of the perceiver. Rather, they are relational phenomena that emerge in the interaction between perceiver and perceived person or situation. The same person in the same context, for example, can exert different impressions on different perceivers, and this happens because the state of the perceiver—from her present feelings to her long-standing values—influences how she is impressed by the other (likewise for atmospheres).

How the other impresses me is often difficult to distinguish from how he is given to me via basic empathy, and indeed the two are often entangled in experience. Physical (*körperliche*) features of the other's body may impress me, but how the other's body appears to me also depends on what the other is experiencing, which is something with which I empathize. Consider, for example, an encounter with, say, a tall, depressed other. I am affected (impressed) by his height, as well as by the sense of gloom and dejection he exudes; the latter, however, are not just physical but *leibliche* expressive features that make me empathize with his experience.

This entanglement of impressions and empathized feelings characterizes, I think, what Stein ([1917] 1989, 68) calls "phenomena of life," such as "growth, development and aging, health and sickness, vigor and sluggishness." For Stein, these are empathized, namely, perceived as foreign experiences: "Thus by his walk, posture, and his every movement, we also 'see' 'how he feels,' his vigor, sluggishness, etc. We bring this co-intended foreign experience to fulfilment by carrying it out with him empathically" (68–69). It seems to me, however, that a more appropriate description of these cases is that the other's body impresses me at the same time with *leibliche* features that are empathized (as is apparent when I perceive the other's sluggishness or vigor, for example), as well as with *körperliche* features that as such are not empathized. Seeing an old face, for example, may strike or impress me primarily as a wrinkled face; whereas seeing an old, hunched lady walking slowly on the pavement involves also basic empathy. Even if in the majority of cases the two modes of experiencing the other come together, it seems important to maintain a difference between grasping the other's subjectivity via empathy and being impressed by the other's features.

7.5   Feeling Close

Basic empathy, as an experience of the other, already provides a certain degree of connectedness with him: I do not merely judge that one is scared when I see fear in his expression; rather, I experience the other as a source of feeling. A stronger degree of connectedness arises, I now want to suggest, when I realize that the other and I *share* a specific feeling, namely, feel the same. The term "empathy" as it appears in everyday talk, as well as much psychology and neuroscience, often refers to this kind of experience. The folk concept of empathy appears to refer to a special way of feeling connected to others, an "emotional resonance" that involves a perceived similarity between self and other. Because I do not think that empathy, in the sense of "grasping experientially" (feeling in) the other's subjectivity, requires specifically the perception of a shared feeling, I call this experience not "empathy" but *feeling close*.

This experience is usually, although not necessarily, prereflective. Stein ([1917] 1989, 16–18) provides a particularly insightful discussion of what I call feeling close. In her example, "A special edition of the paper reports that the fortress has fallen. As we hear this, all of us are seized by an excitement, a joy, a jubilation. We all have 'the same' feeling" (17). In her terminology, in a situation like this, we come to experience a "feeling of oneness" with others. I like this expression, but as Stein points out, in this experience the distinction between self and others remains (hence my preference for "feeling close"). I neither "lose myself" in the others nor incorporate the others' experience into mine in a sort of extended awareness of myself. Rather, I retain an awareness of myself and the others as distinct subjects. At the same time, however, I am also aware, via basic empathy, that the others' feeling is the same as mine. This awareness of sharing a feeling leads to "a subject of a higher level" (17), a "higher unity" (122) between self and other. I do not just experience the other via basic empathy; I am also aware that the other and I feel the same, and this awareness induces a stronger experience of connectedness. It is as if the others' feelings, which I usually experience as nonprimordial (i.e., as belonging to them and not to me), have lost their nonprimordial character and become "live to me" like my own feelings. As Stein continues immediately after introducing the example of the fall of the fortress:

Have thus the barriers separating one "I" from another broken down here? Has the "I" been freed from its monadic character? Not entirely. I feel my joy while I empathically comprehend the others' and see it as the same. And, seeing this, it seems that the non-primordial character of the foreign joy has vanished. Indeed, this phantom joy coincides in every respect with my real live joy, and theirs is just as live to them as mine is to me. Now I intuitively have before me what they feel. It comes to life in my feeling, and from the "I" and "you" arises the "we" as a subject of a higher level. ([1917] 1989, 17)

Note that Stein's example involves a shared intentional object (the fall of the fortress). As such, it is an instance of what Goldie (2000, 193) calls *emotional sharing*. In emotional sharing, two or more subjects have the same feeling toward the same object or event—as when two parents share concern about their child's distress, or when the members of a group feel moved by the same scene or speech (as Goldie points out, the object of the feeling need not be the same particular object but could also just be the same "type" of object, as when two mothers share a feeling of grief for the loss of their child). Emotional sharing as characterized by Goldie, however, is not sufficient for what Stein calls "feeling of oneness." Goldie only emphasizes the presence of a shared object of feeling. For feeling of oneness, there must also be a *recognition* that the other's feeling is the same as mine, which gives rise to a particularly strong sense of connectedness to him.

Furthermore, note that a shared intentional object does not appear necessary for any feelings of closeness altogether, or so I want to suggest. I agree that if I am angry at, say, the government cuts, then seeing that others are angry and knowing that, like me, they are angry at the government cuts makes me feel clos*er* to them than if I did not know what they are angry about. It seems to me, however, that simply sharing the other's attitude while being aware of it can engender feelings of closeness. Suppose that as I see you giggle, I start to giggle myself and find myself amused as a consequence (a case of emotional contagion via mimicry; see sec. 7.8). Even if I do not know what you are giggling about, I now see you giggle and empathize with your amusement while I simultaneously experience myself giggling and amused. Some distance remains between us ("I wonder what's so funny?"), but, I submit, I also feel closer, more connected to you than if I were not giggling and amused myself, or if I were giggling and you were frowning. I shall come back to this point later, when discussing mimicry and social bonding. For now let us just notice that whereas awareness of sharing the intentional object appears to intensify the experience of connectedness, finding oneself simply sharing the same attitude as the other is not immune to feelings of closeness, either.

A special case of feeling close (perhaps the one in which we feel clos*est* to the other) is constituted by feeling *intimate*. There is no clear definition of intimacy (Register and Henley 1992). "Intimate" literally means "inner-most" or "deepest" (in Latin, *intimus* is the superlative of *intra*, "inside"). In ordinary language today, the term is typically associated with sexual encounters, although we also acknowledge that, for instance, friendships can be intimate. Physical contact of sexual bodily parts characterizes the sexual encounter but is not in itself what makes it intimate. Arguably, intimacy comes about with the awareness that something is being disclosed of which others are not usually aware. Intimate friends reveal to each other opinions and feelings that they do not reveal to others.

The sexual encounter has become paradigmatic of intimacy perhaps because in it "inmost" bodily aspects of oneself are disclosed to the other. In addition, in the sexual encounter the shared object of the experience is not something distinct from the participants (as in Stein's example of the fall of the fortress) but *the encounter itself*, which includes oneself and the empathized other; the shared object of the experience is thus "us." Further-more, this "us" involves mutually empathized sensations of extraordinarily close bodies. An intimate sexual encounter therefore appears to involve a twofold breakage of the boundaries with the other: the other's experience is empathized as being shared (which induces a feeling of closeness), and the shared experience in question happens to be partly at least about my and the other's lived bodies entangled in reciprocal sensing-in. This com-plex entanglement may be what makes Scheler ([1923] 1954, 25; italics in original) remark that "in *truly loving sexual intercourse* (i.e., the opposite of the sensual, utilitarian, or purposive act) ... the partners, in an impassioned suspension of their spiritual personality (itself the seat of individual self-awareness), seem to relapse into a *single* life-stream in which nothing of their individual selves remains any longer distinct, though it has equally little resemblance to a consciousness of 'us' founded on the respective self-awareness of each."

The boundaries between feeling close and feeling intimate are not clearly demarcated. In an encounter, feelings of closeness can change into feelings of intimacy when private aspects of the other are revealed, perhaps just momentarily. When feelings of closeness are accompanied by trust and the motivation to disclose, they naturally lead to the development of a more intimate relationship. The process may well involve a "micro-development of intimacy," in which one tentatively nudges the other to disclose, does so oneself, tracks the effects of the attempt, and so on. One particularly intriguing aspect of the process is that one may be surprised by what oneself ends up disclosing; this unpredictable element depends on the fact that each subject is unique in what she brings to the encounter and will thus affect the other (physically and experientially) in her own unique way.

7.6 Sympathy

As some philosophers have pointed out already, empathy ought to be distinguished from sympathy (e.g., Scheler [1923] 1954; Goldie 2000). In ordinary language, the English term "sympathy" is used very much in the sense of "compassion" and "caring." To invite one to have some sympathy for the other is to invite one to care about the other's feelings, and possibly also to show to the other that one cares.

Etymologically, sympathy and compassion both mean "feeling with."[8] Note, however, that if this expression is taken to mean "sharing the same feeling," then "feeling with" does not seem to be required for sympathy. After all, I can feel compassion and care about your grief, panic, or depression without grieving, panicking, or being depressed myself. The expression "feeling *for*" the other thus seems more appropriate to capture what we feel when we care about him and his lived experiences.

Some have argued further that sympathy does not require empathy. According to Goldie (2000), for example, empathy is an imaginative process that necessarily involves "centrally imagining" the other's narrative, as well as assuming a "substantial characterization" of the other's psychological and nonpsychological features. Centrally imagining consists in imagining having the other's experiences from *his* point of view (as opposed to my, or someone else's, or even no one's, point of view). Assuming a substantial characterization of the other consists in taking into consideration his psychological (e.g., kindness), as well as nonpsychological (e.g., height, profession), traits. "Both characterization and narrative are independently necessary for empathy: without the former, there is no possibility of centrally imagining *another*; and without the latter, there is no narrative to experience—at best one might be able only to imagine what it is like to be that other person" (Goldie 2000, 198).

I agree with Goldie that neither characterization nor centrally imagining the other's narrative is necessary for sympathy—indeed, one can care about an other and feel compassion for him without a detailed understanding of the other's condition, history, and nuances of feeling. However, I submit, sympathy *does* require the more basic empathy discussed earlier. At a minimum, it requires an awareness of the other as a locus of experiencing, a lived body. Without that awareness, I may still *care*, but my caring would lack the quality of sympathy or feeling *for*, because it would not be directed at a *subject* (there would be no one for *whom* I can feel). Goldie acknowledges that sympathy requires being aware of the other as a center of consciousness, but does not characterize this awareness as a form of empathy, and more generally does not discuss our basic grasping of the other's subjectivity. Because of this, the wedge he draws between sympathy and the other's experience goes, I think, too deep. For instance, he claims that "it is *entirely mistaken* to assume that … sympathy also involves undergoing difficulties and having feelings *of the same sort* as the other person's"; and "*the whole phenomenology* of sympathy is different from the phenomenology of the experience which is being sympathized with: your feelings involve caring about the other's suffering, not sharing them" (Goldie 2000, 214; my italics; original italics eliminated). The phenomenology of caring and that of sharing do not strike me as *wholly* different. Sympathy involves an empathic awareness of fellow humanness that connects the sympathizer *experientially* with the other. Scheler observed that sympathy presupposes the givenness of the other's experience; the latter can exist without the former, but "experiences of pity and fellow-feeling [*Mitgefühl*] are always additional to an experience in the other which is already grasped and understood" (Scheler [1923] 1954, 8). In other words, in sympathy the other's feeling is grasped and experienced and is therefore present in the sympathizer's experience (although nonprimordially)—indeed, otherwise how could sympathy be a *fellow* feeling? Sympathy that disentangles itself entirely from awareness of the other's experience is not a feeling *for the other* anymore; it is, at best, a lonely subject's desire to be kind.

Note also that perceiving the other's expression is not necessary for sympathy (e.g., I may know that my friend is seriously ill and feel sympathy for him even when he is not showing his sorrow and his illness is not apparent, and more generally outside the concrete encounter). However, seeing or hearing the other's experiences in his face and body is typically a powerful way to arouse sympathy. We may find this regrettable from an ethical standpoint, but it is very much the case that feelings of caring and compassion are more easily awoken in concrete encounters than outside

them. This may be why some Eastern meditative practices aimed at cultivating compassion invite the meditator to visualize someone in distress.
Christina Feldman (2005, 57–58) explains that "the first person you focus
upon in compassion practice is someone who is in the midst of great physical, psychological, or emotional suffering." The instructions for the practice
are: "If possible, visualize that person, their face or their circumstances.
Imagine them in front of you, as vividly as possible, and try to sense every
aspect of that person's distress or anguish." And here is a passage from the
Visuddhimagga (Path of Purification) by Buddhaghosa (fifth century CE) of
the Buddhist Theravadin tradition:

Just as one would feel compassion on seeing an unlucky, unfortunate person, so
he pervades all beings with compassion. Therefore first of all, on seeing a wretched
man, unlucky, unfortunate, in every way a fit object for compassion, unsightly, reduced to utter misery, with hands and feet cut off, sitting in the shelter for the help-
less with a pot placed before him, with a mass of maggots oozing from his arms and
legs, and moaning, compassion should be felt for him in this way: "This being has
indeed been reduced to misery; if only he could be freed from this suffering!" (Bhadantacariya Buddhaghosa 1999, 306)[9]

Goldie (2000, 214) does recognize that empathy may increase sympathy;
specifically, in his view, the imaginative processes constituting empathy
"may make more assured one's thoughts about the other person." The
practices just reported, however, tap not the power of the meditator's
"thoughts" to arouse sympathy but rather her capacity to *experience* foreign
consciousness in the perception of the other's body.

Finally, note that English speakers tend to use "sympathy" as synony-
mous with "compassion." However, we can feel or care for the other in
different ways: we can rejoice in his fortune, regret his grief, worry for
his suffering, hope for his recovery. These different forms of sympathy
can unfold dynamically and change from one to the other in a concrete
encounter, as the other's expressivity and my empathy for him change
and modulate my sympathy. The appearance of a tearful expression on the
other's face expresses sorrow, and as I empathically perceive it, feelings of
compassion mixed with worry for the other and desire to relieve his sorrow
swell into the foreground of my awareness. As the other stops crying and
settles into a more relaxed posture, my sympathy may take on a different
quality, one mixed with relief and hope.

In sum, the distinction between empathy and sympathy is, I think, not
as clear-cut as some may think or want; it is important to differentiate one

from the other conceptually, but experientially sympathy depends on basic empathy, and as such it is itself open to being influenced and modulated in the concrete encounter by the other's attitude and expression. This openness does not imply that one should not attempt to cultivate a capacity to care for others that is not influenced by how the other's body is empathized; yet this will take practice.

7.7   Doing as Others Do

I shall now leave these phenomenological considerations aside for a while, to turn to the empirical results that have been gathered in the laboratory in recent years about how our bodies respond to one another in face-to-face encounters. In particular, we now have ample evidence that humans automatically (i.e., nonconsciously and involuntarily) *mimic* others, namely, copy their facial and more general bodily attitudes.[10]

Chartrand and Bargh (1999) call this phenomenon the *chameleon effect*. A famous study by Meltzoff and Moore (1977), often reported in this context, showed that infants begin to mimic facial gestures of adults (particularly tongue protrusion and mouth opening) shortly after birth. This phenomenon is widely accepted, though some have recently begun to question it, together with the claim that imitation is an innate capacity (e.g., Jones 2009; Ray and Heyes 2011). In any case, mimicry certainly develops and is present in adulthood. Evidence shows that automatic mimicry of facial expressions happens in adults. Using facial electromyography (a technique that records electrical activity generated by muscles when they contract), Dimberg (1982) found that observation of happy and angry faces induces different facial response patterns; in particular, observation of happy faces induces increased activation in the zygomatic major muscle (considered a feature of facial expressions of "positive" emotions), whereas observation of angry faces induces increased activation in the corrugator supercilii muscle (considered a feature of facial expressions of "negative" emotions). Later studies indicated that this kind of facial mimicry does not need to be accompanied by the conscious perception of the other's expression. Dimberg, Thunberg, and Elmehed (2000) obtained the same results by presenting facial expressions of happiness and sadness very quickly, for thirty milliseconds, followed by a picture of a neutral expression flashed for five seconds (this technique is called "backward masking" because only the second stimulus lasts long enough to be consciously perceived, and its perception thus "masks" the perception of the previous, shorter stimulus). Cannon, Hayes, and Tipper (2009) found that mimicry occurs automatically in response to viewing pictures of facial emotion expressions also when subjects are explicitly requested to categorize these pictures according to their color. Harrison et al. (2006) even found that, in the case of sadness, pupils dilate or contract to match the other's pupil size (for further evidence of mimicry of facial expressions, see Blairy, Herrera, and Hess 1999; Hess and Blairy 2001; for recent work indicating that facial mimicry is subject to contextual effects, see Hess and Bourgeois 2010).

Voice, bodily postures, and movements also appear to be automatically reproduced. Newborns respond with distress to other infants' vocalizations of distress, but not to their own (Dondi, Simion, and Caltran 1999; Field et al. 2007). That speakers of the same language who grow up in the same place speak with the same inflection is also evidence of automatic mimicry. Conversation analysts have shown that adult partners come to match each other's conversational rhythms, as measured by length of vocalizations, duration of pauses, and length of talkovers (e.g., Cappella 1991). People even tend to use the same syntax, and the same number and type of words as their conversation partners (Niederhoffer and Pennebaker 2002). Earlier work by Kendon (1970) showed that, in conversation, listeners also mirror the bodily attitude of the speaker. For example, they lean backward when the speaker does so, and they move the left arm when the speaker moves the right one (automatic postural mimicry typically appears to mirror the other in this way, rather than in a "rotational" way, i.e., by imitating left (right) movements with left (right) parts of the body). Berger and Hadley (1975) showed that subjects displayed more muscle activity in the arm when observing arm wrestling rather than stuttering, and more muscle activity in the lips when observing stuttering rather than arm wrestling. In a study by Chartrand and Bargh (1999), participants had to describe some pictures with a confederate of the experiment, who they thought was just another participant. The confederate either moved her foot or touched her face in each session. Examinations of the recordings taken by hidden cameras revealed that participants moved their foot more when the confederate did so, and touched their face more in the other condition. As reviewed by Heyes (2011), ample evidence also indicates that when subjects are engaged in a task that requires them to respond to a cue by performing a specific action A (e.g., opening one's hand), they respond more quickly when they also observe the execution of A rather than of an alternative action B (e.g., closing one's hand). This happens even when the observed actions are "task irrelevant," namely, they have nothing to do with the task the subject is engaged with (e.g., responding to the color of the observed hand stimulus).

There are reasons to believe that, in humans, the capacity to "do as others do" in terms of copying their behavior is mediated by the so-called mirror neuron system. Mirror neurons were first discovered in macaque monkeys, where they were found to activate significantly during the execution of a specific object-oriented action, as well as during the observation of another's execution of the same action (e.g., Gallese et al. 1996; Iacoboni 2009). Mirror mechanisms of this kind are now widely acknowledged to exist in humans, as well (see the overview and discussion in Rizzolatti and Sinigaglia [2006] 2008, chap. 5). Importantly, in humans the mirror system responds not only to object-oriented actions but also to merely mimed actions (Buccino et al. 2001) and to intransitive (i.e., not object-directed) movements, such as a grasping movement when there is no object to grasp (Fadiga et al. 1995; Maeda, Kleiner-Fisman, and Pascual-Leone 2002); also, the human mirror system is responsive to the various temporal phases of the observed movement (Gangitano, Mottaghy, and Pascual-Leone 2001). To provide evidence of a causal relation between mirror neurons and imitation, Heiser et al. (2003) used TMS (transcranial magnetic stimulation) to temporarily disrupt activity in human mirror neural areas (specifically, the left inferior frontal gyrus).[11] They asked subjects either to just press buttons on a keyboard (control condition), or to press buttons on a keyboard while imitating someone else doing so (imitation condition), or to press buttons on a keyboard by following a red dot appearing on it (visuomotor condition). They found that TMS-induced hypofunctionality of the target brain areas disrupts the ability to imitate, but not to perform the movement in the visuomotor task. More recently Catmur, Walsh, and Heyes (2009) also showed, using TMS, that temporarily disrupting activity in the same neural area selectively impairs automatic imitation of index and little finger abduction movement. Finally, evidence also indicates that the same neural areas in the human brain activate significantly during the observation of a number of facial expressions of emotion, as well as during the imitation (Carr et al. 2003) and execution (van der Gaag, Minderaa, and Keysers 2007) of the same expressions. Perhaps these mirror areas are involved in mediating facial mimicry; indeed, the amount of facial movement during the (intentional) mimicry of emotion expressions appears to correlate with activity in mirror areas (Carr et al. 2003; T. Lee et al. 2006). Note, however, that these data remain correlational, and it is not possible to apply TMS to the anterior insula or amygdala, as these areas are too deep in the brain.[12]

7.8   Do We Mimic Others to Read Their Minds?

But why do we do as others do? What is the function of mimicry? A popular interpretation is that mimicry is involved in mind reading, namely, in the attribution of mental states to others to explain and predict their behavior. This interpretation has been proposed in particular for the imitation of facial expressions of emotions. We can distinguish two versions of it. According to one, mimicry enables mind reading via *emotional contagion* (see E. Hatfield, Cacioppo, and Rapson 1994; E. Hatfield, Rapson, and Le 2009). The proposal here is that, by mimicking the other's attitude (his angry facial expression and bodily stance, e.g.), one also comes to *experience* what the other does via bodily feedback (primarily from one's own face, but also from voice and posture). For clarity, I shall refer to this process specifically as *phenomenal* contagion. As Goldman and Sripada (2005, 205) remark, this interpretation is consistent with a "reverse simulation model," according to which the observer first comes to experience the other's feeling via mimicry and feedback (phenomenal contagion), then classifies her own feeling as one of happiness, anger, and so on, and eventually attributes it to the other (an earlier version of this account can be found in Lipps 1907; see Zahavi 2012).[13] According to another, more recent interpretation, mimicry is an *embodied simulation* of the other's emotional state that may or may not lead to experiencing the same emotion as the other (Niedenthal et al. 2010). More specifically, the proposal here is that mimicry is the simulation of an emotional state that, together with the belief that this state has been caused by the observation of the other's facial expression, provides (subpersonal) information about the other's emotional state.

I think that both versions of this simulationist interpretation have problems. Importantly, evidence from studies of facial emotion recognition indicates that whereas subjects tend to mimic the expressions they are observing (as we saw), mimicry is not *necessary* for recognizing them as expressions of specific emotions (see the reviews and discussions in Hess,

Blairy, and Philippot 1999; Atkinson 2007; Heberlein and Atkinson 2009; Niedenthal et al. 2010). Some studies with healthy subjects failed to find any relation between facial emotion recognition and mimicry (Blairy, Herrera, and Hess 1999; Hess and Blairy 2001). Moreover, it has been shown that an inability to mimic facial expressions does not imply an inability to recognize the expressed emotions. Notably, patients with Moebius syndrome, whose face is congenitally paralyzed, can still recognize emotional facial expressions (e.g., Bogart and Matsumoto 2010).

On the other hand, evidence suggests that mimicry *facilitates* recognition. In Niedenthal et al.'s (2001) study, subjects played with computerized morph movies of the same person changing facial expression from happy to sad, and vice versa. The first frame of the movie showed a face clearly expressing either sadness or happiness, and subjects were asked to stop the movie at the frame in which they no longer detected the initial emotional expression (they used a sliding bar at the bottom of the screen to morph the movie). In addition, while doing so, some subjects were asked to hold a pen horizontally between their teeth and lips to prevent them from mimicking the observed facial expressions.[14] Other subjects were left free to mimic (and thus presumably did so, based on existing evidence for spontaneous mimicry). Results showed that the subjects who were prevented from mimicking stopped the morph later than subjects who were left free to mimic, confirming the experimenters' hypothesis that mimicking facilitates the recognition of emotional facial expressions (the idea being that subjects who were left free to mimic received information from their own face that made them identify changes in the movie earlier than in the absence of such information). Similarly, Stel and van Knippenberg (2008) found that female (but not male) subjects are slower to recognize the positive or negative character of a facial expression when they are prevented from mimicking it. Neal and Chartrand (2011) injected some subjects with Botox to paralyze their facial muscles and found that they were slower at recognizing expressions (in terms of matching pictures of eyes with one of four given adjectives) compared with subjects injected with Restylane, which does not paralyze muscles. Moreover, they found that enhanced facial feedback (induced by spreading a gel on the face that tightens the skin and in so doing amplifies sensations from the facial muscles) facilitates (speeds up) recognition.

These results are interesting, but they can be interpreted in a nonsimulationist way. Mimicry may be functioning here simply like a prime that speeds up the subjects' response when they are asked to interpret facial expressions (very much like, in the Stroop effect, reading words such as "green," "red," and "blue" is facilitated if the words themselves are colored in green, red, and blue respectively, and is slowed down if the words are colored differently). In this interpretation, the presentation of a facial expression (or a part of it, such as the eyes) activates a recognition process (which could be an association pattern) whose completion is facilitated by the generation of a congruent response in the observer. When this congruent response is blocked, the recognition process takes longer. Importantly, the congruent response here need not be a "simulation" in the sense of a copy of the other's state in oneself specifically for the purpose of recognizing his expression. The congruent response may be generated irrespective of this purpose (see the next section for a specific proposal), but once activated, it has the effect of speeding up the recognition process.

Note also that the first version of the simulationist interpretation—the one according to which mimicry mediates mind reading via phenomenal contagion (E. Hatfield, Rapson, and Le 2009)—is phenomenologically problematic. It just does not seem to be the case that recognizing the other's expression involves feeling what the other does. I can see the other's disgust in his face without feeling disgust myself. Likewise for anger, joy, suffering, and so on. Indeed, seeing the other's facial expression can induce quite different experiences in me; for example, I may feel fear at the other's anger, contempt at the other's fear, or envy at the other's joy (see also Zahavi 2008).[15]

This is not to say that no experiential congruence is ever present, and that this congruence does not have any effect on my interaction with, and understanding of, the other (it seems to me that it is indeed the case that, on some occasions, when I see someone making a disgusted expression, I feel disgust myself, or something very akin to it). As we shall see in the next section, empirical evidence indicates that phenomenal contagion does take place when people observe others' expressions; and, as I shall argue, phenomenal contagion may thus affect how we experience the other.

Finally and more generally, I think that questions regarding how we feel others when we face them should be explored more rigorously in the laboratory with the first- and second-person methods delineated in the previous chapter (and ideally also integrated with third-person ones), rather than just stating that shared feelings occur during recognition, or concluding it from a coarse measure of experience. To understand the nature of these feelings, it does not seem enough to ask subjects to rate, on a numerical scale, how much of an emotion they experience when they see another's expression. It seems important to explore the nature of their experience along various qualitative dimensions, including how close or connected one feels to the other. To my knowledge, no study has carefully compared what subjects experience when they themselves feel a specific emotion and when they observe it in the other. Neuroscientific studies claiming that observing the other's expression involves a congruent feeling exhibit the familiar reluctance to explore first-person experience in detail. A much-cited study by Wicker et al. (2003), for example, found that the anterior insula is significantly active when one observes others' facial expressions of disgust as they inhale an odorant, as well as when one experiences disgust oneself when inhaling the same odorant. On the basis of this result, Wicker et al. (2003, 655) claim that "to understand the facial expression of disgust displayed by others, a feeling of disgust must occur also in the observer." If we take a closer look at this study, however, we see that subjects were asked to report (rate) their experience only after they inhaled the odorants. They were not asked also to report their experience while or immediately after observing the facial expressions of others—so we do not really know whether subjects in this condition also felt the emotion they saw in the other (or at least something similar to it, and if so, in which sense). Morrison et al. (2004), in a study of pain observation and experience, asked subjects to report (rate) their experience both after experiencing a painful stimulation and after observing others being subjected to a painful stimulation. However, the experimenters asked subjects to rate specifically how unpleasant they felt only in the first case; when observing others, subjects only had to rate how unpleasant the *observed pain* looked. Thus again it remains unclear whether subjects, when observing others, felt pain themselves (let alone, if they did, what the nature of this pain was). In yet another study, Singer et al. (2004, 1157) point out that neural activity involved in one's own response to observing the other's pain does not involve "the whole pain matrix" but only activity related to "affective" areas. Presumably this reflects a difference in subjects' experiences, although again these were not explored in any detail. It seems to me that a more rigorous application of first- and second-person methods in these experiments, as well as in experiments of mimicry, is needed to clarify the nature of the experience of "vicarious" emotions and pain, thereby helping to better understand the role of phenomenal contagion in our interactions with others.

7.9   Mimicry as a Mechanism for Social Bonding

I now want to draw attention to an interpretation of the function of mimicry that characterizes it not as a mechanism for mind reading but as one for *social bonding*. This interpretation has been relatively neglected in the domain of social cognition, perhaps because of the predominance in this field of the concern with how we read or infer other people's mental states.

By now, however, we have ample evidence that mimicking others facilitates interaction, increases liking among participants, and promotes prosocial behavior more generally. Interest in this role of mimicry began forty years ago, and today there is strong empirical support for it (see Chartrand and van Baaren 2009 for an overview). Early correlational evidence showed that during a psychotherapy session the postures of client and therapist tended to become more similar, and this convergence was positively correlated with an increase in rapport (Charney 1966). In a later study, Chartrand and Bargh (1999) found that perceiving attitudes in the other similar to one's own increases liking and feelings of rapport with him. Recall that in one of Chartrand and Bargh's studies, participants had to describe some pictures in collaboration with another participant, who was in fact a confederate in the experiment. In addition to finding, in one study, that participants automatically and unconsciously mimicked the confederate (see earlier), in a related study they found that when the confederate mirrored the posture, movements, and mannerisms of the participants (without them noticing), they rated the confederate as more likable, and their interaction with her smoother, than when she just sat in a relaxed posture.

Subsequent studies have shown that people who are mimicked are more trustful and more likely to help others (the mimicker, but not only); they also report increased rapport more generally. These effects always occur when the mimicked person does not notice that she is being mimicked (for a review, see Lakin and Chartrand 2013). Also, people who have an affiliative goal automatically mimic the behavior of others more; automatic mimicry is even more frequent when affiliation has previously failed, and in those previously excluded from a social activity (Lakin and Chartrand 2003, 2013; Lakin, Chartrand, and Arkin 2008; Chartrand and van Baaren 2009). Conversely, when people do not want to affiliate (because, e.g., they perceive the other to be socially stigmatized), they mimic less (L. Johnston 2002). Finally, we have evidence for a reversed causal direction between automatic mimicry and rapport: subjects manipulated into liking another mimic him more, and those manipulated into disliking him mimic him less (Likowski et al. 2008).

These results indicate that a (if not the) function of mimicry is to facilitate social bonding. This interpretation has a straightforward possible explanation, namely, that someone who "does as I do" appears more predictable and less threatening than someone who does not (at least in the absence of further information about him). In addition, unlike the simulationist interpretation, it resonates with lived experience. Let me elaborate on this point.

The studies just mentioned focused on *covert* mimicry—in particular, in cases in which the mimicked person does not notice that she is being mimicked, as well as in cases in which the mimicker unconsciously mimics others. Indeed, the experimenters are particularly keen to emphasize that it is covert mimicry that produces interesting social effects, and when one becomes conscious that one is being mimicked, mimicry loses its social-glue effect. Yet it is not clear why mimicry ought to remain covert to exert its bonding spell. At least one study so far has found that intentionally (consciously) mimicking others also enhances prosocial behavior in the mimicker, as measured in terms of how much money was donated to a charity (Stel, van Baaren, and Vonk 2008). Also, we know from therapeutic techniques, such as music therapy, that overtly imitating and matching the other is an effective way to indicate that one is paying attention to the other, and to "resonate" experientially with him, thus establishing rapport (Gardstrom 2007, chap. 7; see also the next section). Admittedly, the therapist needs to use these techniques skillfully, or otherwise the client may feel ridiculed, but the point is that in some contexts *overt* mimicry appears to importantly contribute to the establishment of an affective bond.

It may well be that an important function of mimicry is precisely to make our experiences converge via phenomenal contagion, so that we feel more connected to one another. There is indeed evidence (mainly indirect) that mimicry leads to catching the other's experience, at least in some contexts. Subjects not only mimic the other's emotion expression but often report congruent experiences (Lundqvist and Dimberg 1995; Blairy, Herrera, and Hess 1999; Wild, Erb, and Bartels 2001; Hess and Blairy 2001; Stel, van Baaren, and Vonk 2008). Whereas some studies found no evidence that mimicry and phenomenal contagion are related (Blairy, Herrera, and Hess 1999; Hess and Blairy 2001), independent evidence suggests that producing facial expressions can lead to experiencing the corresponding emotions (Adelmann and Zajonc 1989; McIntosh 1996; Soussignan 2002; Davis et al. 2010). Hence it seems safe to assume that doing as others do can induce convergent experiences (see also Atkinson 2007). This convergence may be what induces increased rapport and liking, and it can do so while remaining prereflective, tacit, but also as an overt phenomenon that also increases feelings of connectedness; in particular, the realization that I feel what the other does will make me feel close to him in the sense specified earlier (sec. 7.5).

We know from organizational psychology that emotion experiences spread within groups. Barsade (2002) talks of a "ripple effect" and says that everyone in a group is a "walking mood inductor." She has provided evidence that a person's pleasant attitude (such as smiling) in a group affects the feelings of other people in the group, with subjects typically reporting more pleasant feelings than those in a group with someone behaving unpleasantly (no smiles, slouching in the chair, speaking with a low tone of voice). We can speculate that mechanisms of mimicry happen frequently within groups and may be partly responsible for how people come to feel like others around them (this would have to be verified empirically; as Niedenthal and Brauer [2012] point out, there is little controlled research on emotional contagion within groups). It is likely that emotional ripple effects within groups will depend on the internal structure of the group itself, such as its more or less hierarchical organization, and already existing bonds (recall that how much one mimics others depends itself on how much one already likes others and wants to affiliate). Irrespective of these complications, notice for now that the fact that we tend to catch the other's blues, and not just his good moods, can be explained by reference to the experience of closeness that feeling like others can foster, irrespective of how others feel (see also Niedenthal and Brauer 2012).

Everyday as well as socioanthropological considerations also indicate that moving in synchrony with others can feel particularly good and help alleviate unpleasant feelings. Anyone who has participated in a group exercise class (from aerobics to tai chi) is likely to be familiar with the feeling of togetherness that one experiences when everyone's movements are synchronized, as well as with the feeling of discordance that arises as soon as oneself or someone else falls out of sync with the others. Moving in synchrony with others is a powerful experience in which one feels that one's own activity is somehow supported and rendered "lighter" by the movement of the group. No doubt in some cases this has to do with the fact that watching the others' movements helps one remember how to move next (when one does not quite remember the next step of a choreography) and thus facilitates one's performance; but even when one already knows how to move, and arguably even *more so* in this case, the experience of moving in and with a group can be particularly intense and meaningful.

A vivid account of just such an experience is provided by the historian William McNeill (1995, 2) as he recalls "strutting around" in the desert heat when training during his military service in Texas:

> Marching aimlessly about on the drill field, swaggering in conformity with pre-scribed military postures, conscious only of keeping in step so as to make the next move correctly and in time somehow felt good. Words are inadequate to describe the emotion aroused by the prolonged movement in unison that drilling involved. A sense of pervasive well-being is what I recall; more specifically, a strange sense of per-sonal engagement; a sort of swelling out, becoming bigger than life, thanks to par-ticipation in collective ritual. ... A state of generalized emotional exaltation whose warmth was indubitable, without, however, having any definite external meaning or attachment. ... Moving briskly and keeping in time was enough to make us feel good about ourselves, satisfied to be moving together, and vaguely pleased with the world at large.

He calls this phenomenon "muscular bonding" and identifies it in a variety of contexts—from community dancing to religious rituals—arguing that throughout human history, moving together in coordination has con-tributed to creating and maintaining social cohesion, fostering feelings of togetherness and reciprocity. That these experiences feel good is also shown by the existence of collective chanting and moving together during the per-formance of otherwise strenuous or boring activities. We can speculate that these practices not only generate feelings of closeness but also allow people to follow through their natural tendency to do as others do, without inhibi-tions or restraints. In other words, contexts of muscular bonding may well be contexts in which imitating motor tendencies are allowed to "go wild," thus contributing to a feeling of exhilaration.[16]

One may remark at this point that strutting around, chanting together, and so on, do not involve any mimicry; they are merely instances of "mov-ing together" that occur because participants move at the same rhythm, and thus cannot tell us anything about the experience of mimicking or being mimicked. However, if it is indeed the case that moving together is accompa-nied by feelings of connectedness, then to the extent that mimicry leads to moving together, it will also come with such feelings. The point I intended to make is that given that in aerobics classes, marching drills, collective dances, rituals, and so on, one is *aware* that others are moving as one is, it does not seem that mimicry needs to remain *covert* to exert its bonding spell.

7.10 Beyond Strict Mimicry

The bonding power of mimicry may be what grounds more complex forms of "matching" the other's actions and expressions, which have also been shown to promote rapport and feelings of closeness, even intimacy. Consider what Stern (1985) calls *affect attunement*. In this mode of interaction, participants do not exactly copy the other but reproduce cross-modally some of the features of his expressivity. Stern illustrates the phenomenon with different examples of mother-child interactions:

A nine-month-old girl becomes very excited about a toy and reaches for it. As she grabs it, she lets out an exuberant "aaaah!" and looks at her mother. Her mother looks back, scrunches up her shoulders, and performs a terrific shimmy with her upper body, like a go-go dancer. The shimmy lasts only about as long as her daughter's "aaaah!" but is equally excited, joyful, and intense. ...

An eight-and-one-half-month-old boy reaches for a toy just beyond reach. Silently he stretches toward it, leaning and extending arms and fingers out fully. Still short of the toy, he tenses his body to squeeze out the extra inch he needs to reach it. At that moment, his mother says, "uuuuuh ... uuuuuh!" with a crescendo of vocal effort, the expiration of air pushing against her tensed torso. The mother's accelerating vocal-respiratory effort matches the infant's accelerating physical effort. ...

A nine-month-old boy is sitting facing his mother. He has a rattle in his hand and is shaking it up and down with a display of interest and mild amusement. As mother watches, she begins to nod her head up and down, keeping a tight beat with her son's arm motions. (Stern 1985, 140–141)[17]

Stern interprets these interactions as facilitating mind reading. He sees them as enabling the participants to access "internal" feelings behind external behavior, namely, as a way of getting "inside of other people's subjective experience" (138). "Mere" mimicry, he claims, cannot achieve this; when one is being mimicked—his argument goes—one cannot be sure that the other is sharing one's experience or merely reproducing one's behavior. Note, however, that the same argument could be applied to the behavior displayed in affect attunement. If one takes feelings to be hidden behind behavior, then how can one be sure that the other's behavior is manifesting any feeling?

If, however, we leave aside Stern's assumption that feelings are internal experiences behind behavior, we can interpret the interactions just described instead as bodily ways of enhancing feelings of closeness between participants that capitalize on the bonding power of mimicry but also add an element of surprise, a "variation on the theme" (where the theme mainly comes from the child, and the variations from the mother) that preserves feelings of connectedness but also solicits the interest of the mimicked person. Affect attunement is not just mimicry, but as Stern acknowledges, it is nevertheless based on "matching" the other's bodily (facial, vocal, gestural) attitude in various aspects—primarily intensity, shape, and beat. We can thus see the phenomenon as a more elaborate form of mimicry in which different modalities are recruited, thus making the interaction more engaging and more likely to be sustained.[18]

Some therapeutic practices explicitly recommend something very similar to "affect attunement" to enable interacting and relating affectively and even intimately with people who have severe communicative difficulties. One such practice is the "intensive interaction" method (also known as "augmented motherhood"; see Ephraim 1986), which has been used effectively to engage with people who have severe autistic disorders. Phoebe Caldwell (2006) provides several touching examples from her experience as a therapist, illustrating that doing as others do can be a compelling and effective way to draw severely autistic people into an active and intensely affective interaction, even in cases where any other attempt to communicate with them has previously failed. Importantly, she often initiates an interaction by reproducing or mimicking the other's behavior (bodily stance, movements, breathing pattern). This strategy is used to simplify the autistic person's world, which is typically characterized by a sensory overload that causes great anxiety and makes the person withdraw from stimulation; reproducing the other's behavior provides a stimulus that is easily recognizable and perceived as safe, because it is predictable and familiar. This simplified and secure environment is one in which the autistic person can (finally) pay attention to the other's attitude, recognize its affinity with the person's own, and achieve an experience of mutual understanding and connectedness (see also Zeedyk 2006). Caldwell, however, also emphasizes that once rapport is established, it is important to add elements of variation to the encounter, to create a sense of expectancy and increase alertness, which fuels the interaction: "Once our partner knows that when they make an initiative they will get a response, we start to build up a conversation, taking turns and using their sounds and movements in a creative way. In order to widen our engagement, we no longer copy our partner exactly but use elements of their language put together in different ways to respond to their initiatives. This creates more surprise" (Caldwell 2006, 160). For example, she recounts her interaction with a woman who was banging her feet loudly on the pavement. Caldwell initially stayed behind her and copied her behavior until the woman gave sign to have noted her. After thus building up the woman's expectations, on a next step Caldwell placed her foot quietly down, which made the woman swing round immediately, laughing, "sharing the joke" (126).

Analogous techniques are used with autistic people (and not only) in music therapy. In improvised music making, the music therapist and the client engage in a musical conversation by playing together. The therapist uses various techniques to facilitate the interaction, most of which include matching the client's music in some respect, such as rhythm, intensity, and melody. Matching techniques are also called "techniques of empathy" (Gardstrom 2007, chap. 7), and their purpose is to establish rapport and intimacy between therapist and client; the therapist uses matching techniques to make the client more aware of what he is doing at a given moment, to make him feel that his contribution to the conversation is being endorsed, to match the emotional character of his music, and to give structure to the interaction when it becomes too chaotic and fragmented. In particular, imitation (here, echoing some aspects of the client's music after he has played it) and synchronization (simultaneously playing the same phrase as the client's) are often used at the beginning of a session to initiate a relationship, convey acceptance, and encourage self-awareness—with the caveat not to overdo it, to avoid making the client feel derided. Once rapport is thus established, variations and novel elements can be brought into the session (breaking the established rhythm, introducing a new melody) to avoid excessive rigidity and encourage the client's autonomy; the aim is to move to a more diverse interaction in which the participants, however, remain reciprocally attuned (although the aim of any session should remain flexible and could shift as the interaction unfolds).

It looks as if imitation and coordination even work as a means of communicating with nonhuman animals. See, for example, Barbara Smuts's (2001) account of coming to be accepted within a community of baboons.

She emphasizes that her relationship with the baboons she was studying changed dramatically when she stopped trying to make herself "invisible" by ignoring their attempts to communicate with her. Rather, they accepted her as part of the group once she started responding to them by "sending back" to them their signals (295) or in other ways that she had picked up from them. She adopted their routines and coordinated most of her activities with theirs, eventually coming to feel a deep and primordial sense of belonging to the group. Smuts also describes how she fine-tuned her interactions with her dog, largely via "synchronous and complementary movements" (304) such as stretching together in the same way while facing each other in the morning.

Perhaps these broadly imitative practices are best seen as an intermediate step along a bonding spectrum, with strict mimicry at one end and *complementary* actions at the other end—such as leaning backward when your dance partner leans forward in ballroom dancing, or opening your hand to receive an object that someone passes to you with a closed hand. These sorts of actions do not retain any imitative element, yet they still require coordination and matching the other's rhythm. A capacity for coordination in turn opens up the space for more complex forms of turn taking—as in waiting for your dance partner to complete her pirouette before proceeding to the next figure. Maybe mimicry is what makes it possible to develop such complex forms of bodily interactions in the first place, by enabling us to attune to others, to bond with them via bodily similarity and action matching, and from this shared bodily affective space to move on to increasingly more intricate forms of attunement, with added variations, contrasts, and oppositions, and eventually a capacity for sustained and diverse engagements with others over time.

7.11 Conclusion

This chapter has explored the various ways in which we, as living bodily beings, experience one another in concrete encounters. I distinguished the capacity to directly perceive the other's subjectivity and emotions in his body and expressions (what I called basic empathy) from the phenomena of impressions, feelings of closeness, intimacy, and sympathy. I also illustrated and discussed existing evidence that we tend to mimic others' attitude when we face them, and also that mimicry appears to make us like one another better and even enhances prosocial behavior. I then linked this evidence to previous phenomenological considerations, suggesting that a function of mimicry is to make us converge experientially, and thus to foster feelings of closeness. Finally, I speculated that this function may be what grounds more varied and reciprocal forms of bodily interactions that have also been shown to promote closeness and even intimacy. Arguably, these interactions still exploit the bonding function of imitative aspects of the relationship while also adding elements of surprise and novelty, and eventually enabling a capacity for more complex complementary actions and turn taking.

Epilogue

The chapters of this book have addressed several topics in affective science (primarily the psychology and neuroscience of emotion) from an enactive perspective. Of the various themes that make up this complex framework, I have emphasized the deep continuity of life and mind; the autonomous and adaptive nature of organisms (including their immanent purposefulness and their temporal and self-organizing character); the coupling of brain and bodily processes; the lived or experiential dimension of our embodiment; the need to integrate first-, second-, and third-person methods in the scientific study of consciousness; and finally the bodily nature of our encounters with others. I have used these themes as a springboard to make a variety of points about the nature of affectivity, emotional episodes, moods, appraisal, emotion experience, and their relation to bodily feeling, affective neuroscience, and our experience of others in the concrete encounter.

In a nutshell, I have argued that affectivity is a pervasive dimension of the mind, deeper and broader than the emotions and moods of the affective scientist; that emotional episodes are best conceptualized as self-organizing dynamical patterns of the organism (rather than as affect programs, psychological constructions, or component processes driven by a separate process of appraisal); that the conceptual tools of dynamical systems theory can also be used to characterize moods and their relationship to emotional episodes; that the process of appraisal, from an enactive perspective, is not a purely cognitive and wholly heady phenomenon separate from the bodily components of emotion, but is enacted by the organism in virtue of its organizational properties, including the deep interconnectivity and coregulation of brain and body; that the experience of appraisal is also not clearly separate from the rest of emotion experience, including bodily feelings; that the body can enter emotion experience in many different ways, not just as an intentional object, but as that through which something else is experienced, and in different degrees of "self-luminosity"; that affective neuroscience ought to be augmented by a neurophenomenological method that integrates the already well-developed third-person technologies for recording brain and bodily activity with first- and second-person methods for generating first-person data about emotion experience; that our concrete encounters involve different ways in which we experience or feel others; and finally that our well-documented tendency to do as others do, to mimic their expressions, postures, and actions, may be a basic mechanism to foster social bonding by making us converge experientially and thereby promote feelings of closeness while at the same time grounding more complex forms of interaction and affective interconnectedness.

Affectivity is a complex phenomenon that can be addressed from many different angles, and how one characterizes it has implications that go beyond the immediate concerns of affective science narrowly conceived. As the conceptual apparatus of enactivism bears further fruit, I believe that it will be possible to address even more facets of this central dimension of the mind. For now, my aim has been to show that the enactive approach already offers a host of resources for thinking about affectivity and emotion in novel and fruitful ways. By exploiting and elaborating on these resources, I hope to have contributed further to our appreciation of the mind as a thoroughly living and lived bodily phenomenon.

Notes

Introduction

1. Throughout the book, I use the term "body" to refer to the organism "minus" the brain (and, relatedly, I use the term "organism" to refer to the brain and body together). By "brain" I refer only to a part of the central nervous system—the one that, in vertebrates, is located within the skull (in vertebrates, the central nervous system also includes the spinal cord). I often follow convention in using "neural activity" in place of "brain activity," although it is important to remember that brain activity does not reduce to neural activity but includes biochemical activity; conversely there is "neural activity" going on in the body as well, in the peripheral (somatic) nervous system, as well as the autonomic or visceral one (whose divisions—sympathetic, parasympathetic, and enteric—all include a host of neurons and ganglia).

2. Most of the embodied-embedded literature in philosophy of cognitive science focuses on cognition only, with no discussion of its affective dimension or at least of its relation to emotion (see, e.g., A. Clark 1997; Noë 2004; Wheeler 2005; Chemero 2009; Shapiro 2011). As for the enactive approach, Thompson (2007) dedicates a chapter to emotion, and in another he extensively discusses empathy (see also Thompson 2001). He also often emphasizes the affective nature of cognition, and the integration of cognition and emotion (see also Colombetti and Thompson 2008; Thompson and Stapleton 2009). Yet much more, I think, can be said about affectivity from an enactive perspective, as this book hopes to show.

1   Primordial Affectivity

1. Admittedly, in practice moods are not always clearly differentiated from emotions (see Fox 2008, chap. 2, for a useful overview). The elicitation of emotion in the laboratory, for example, is called "mood induction" and is sometimes effectuated with procedures that, indeed, elicit what look prima facie more like moods than

emotions—as when subjects are asked to recall events from their past to self-induce sadness or joy. The study of mood disorders, such as depression and anxiety, is also an important subject area in affective science.

2. Note that unlike emotions and moods, *passions, affections,* and *sentiments* have fallen off the contemporary (scientific, and also largely ordinary) map of the affective mind. Because in this book I deal primarily with current work in affective science, I will not discuss these further constructs. However, for a history of these notions and their relation to the category of emotion, see Rorty 1982; Dixon 2003; and Charland 2010.

3. Further authors who could have been discussed in this chapter, e.g., are Schopenhauer, Ribot, Bergson, Erwin Straus, and Jonas.

4. This section of the chapter builds on arguments previously explored in Colombetti 2010. There, however, I did not distinguish between affectivity and emotion.

5. The Roman numeral indicates the part of the book, and the Arabic numeral its proposition. I use this notation instead of page numbers to facilitate finding the relevant passages in different editions of the *Ethics*. When quoting, I use the edition published by T. Fisher Unwin in 1894.

6. Descartes discussed the division of mind and body in several works, most notably *Meditations on First Philosophy* ([1641] 1996). This work, however, does not refer to the pineal gland, whose role is mentioned in *The Passions of the Soul* ([1649] 1989) and *Treatise of Man* ([1664] 2003).

7. Scholars debate whether parallelism, aspect dualism, or even epiphenomenalism (just to mention some possibilities supported by the text) are better characterizations of Spinoza's account of the mind—body relation. For a discussion of various interpretations, see, e.g., Delahunty 1985.

8. Spinoza uses the term "ideas" in different ways. Importantly, he distinguishes between "adequate ideas," which are produced in the mind by the activity of the mind itself, and "inadequate ideas" or "images," which are left in the mind by experience (e.g., in perceiving, imagining, hallucinating, dreaming).

9. This interpretation is along the lines of Jonas 1965. Jonas argues that Spinoza's metaphysics enable an account of living organisms as self-maintaining and immanently animated that is precluded by Cartesian mechanism and dualism (see also Hampshire 1951). Toward the end of his paper, Jonas talks of "Spinoza's insight into the essentially dual character of the organism: its *autonomy* for itself, and its *openness* for the world: spontaneity paired with receptivity," where receptivity is not just the passive reception of stimuli from outside but the complement of spontaneous striving: "The affectivity of all living things complements their spontaneity; and while it seems to indicate primarily the passive aspect of organic existence, it yet provides … the very means by which the organism carries on its vital commerce with the envi-

ronment, that is, with the conditions of its continued existence. Only by being sensitive can life be active, only by being exposed can it be autonomous" (Jonas 1965, 56). This idea is further elaborated in Jonas ([1966] 2001), where he also talks of the *concern* that organisms have for their continuation.

10. Some have argued that *any* kind of feeling disappears altogether in Spinoza's account, which has thus been criticized for overintellectualizing the emotions (see G. Segal 2000). Yet this charge seems excessive, for even if it is the case that Spinoza discusses emotions in relation to "ideas," this term in Spinoza can refer to thoughts as well as feelings; and it is apparent from reading the *Ethics* that feelings are often at stake in much of Spinoza's discussion of how we are affected by the passions. See also E. Marshall (2008) for the argument that in Spinoza ideas, as expressions of the conatus, have "power," and feelings enter into his account as experiences of the mind moving to higher or lesser degrees of power.

11. The phenomenological relevance of this distinction was noted already by Scheler ([1913–1916] 1973). In Scheler, however, the *Leib* is sometimes also just the *living* body (living *Körper*).

12. For a brief introduction, in English, to Maine de Biran's philosophy of the body, see Gaines 1990.

13. Merleau-Ponty's ([1945] 1962) account of the lived body, for example, although undeniably rich and multifaceted, focuses on its ecstatic or world-oriented character (for a criticism of this tendency, see Shusterman 2008, chap. 2; Shusterman talks of a "somatic attention deficit" in Merleau-Ponty. Similarly Sartre [1943] 1958; see also my discussion in chap. 5). Husserl's discussion of *Empfindnisse* (sensings) in the second volume of *Ideas* comes closer to Biran's notion of the body. Husserl coined the neologism *Empfindnis* from *Empfindung* (feeling, sensation) and *Erlebnis* (lived experience) to refer specifically to the way sensations are experienced in the body. Kinesthetic sensations also play an important role for Husserl in constituting the lived body (see Welton 1999 for an introduction to Husserl's notion of *Empfindnisse*; for various differences between Husserl's and Merleau-Ponty's conceptions of the lived body, see Carman 1999; see also Zahavi 1999).

14. Although not published until 1965, Henry's essay was written in 1948 and 1949, when the author was not familiar with Merleau-Ponty's work. In the preface, Henry emphasizes that his views are "totally different" from Merleau-Ponty's, because he does not attempt to characterize life in terms of transcendence; on the contrary, he characterizes life and embodied subjectivity in terms of pure immanence. Henry, like Maine de Biran, is interested in the phenomenon of an "immediate internal apperception," which characterizes our embodiment as a force, and an "immediate pathos." Arguably this affective dimension is less present in Merleau-Ponty, who, as mentioned in the previous note, focuses more on the world-oriented motor intentionality of the lived body.

15. For further discussions, in English, of Henry's work, see Zahavi 1999 and the recent collection of essays, Hanson and Kelly 2012. .

16. The other two constituents of care are understanding (*Verstehen*) and discourse (*Rede*). Approximately, understanding refers to the field of activities in which tools appear to Dasein in their functionality; discourse refers to the articulation of how things show themselves to Dasein.

17. Macquarrie and Robinson (see Heidegger [1926] 1962) translate *Befindlichkeit* as "state-of-mind"; however, this translation, as others have complained, is misleading, because it suggests a private, enclosed psychological state, and Heidegger strongly rejected the Cartesian view of existence as subjectivity and interiority. *Befindlichkeit*, in fact, emphasizes the world-dependent nature of existence, the fact that we are "thrown" into the world and "find ourselves" in it as a consequence. A better translation is "situatedness" (e.g., Guignon 2003), but this term loses the affective connotation entailed by the German term. Stambaugh (Heidegger [1926] 1996) translates *Befindlichkeit* as "attunement," which is also better than "state of mind"; however, "attunement" also means *Stimmung* (translated by Stambaugh as "mood"; see my discussion in the text). I shall therefore stick to the original German.

18. This is in line with the general treatment of Dasein in *Being and Time*, which explicitly leaves aside the question of its embodiment. But see, e.g., Overgaard 2004 for the argument that Heidegger does not explicitly talk about the embodiment of Dasein to avoid furthering the analytic view that Dasein can be divided into mental and bodily components.

19. This work is the English translation of a collection of essays published posthumously in Czech in 1995. These essays are compilations of students' notes from lectures Patočka gave in 1968–1969 at Prague's Charles University, after being banned from teaching for several years by the Communist regime (Patočka was Václav Havel's mentor and died after two months of police interrogation).

20. More recently Ratcliffe (2008) has also pointed out that Heidegger's account of mood does not clarify its relationship to the feeling body. Ratcliffe's own proposal is to adopt a different term, *existential feelings*, to designate a variety of ways in which we find ourselves bodily in the world. Existential feelings, like Heidegger's moods, are preintentional background orientations that function as preconditions for other states. Importantly, however, Ratcliffe also emphasizes a role for the "feeling body" in existential feeling, where the body is not an object of awareness (a felt body) but rather that *through which* the world is felt or lived. I come back to Ratcliffe's existential feelings later in the book (chaps. 3 and 5).

21. I recount here in highly condensed form the main points of a complex discussion woven by Thompson (2007, esp. chaps. 3, 5, 6). I refer the reader to this work for a history of the theory of autopoiesis, its relation to Kant's notion of natural purposes in the *Critique of Judgment*, a review of attempts to create minimally auto-

poietic systems, a discussion of the relationship between autopoietic and autonomous systems, and more. A useful summary of the most salient points for present purposes can be found in Thompson and Stapleton 2009. See also Thompson 2011b for an updated discussion.

22. This would seem to indicate that autopoiesis is not necessary for autonomy, in tension with other passages in Thompson 2007 (see Wheeler 2011 for a detailed analysis). Indeed, Thompson (2011b, 215) has recently admitted to being unsure of this point. His latest view is that autopoiesis may be necessary for autonomy in the sense that autonomy may require autopoietic components as constitutive parts, and that as a matter of fact, all known autonomous systems have autopoietic elements (i.e., cells) as components. He also points out that it is hard to see how adaptive autonomy could be realized without "something like a *metabolism*" or "put another way … *without something like an autopoietic organization for the constituents that make up the sensors, effectors, and the adaptive mechanism that links them*" (Thompson 2011b, 216; italics in original). I shall not address this complex issue here. For present purposes, what matters is the enactive account of the relationship between autonomy, adaptivity, and sense making illustrated in the main text (that is, the claim that autonomy and adaptivity are individually necessary and jointly sufficient for sense making), which I believe would hold even if autopoiesis turned out not to be necessary for autonomy.

23. Maturana and Varela (1980) had explicitly banned any talk of purposes and teleology from the autopoietic system. As Thompson (2007) explains, however, this ban applied to "extrinsic" purposes, namely, to the idea that living systems may serve some end or purpose external to them, imposed from the outside. Thompson also recounts how Varela later came to accept the view that the autopoietic organization is intrinsically teleological—a view he eventually explicitly defended in Weber and Varela 2002.

24. For more about the relation between Jonas and the enactive approach, see Weber and Varela 2002; Di Paolo 2005; and Thompson 2007, chap. 6.

25. Or at least this is my gloss in the attempt to make the enactive claim that all living systems are cognitive more palatable, given its counterintuitive flavor. A common reaction to this claim is to deny that simple living systems are cognitive or sense making, because cognition must involve representations. Yet this reaction disregards the arguments just summarized in the main text. The enactive approach does not simply assert that all living beings are sense making and that sense making is cognition, but provides reasons to see them as such (see also Thompson 2007, 158–165).

26. The structure of sense making is indeed much like the one of Dasein: it is intrinsically purposeful, concerned with its existence, world dependent, and world related, and the Umwelt it enacts depends on its specific needs and purposes. Yet Dasein is, importantly, also conscious and capable of reflection. From an enactive perspective,

the primordial capacity for sense making is best understood as itself grounding or making possible Dasein's care for its existence, and accordingly its moods (see also chap. 3).

27. When and why this happens is, of course, a hard question, and I shall not address it here. Just note that the enactive approach favors accounts according to which consciousness dawns as a primitive form of bodily self-awareness. Thompson (2007, 161) suggests that consciousness appears initially in the form of *sentience*, namely, "as a kind of primitive self-aware liveliness or animation of the body," akin to Maine de Biran's experience of movement and effort. This is along the lines of, e.g., Damasio's (1999, 2010) and Panksepp's (1998b) proposals that the simplest forms of consciousness entail a minimal, nonreflective sense of being a bodily self embedded in the world. In their accounts, this form of consciousness requires a nervous system with the capacity to map the self-regulatory activity of the organism.

28. "Valence" is not always used in affective science to refer to pleasantness—unpleasantness. Sometimes it refers more generally to the positive or negative character of an emotion, sometimes to its direction of behavior (approach or avoidance), sometimes to its adaptive or maladaptive character, and more. See Colombetti 2005 for an overview and discussion of the different meanings of this term.

29. Damasio also talks of "background feelings," but I will postpone discussion of these until chapter 5.

30. I say "roughly" because there is in fact more than one formulation of this hypothesis (see Colombetti 2008).

2   The Emotions: Existing Accounts and Their Problems

1. The superordinate English term "emotion" differs here from the Italian *emozione*—just to mention my native language. The Italian word is narrower in range and refers primarily to specific stirrings or excitements. In Italian more enduring states are called *sentimenti*, which are not the same as the English *sentiments*—a term that is rarely used in ordinary language today. See Wierzbicka 1995 for this and other comparisons.

2. The terms "physiological" and "autonomic" activity are used interchangeably in affective science, usually to refer to visceral changes induced by the sympathetic division of the ANS. The ANS is made of peripheral nerves and ganglia that innervate the viscera and other internal organs that are not under voluntary control (e.g., it regulates heartbeat, sweating, tears, digestion, and salivation). Traditionally, the sympathetic division of the ANS has been taken to excite or arouse the organs under its control, whereas the parasympathetic division has been taken to have an inhibiting and calming influence. Today it is acknowledged that both divisions act together to maintain homeostasis, and their reciprocal influences affect health and emotion (see Berntson and Cacioppo 2009). This is a relatively recent change of perspective,

however, and the expression "physiological arousal" still often refers primarily to the excitatory effects of the activity of the sympathetic nervous system.

3. See also Cosmides and Tooby 2000; Panksepp and Watt 2011; Levenson 2011. Their lists of basic emotions differ from one another, but they all characterize basic emotions as adaptations.

4. This list has changed over the years. A revised one has been proposed recently by Ekman and Cordaro (2011, 365), in which "distinctive appearance developmentally" has been eliminated (presumably in light of evidence that I discuss in the next chapter) and replaced by "11. Refractory period filters information available to what supports the emotion. 12. Target of emotion unconstrained. 13. The emotion can be enacted in either a constructive or destructive fashion." For present purposes we need not dwell in too much detail on these changes and their reasons. What matters is the existence of a number of features that have been proposed as distinctive of basic emotions.

5. PET and fMRI provide indirect measures of neuronal activation in different brain areas by measuring local increases in blood oxygenation and blood flow, respectively. Significant activation refers to activation found to be particularly intense in a specific experimental condition, compared to some other control condition. In studies of emotion, the experimental condition often involves responding to specific emotional stimuli (facial expressions of fear, anger, happiness, etc.; disgusting, saddening, happy, etc., pictures, films, music clips, scripts), whereas the control condition is usually a "neutral" condition (e.g., a neutral facial expression, a neutral film). Brain activity in both conditions is recorded and then compared statistically to extrapolate which brain areas respond significantly more in the emotional condition. Using neutral stimuli that match the kind of stimuli used in the experimental condition—e.g., neutral facial expressions compared to emotional facial expressions—allows one more rigorously to discriminate the specific effect of emotion. (The notion of "neutral" stimuli is, of course, problematic, and I would argue that there are no absolutely neutral stimuli. Yet some stimuli can certainly be more salient than others.) Some fMRI and PET studies compare activations across the whole brain; others focus only on "regions of interest" and look at whether specific brain regions respond selectively in some conditions compared to others. Phan et al. (2002) focused their analysis on twenty regions of interest, whereas Murphy, Nimmo-Smith, and Lawrence (2003) included only studies that had looked at activation across the whole brain. In addition, Murphy and colleagues included only studies that used matched neutral control stimuli.

6. The debate is ongoing. As I write, a new meta-analysis of neuroimaging studies by Barrett and collaborators has just been published (Lindquist et al. 2012). Like previous studies, it concludes that no evidence points to the existence of brain regions that are always and only significantly activated when a specific emotion occurs; yet it also indicates that some brain areas are more consistently activated than others in the perception or experience of specific emotions—notably the amygdala in the

perception of fear and the experience of disgust, and the insula in the perception and experience of disgust. Lindquist et al. (2012) interpret this result as rejecting the "locationist" view that the emotions they looked at (the same five as the previous analyses) map in a one-to-one way onto distinct brain areas, and rather as being consistent with their own proposal that distinct brain areas underpin basic psychological components that do not have specific emotion functions. In their view, the amygdala, for example, is not dedicated to fear, but its main function may be to detect novelty, which may be why it activates consistently in the perception of fear and the perception and experience of disgust. Similarly for the insula, as well as for other brain areas that, in their analysis, do not turn out to activate preferentially for any specific emotion. This is a plausible interpretation, but importantly it is consistent with the hypothesis that different emotions may correspond to different recurrent patterns of neural activity involving activations in brain areas that are not "dedicated" to any specific emotion but nevertheless reliably associated with it in specific contexts (see also Scarantino 2012). Indeed, few if any affective neuroscientists today would subscribe to the view that individual brain areas have *dedicated* specific emotional functions.

7. See, however, Matsumoto and Ekman 2009, 72: "The existence of basic emotions does not argue against other types of emotions; nonbasic emotions are important for a rich and varied emotional life."

8. Ekman, however, also asserts the existence of affective phenomena that are not adaptations. He claims that there are "affective states" other than (basic) emotions, such as "a mood, an emotional trait, an emotional disorder, et cetera," that "do not possess universal, distinctive signals, nor is it certain that they have distinctive antecedent events" (Ekman and Cordaro 2011, 365–366).

9. The cortex is the part of the brain traditionally associated with executive functions, including explicit deliberation. The limbic system is sometimes also called "the emotional brain" and refers to a set of neural structures (such as the amygdala, hippocampus, fornix, etc.) sandwiched between the oldest "reptilian" brain, constituted mainly by the thalamus and responsible for basic regulatory and homeostatic functions, and the newer cortical and neocortical areas. This classification, which was proposed already in the 1940s by Paul MacLean, is still influential, though it has also been questioned—most notably by LeDoux (1996), who believes that the limbic system is not anatomically well defined. In chapter 4 we shall look at alternative views of "the emotional brain" that do not constrain it within specific neural areas.

10. More precisely, I think that rigorous first- and second-person methods, rather than quick introspective remarks, should be developed to assess the claim that some emotion experiences include other ones as parts. In addition, if one's aim were to establish whether some emotions are building blocks of other ones, then first- and second-person methods should be augmented and integrated with third-person methods (for more detail, see the outline of what I call a "neuro-physio-phenomenological method" in chap. 6).

11. One complication here is that although Russell's and Barrett's models are similar in many respects, they are also different, but their differences are not particularly explicit or obvious. For present purposes, I will treat them as broadly similar, unless otherwise specified.

12. I am also dissatisfied with the radical nature/nurture dichotomy they assume, but I shall leave this issue aside here.

13. Russell, for his part, in some passages at least, seems to grant that emotional episodes arise as coherent patterns *independently* of mental scripts. For example, he claims that one realizes that one is scared when various components "form into a perceptual Gestalt with a specific meaning" (Russell 2005, 34), and one recognizes that these components match the mental script for fear. Russell also believes (personal communication) that it is possible for someone to be in a specific emotional state without knowing it. For example, he thinks that all the components of an episode of anger may occur *save* the recognition, on the subject's part, that what is going on matches the anger script; an outside observer, however, would still be able to recognize the episode as one of anger.

14. In a more recent version of their psychological constructionist model, Lindquist et al. (2012) emphasize the "situated" nature of the categorization process, and its reliance on the history of the organism's interactions with the world. This account thus at times appears to acknowledge a more prominent role of "biology" in structuring various processes into emotions (and comes closer to the dynamical systems approach I defend in the next chapter). Yet they also reiterate that "emotion words that anchor emotion categories work hand in hand with conceptualization. ... Emotion words are central to our model because we assume that the instances of any emotion category (e.g., anger) that are created from affective feelings don't have strong statistical regularities in the real world or firm natural category boundaries. ... In our view, emotion categories are abstract categories that are socially constructed. ... As with all abstract categories, in the absence of strong perceptual statistical regularities within a category, humans use words as the glue that holds the category together" (Lindquist et al. 2012, 125).

15. The idea that specific components of expression—e.g., brow furrowing or raised upper eyelid—reflect different appraisals was already advanced by Darwin ([1872] 2007). Ortony and Turner (1990) also discuss it in some detail.

3   Emotional Episodes as Dynamical Patterns

1. I provide here only a very brief overview of some of the main concepts of DST (see also A. Clark 2001, 120–128; Wheeler 2005, 90–96). For more detailed introductions, see, e.g., Abraham and Shaw 1992; Kelso 1995.

2. The latter direction of influence is sometimes also referred to as "downward causation." In the context of self-organizing systems, this kind of influence is best

understood as "the influence of the system's topological organization on its constituent processes. ... 'Downward' is thus a metaphor for the formal or topological influence of a whole with respect to its parts" (Thompson 2007, 426). As such, downward causation in self-organizing systems is simultaneous with (rather than a preceding step to) "upward causation," so to speak, namely, with the influence the system's components exert on the macrolevel pattern; it refers to an "interconnectedness or relatedness among processes" (427). For a more detailed discussion, see Thompson 2007, 417–441. See also Juarrero 1999, chaps. 9 and 10.

3. Clark's favored notion of emergence is not limited to collective self-organization; emergent phenomena for him include "the effects, patterns, or capacities made available by a certain class of complex interactions between systemic components. Roughly, the idea is to depict emergence as the process by which complex, cyclic interactions give rise to stable and salient patterns of systemic behavior" (A. Clark 2001, 114). This broad notion of emergence as "interactive complexity" is meant to cover collective self-organizing phenomena (such as the Rayleigh-Bénard instability), but also phenomena involving simple kinds of feedback loops in repeated linear interactions—as when a process sequentially influences a second one, which in turn influences the first one, and so on, generating behavior that is not "pre-designed" into the system (for more detail, see A. Clark 2001, 112–117).

4. Models, overviews, and critical evaluations of the approach can be found, e.g., in A. Clark 1997, 2001; van Gelder 1998; Giunti 1997; Juarrero 1999; Keijzer 2001; Thelen et al. 2001; Wheeler 2005; R. D. Beer 2000, 2003; Thompson 2007; Chemero 2009; Shapiro 2011.

5. Enactivism is often associated with radical antirepresentationalism, but this point needs to be qualified. Varela, Thompson, and Rosch (1991, esp. chap. 7) clearly rejected the ontological assumption of the symbolic approach in cognitive science, according to which the mind is something "internal" and the world is "external" to it, and the mind represents objective features of the world. However, enactivism does not deny that the nervous system, for example, exhibits patterns of activity that occur reliably in a certain context, and even that these patterns can be seen as "embodying meaning" for the organism. As Thompson (2007, 368) writes, "When a stimulus arrives, the activated receptors transmit pulses to the sensory cortex, where they induce the construction by nonlinear dynamics of an activity pattern in the form of a large-scale spatial pattern of coherent oscillatory activity. This pattern is not a representation of the stimulus but an endogenously generated response triggered by the sensory perturbation, a response that creates and carries the meaning of the stimulus for the animal. This meaning reflects the individual organism's history, state of expectancy, and environmental context." An important feature of enactivism is that these meaning-embodying patterns need not be confined to the nervous system. To quote Thompson again: "If we wish to use the term *representation*, then we need to be aware of what sense this term can have for the enactive approach. Representational 'vehicles' (the structures or processes that embody meaning) are

temporally extended patterns of activity that can crisscross the brain-body-world boundaries, and the meanings or contents they embody are brought forth or enacted in the context of the system's structural coupling with its environment" (58–59, italics in original). I interpret these passages as implying that enactivism need not exclude *any* kind of representational talk, provided it is clear that "enactive representations" are not internal items representing an external objective world, but self-organizing structures of an autonomous cognitive system, which bring forth (enact) specific meanings. (See also Foglia and Grush 2011, and the response in Thompson 2011b; see Hutto 2011 for the point that representational talk comes in many varieties, some of which appear less in tension with enactivism than others—although Hutto himself is a staunch antirepresentationalist.)

6. "Intentional" here means "goal oriented"; this use of the term is closer to its everyday meaning and is common among psychologists and neuroscientists. It is important not to confuse it with its other use, more common among philosophers, which refers to the "directedness" or "aboutness" of mental states (from the Latin *intendere*, "to tend toward"). I use the term in this second sense later in the chapter, in the section on moods.

7. See also Edelman's theory of "neural Darwinism" or "neuronal group selection" (e.g., Edelman 1987), according to which neural development consists in (1) the early establishment of connections between growing neurons on the basis of the associationist principle that "neurons that fire together wire together," (2) the selection of some connections over others on the basis of environmental stimuli, and (3) the establishment of a large number of reentrant connections both locally and over long distances.

8. See also chapter 7 for more empirical evidence illustrating affective and expressive reciprocal influences between caregiver and child.

9. It is worth pointing out that supporters of BET themselves have recently acknowledged that the notion of affect programs is problematic, and have at least tried to distance themselves from it. Ekman (2003, 66), e.g., writes that "affect programs are, like the emotion databases, a metaphor, for I do not think there is anything like a computer program sitting in the brain, nor do I mean to imply that only one area of the brain directs emotion." Yet at the same time he does not seem ready to replace this metaphor with a different one; as he adds in a footnote, "It is more popular today to use connectionist models. I don't disagree with those formulations, but they are more difficult to understand, and for my purposes here I believe the computer metaphor of a program and instructions is more useful" (247).

10. The dynamical systems perspective, in other words, is consistent with the developmental systems approach in philosophy of biology (e.g., Griffiths and Gray 1994; Oyama 2000), which is another important constitutive strand of the enactive approach (see the extensive discussion in Thompson 2007). I have chosen not to present this approach here, to avoid digressing too much from debates in affective

science. I shall only point out that, in the philosophy of emotion, Griffiths (1997, 132–136) explicitly draws on a developmental systems approach to emphasize what he calls the *heterogeneous construction* of the emotions. At the same time, however, he endorses BET's notion of affect programs and talks of heterogeneous construction only in relation to the higher cognitive emotions. The present dynamical account begs to differ, in that it explicitly applies a dynamical-developmental conceptualization to *all* emotions (including the alleged basic ones) and rejects the notion of an affect program altogether. It thus makes space for the variability and context dependence of *all* emotions, not just the alleged nonbasic ones.

11. The adjective "discrete" comes from the Latin *discretus*, which is the past participle of *discernere* (to discern). *Discernere* itself comes from the Latin verb *cernere*, which means to separate and divide, but also to distinguish, to see clearly, to recognize (and also to deliberate); and from the Greek prefix *diá*, which denotes separation and interruption. Etymologically, then, we can say that the primary meaning of "discrete" is "separate," but it also means "distinguished," "recognized," "identified."

12. Dimensional models are often misleadingly characterized by their critics as implying that emotions are not differentiated from one another. See, e.g., the following passage by Ekman (1999, 45): "There are a number of separate emotions, that differ one from another in important ways. ... This basic emotions perspective is in contrast to those who treat emotions as fundamentally the same, differing only in terms of intensity or pleasantness."

13. Admittedly, much more is known about the neurochemistry of depression and anxiety than of "ordinary" moods such as grumpiness and the blues.

14. My account here is similar to the one proposed by Lewis (2000, 48), in that he also characterizes moods as self-organizing patterns of the organism that involve a modification of "the entire state space ... for a period of hours, days, or weeks" (see also Thompson 2007, 379). Lewis also characterizes moods as "goal-oriented" states that entrain the organism into a highly coherent or orderly form, which persists until action is taken to dissolve it. Note, however, that whereas moods may depend on the thwarting or realization of specific goals, not all moods feel directed toward specific aims. Quite the contrary, sometimes moods are lived more as diffuse alterations in experience with no specific directedness—as when one feels cheerful or irritable.

15. A similar story could also be told about the relationship between personality or character traits, and moods. Personality or character traits can be seen as the consolidation, over one's life span, of certain landscapes of attractors and repellors corresponding to specific moods. I shall not discuss this complex phenomenon here, however (for relevant discussions, see Lewis 2000; Goldie 2000).

16. Note that acknowledging the intentional character of the emotions is not at odds with the dynamical systems approach endorsed here, and the enactive

approach more broadly. Some people may raise this worry if they assume, as many do, that intentionality requires internal mental representations, and that a dynamical/enactive approach must reject any kind of representational talk. Both assumptions are misguided, however. First, to acknowledge that an experience is intentional does not necessarily imply that it involves internal mental representations. This conception of intentionality is certainly widespread in philosophy of mind, but it is not the only available one. In the phenomenological literature and the enactive approach, one finds accounts of intentionality that characterize it primarily as a nonrepresentational "act" directed toward objects in an unmediated way (see Thompson and Zahavi 2007; Thompson 2007, 22–27; Gallagher and Zahavi 2008, chap. 6). Second, as mentioned earlier, the dynamical systems approach is not necessarily antirepresentational, and the enactive approach acknowledges the existence of recurrent self-organizing patterns of physical processes that carry meaning for the organism. Indeed, as Thompson (2007, 26–27, 159) discusses, event directedness from an enactive perspective corresponds to a specific self-organizing configuration of the organism (an attractor), which is at the same time a specific mode of relating to the world: external events are "a function of the system's own activity. Their meaning or significance corresponds to an attractor of the system's dynamics (a recurrent pattern of activity toward which the system tends), which itself is an emergent product of that very dynamics" (27).

4   Reappraising Appraisal

1. Nisbett and Schachter (1966) did remark that, in everyday life, emotions are not usually generated by first experiencing a state of unexplained arousal and then attaching a label to it. Instead, in their view, cognitive or situational factors usually trigger physiological changes in the first place and label them from the beginning, so that physiological arousal does not remain unexplained. However, this concession still implies that arousal needs to be interpreted by cognition and does not come "with its own label," so to speak; in this sense, then, the view remains phenomenologically implausible.

2. In a different paper, Scherer (2000, 87; italics in original) writes: "Appraisal is seen as the initiator and driver of the synchronization process but *also* as being *driven by it*. As is usually the case in self-organizing systems, there is no simple, unidirectional sense of causality." In this paper, the arrows in the model go from the appraisal component to the other emotion components, as well as "directly" back to the appraisal. However, as noted in the previous chapter, appraisal in the CPM is otherwise usually depicted as very much the pilot of the emotional ship: it drives the interaction of the other emotion subsystems and shapes their patterning; moreover, each SEC is hypothesized to kick in sequentially, in a specific order.

3. See also R. D. Beer 2000 for a short introduction to the dynamical systems approach in cognitive science that discusses both these models. Further discussions can be found in Chemero 2009 and Shapiro 2011.

4. Thompson (2007, 46) writes: "Any nervous system operates according to a basic 'neurologic,' a pattern that continues and elaborates on the biologic of autopoiesis." Note that it is not straightforward whether the nervous system is also an *adaptive* autonomous system and hence a cognitive, sense-making system. Yet even if it were a cognitive system in this sense, its Umwelt would be very different from the one enacted by the organism. It would care about things like maintaining homeostasis between cell assemblies, distributing flows of synaptic activity, creating and responding to large-scale organization, and so on (likewise for other subsystems of the organism that turned out to be autonomous and adaptive). So it would be a sense-making (cognitive) system within a larger and more complex one, but the sense making (cognition) of the larger system would not reduce to that of the smaller system (I am indebted to Ezequiel Di Paolo here for this point).

5. The idea that the nervous system is tightly coupled with other organismic systems has been stressed in other quarters, as well. Pert (1997), for example, claims that the nervous, endocrine, and immune systems can be seen as one whole system, which she calls a *psychosomatic network*. As she points out, these systems communicate with one another via the same family of molecular messengers, the peptides, which are small proteinlike structures (amino acids) that bind selectively to specific receptors distributed across brain and body. Peptides in the immune and endocrine systems reach the brain through the brain-blood barrier by binding with receptors on the surface of the brain to affect the permeability of its surface membranes and propagate a signal that is picked up by other peptides and receptors deep in the brain. Importantly, different peptides contribute differently to emotion and moods, among other things (which is why Pert calls them "molecules of emotions"), in the form of hormones, neurotransmitters, and neuromodulators. Consistent with this integrated view, the traditionally separate fields of neuroscience, endocrinology, and immunology are now converging, and today "psychoneuroendocrinologists" and "psychoneuroimmunologists" study how brain and body modulate each other, and how they react together to social and environmental changes (e.g., Segerstrom 2012).

6. My summary in this paragraph is based primarily on Thompson's (2007, 366–370) useful overview of Freeman's model.

7. An oscillatory pattern is a pattern of synchronous activity of a large number of neurons, which can be observed with an electroencephalogram (EEG). See also chapter 6.

8. This account is consistent with various lines of evidence. For example, as Sander, Grafman, and Zalla (2003) mention, we know that the amygdala is densely interconnected with many other parts of the brain, both cortically and subcortically (see also Pessoa 2008, 2010). In particular, neurons within the amygdala project directly to all cortical stages along the ventral visual system (LeDoux 1996; Vuilleumier 2005), indicating that stimuli that reach the amygdala from this system have already been influenced by the activity of the amygdala, in a process of circular causation.

Studies of emotion and attention have shown that salient stimuli, such as fearful faces or other threat-related stimuli, enhance neural activation compared to neutral stimuli, and this enhancement correlates with amygdala activity (see Vuilleumier 2005 for discussion and references). Evidence also suggests that presentation of fearful faces enhances activity in the primary visual cortex already at the earliest stage of visual processing, namely, 65–90 milliseconds after stimulus presentation (Pourtois et al. 2004; for an overview of these and related studies, see Fox 2008, chap. 6).

9. Although Barrett and Bar mention "sensations from the body" in the quoted passage, their view need not imply that the state of the body is felt.

10. Note that Dewey uses the term "reflection" here differently from how it is used in phenomenology. When he says that perception and appraisal are discriminated "in reflection," he means that the discrimination is a conceptual act that comes after a certain experience has taken place, and that imposes an artificial and distorting distinction that does not belong to the experience. In phenomenology, on the other hand, "reflection" usually refers to the act of articulating and bringing to light the tacit (or "prereflective"; see chap. 5) structure of lived experience. From the perspective of phenomenology, then, reflection, when carried out properly, does not distort lived experience (see also chap. 6).

11. See also Frijda's (1993, 358) point that appraisal can be, as he puts it, part of the content of emotion experience: "It can be argued that an emotional experience consists, in part, of the perception of the emotional event as appraised by the subject. One can say that an experience of joy is the experience of an event appraised in a joyful way, for instance as beneficial and within reach."

12. See Hutto 2012 for a discussion of Prinz's theory in relation to some enactive ideas, in particular for the proposal to reframe Prinz's view of embodied appraisal in a nonrepresentational "teleosemiotic" context, arguably more akin to the enactive approach.

5   How the Body Feels in Emotion Experience

1. Note that James (1884) began by claiming that his discussion would apply only to emotions "that have a distinct bodily expression" (189), and he would "leave entirely aside" other types of emotions, such as pleasure and displeasure in, for example, watching colors and hearing sounds, and the intellectual delight in solving a problem. At the end of his discussion, however, he came back to these phenomena and appeared clearly reluctant to acknowledge that they are emotions: "We have then, or some of us seem to have, genuinely *cerebral* forms of pleasure and displeasure. ... But a sober scrutiny of the cases of pure cerebral emotion gives little force to this assimilation. Unless in them there actually be coupled with the intellectual feeling a bodily reverberation of some kind, ... our mental condition is more allied to a judgment of *rights* than to anything else. And such a judgment is rather to be classed among awareness of truth: it is a *cognitive* act" (201–202, italics in original).

2. This chapter brings together distinctions drawn in Colombetti 2011 and Colombetti and Ratcliffe 2012. The main difference with Colombetti 2011 is that here I make room for bodily feelings in which the body is an intentional object of awareness without thereby being "objectified." Bodily subjectivity, in other words, can here be an object of awareness (as also discussed in Legrand and Ravn 2009). In addition, in this chapter I have dropped the terminology of "noetic" and "noematic" bodily feeling adopted in Colombetti and Ratcliffe 2012, to avoid potential confusions due to different uses of these terms in Husserl's work (Husserl famously used the terms *noesis* and *noema* to refer, respectively, to the ego-pole and the object-pole of object-directed intentional experiences).

3. To be precise, the term *Leib* in ordinary German refers more broadly to the *living* body, as opposed to lifeless matter. Indeed, in phenomenology as well, the term is sometimes translated as "living body" rather than "lived body." The term "lived body" seems to me better to capture the connotation of "experienced body," and I prefer it to "living body" here. As mentioned in chapter 1, the phenomenological relevance of the *Leib/Körper* distinction was noted by Scheler ([1913–1916] 1973) and further emphasized and developed by others, Husserl in particular (see Husserl [1952] 1989). Merleau-Ponty ([1945] 1962) makes the same distinction with the terms *corps objectif* (objective body) and *corps propre* or *corps vécu* (proper or lived body).

4. See also Legrand and Ravn 2009 for the point that what they call the "body-as-subject" can be an object of experience. Likewise Shusterman (2008) extensively argues that cultivating awareness of one's own body does not amount to self-objectification.

5. Of course, not only English speakers have bodily expressions and metaphors for emotion experience. Kövecses (2000) reports examples from several other languages.

6. For Sheets-Johnstone (1999), emotion experience is actually "inherently" kinesthetic, namely, it *necessarily* involves an experience of bodily movement, or at least of possibilities for bodily movement; conversely, each bodily movement is also inherently affective. As she also puts it, emotion experience and movement are "experientially intertwined" (264) and "mutually congruent" (265). Hence, like James, she thinks that emotion experience necessarily involves bodily feelings (although she emphasizes kinesthetic over visceral sensations). As mentioned in the introduction, I am not concerned with this constitutive claim. We can just acknowledge here that we often experience kinesthetic sensations in emotion, and we often perceive movement as affectively laden.

7. A reminder that interoception refers to the perception of internal states of the body, as it occurs, e.g., in pain, perception of bodily temperature, itch, visceral sensations (e.g., gut movements), vasomotor activity, hunger, and thirst. The interoceptive system appears to be anatomically distinct from the proprioceptive one; the

interoceptive system is associated with autonomic motor control, whereas the pro-prioceptive one is part of the exteroceptive system (Craig 2002).

8. But see Sass 2004 for the interesting alternative suggestion that whereas some emotional aspects are indeed diminished in schizophrenia, other aspects are exaggerated (in some forms of the condition, at least). Anxiety and consternation are often present, as well as feelings of desolation, but also wonder, awe, and even complex feelings of the "sublime," namely, of something so great (physically, morally, or aesthetically) as to be beyond measurement. Sass relates these experiences to bodily alienation and disorders of prereflective self-awareness.

9. Admittedly, it is possible to step back from a window and inspect it (in this case, the window is an intentional object of experience). To clarify, my suggestion here is that background bodily feelings are *always* like colored windows through which one sees the world, and never like "inspected" windows. Of course, however, if one draws attention to how one's body feels in emotion experience, one's body will become an intentional object of awareness and cease to be a background medium through which something else is experienced.

10. Gurwitsch (1964) presents his distinction as an elaboration and refinement of James's ([1890] 1950, chap. 9) notion of *fringes*. Broadly speaking, Jamesian fringes correspond to Gurwitsch's thematic field; they are a dimly felt domain of relevancy or affinity.

11. Sartre's view here is a matter of debate and interpretation, but see the following remarks: "What then is this pain? Simply the translucent matter of consciousness, its *being there*, its attachment to the world, in short the peculiar contingency of the act of reading. ... Pain as a contingent attachment to the world can be existed non-thetically by consciousness only if it is surpassed. Pain-consciousness is an internal negation of the world; but at the same time it exists its pain—*i.e.*, itself—as a wrenching away from self. Pure pain as the simple 'lived' cannot be reached" (Sartre [1943] 1958, 333; italics in original).

6   Ideas for an Affective "Neuro-physio-phenomenology"

1. EEG measures the brain's spontaneous electrical activity with several electrodes placed on the scalp. Whereas fMRI and PET can identify which specific brain areas are significantly involved in a mental task (see chap. 2), EEG can track the unfolding of large-scale neural activity over time, in the form of patterns of synchronization and desynchronization across neural populations distant from one another.

2. Unfortunately Lutz et al. (2002) do not say much more about the training session. For more details about the method of open questions, see the work of Claire Petitmengin (Petitmengin-Peugeot 1999; Petitmengin 2006). I talk more about this method later, when presenting my own ideas for a neuro-physio-phenomenology of affect.

3. This does not imply an *identity* between the two; see next section for the difference between "neural correlates" and "dynamical neural signatures" of consciousness.

4. Another useful term here is proposed by Gallagher (2003), who talks of *front-loading phenomenology*. As he puts it, phenomenological insights need to be front-loaded into the experimental design; namely, they need to influence how the experiment is set up from the beginning. One example is the search for distinct neural mechanisms underpinning the phenomenological distinction between sense of agency and sense of ownership (see Gallagher and Zahavi 2008, 38–40). Although Gallagher and Zahavi (2008) present neurophenomenology and front-loaded phenomenology as two different nonreductionist approaches to naturalizing phenomenology, arguably the two are not really distinct, and neurophenomenology always involves front-loaded phenomenology, namely, it always involves using phenomenological analyses to influence experimental design (thanks to Evan Thompson for pointing this out).

5. See also Petitmengin and Bitbol 2009, 397–400, for a (brief) discussion of how this methodology of covalidation and search for internal consistency (rather than correspondences) is characteristic of the natural sciences.

6. Varela (1996, 342) mentioned emotion in passing, noticing that neuroscientific studies of emotion "are entirely based on verbal protocols, and the questions of competence for emotional distinction and the patterns of relation between mood, emotion and reasons need to be addressed explicitly at this stage of research." Thompson (2007, chap. 12) provides a more extended discussion of emotion; however, his account does not draw on existing neurophenomenological experiments but consists in a theoretical synthesis of phenomenological and neuroscientific considerations. In particular, he suggests that there is a correlation between the protentional or forward-looking nature of consciousness (as discussed by Husserl), which is at the same time emotional (or rather, as he emphasizes, e-motional, "moving outward"), and life's intrinsic purposiveness. However, as will become clearer, I think that a lot more can and should be said about the experiential dimensions of emotion, and on how to investigate the nature of its relationship to the living organism. Thompson's discussion is relevant in the present context as an outline for a neurophenomenological account of affectivity broadly understood (see chap. 1). Yet as I see it, an affective neurophenomenology should also be developed that is sensitive to the variety of our affective states, including what differentiates among emotion experiences, for example, and the various ways in which the body is felt in them.

7. Of course, Antonio Damasio has, most notably, written much about the neuroscience of emotion and feeling (e.g., Damasio 1994, 1999, 2003, 2010). In saying that affective neuroscience has so far largely neglected emotion experience, I do not mean to downplay Damasio's important contributions. However, Damasio's work on consciousness and feelings is exceptional. The majority of neuroscientific studies

of emotion eschew questions about experience (even if, arguably, the situation is now gradually changing; see the main text for details). In addition, Damasio's books primarily bring together state-of-the-art knowledge about brain lesions and consciousness with his own hypotheses about the nature of emotion and feeling. They do not concern laboratory experimentation per se, including specifically the question of how to integrate the study of emotion experience into neuroscience. There are some exceptions (e.g., Damasio et al. 2000), which I discuss in the main text.

Another eminent affective neuroscientist interested in consciousness is Jaak Panksepp. He is best known for his work on what, he argues, are primary affective systems in the mammalian brain, which are also responsible for emotional feelings (see for example Panksepp 1998a, 2005). Panksepp certainly believes that neuroscientists should pay more attention to emotion experience, and not just in humans. However to the best of my knowledge his work has focused mainly on the study of animal brains, and not on the development of first- and second-person methods for the study of emotion experience in human subjects (but see Panksepp and Trevarthen 2009 for the proposal to integrate affective neuroscience with cultural studies of music and emotion).

8. Each grade of the symptom is described with a whole sentence. E.g., for "sadness" the subject has to circle one of the following: "0. I do not feel sad; 1. I feel sad much of the time; 2. I am sad all the time; 3. I am so sad or unhappy that I can't stand it."

9. Critchley et al. (2004) did not find a relationship between how good subjects are at detecting their heartbeat online and their bodily self-awareness as reported with Porges's questionnaire. They commented twice that this result is "interesting" and even "intriguing." I do not find this result surprising, however, given the general nature of the questionnaire.

10. In fact, they refer to Kahneman 1999, and *only* to this paper. This work, however, is critical not of self-reports altogether but only of retrospective global judgments about one's general affective condition (one of happiness, in this case). In this paper, Kahneman reports the results of a study in which he "beeped" subjects during the day and asked them to report on their current state of happiness. This method is precisely the one advocated by those who think that it is important to collect first-person data and revive introspection (see Hurlburt 2007).

11. See also Price, Barrell, and Rainville 2002 for the explicit recommendation of self-observation in the first stage of the experiential study of pain.

12. For further considerations about mixed feelings, see Colombetti 2005. Note that early introspectionist psychologists were also particularly interested in hedonic tone and devised ingenious experiments to understand, for example, whether pleasures could be added together, or whether pleasure could be added or subtracted from an activity without otherwise changing it (see Beebe-Center 1932). It may be interesting to revive some of their research questions and findings, compare them with the current state of the art, and try to refine their methods.

13. Note that, consistent with my critique of BET (chap. 2), I am not here advocating a privileged focus on a limited number of emotions. Among other things, the approach recommended here may lead to a better understanding of emotions that are often left out of the scientific enterprise because of their purported nonbasic nature, and thus the assumption that it is more difficult to identify their neural and bodily concomitants.

14. Teroni and Deonna (2008), for example, provide a useful extended discussion of various criteria used in philosophy and psychology to distinguish between shame and guilt. Their analysis, however, includes few experiential considerations. Similarly for Ben-Ze'ev's (1990) discussion of envy and jealousy.

15. This openness on the part of the questioner, and the invitation to let the reports be guided by the subject as much as possible, is a fundamental tenet of qualitative approaches in psychology, like grounded theory, interpretative phenomenological analysis, narrative psychology, discourse analysis, and others (see the papers in Smith 2008). These approaches differ in method, but they all invite the experimenters to let their analyses and interpretations be guided as much as possible by what subjects report. Even if one denies that it is possible to adopt a theory-free stance toward experiential reports, there is a difference between looking for specific dimensions (e.g., pleasantness, bodily sensations, loss of control) when one reads or listens to a report, and looking for dimensions that the report itself presents as particularly salient or relevant. This difference is akin to the one between the mainstream neuropsychiatric approach, which looks for specific "experiential symptoms" (hallucinations, delusions, etc.) to classify a mental disorder, and phenomenological psychopathology, which aims to describe and analyze the patient's experience on the basis of what the patient says (see Colombetti 2013 for a comparison between neurophenomenology and phenomenological psychopathology).

16. A number of examples illustrating further possible intersubjective methods can be found in Petitmengin 2009.

17. Thanks to Claire Petitmengin for making these forms available to me, together with the interviews described in the next paragraph.

18. MEG (magnetoencephalography) records the magnetic fields produced by electric activity generated in the brain. MEG is now usually preferred to EEG because it has better spatial resolution (in addition to much better temporal resolution than PET and fMRI).

19. In the only study of this kind that I am aware of, Dan Glauser and Scherer (2008) presented subjects with various images and asked them to press a button if they felt an emotion following such presentation and to do nothing if they felt no emotion. The experimenters looked at beta and gamma waves in both conditions and, contrary to their hypothesis, found stronger oscillatory activity in both wave types when subjects did *not* report experiencing an emotion.

20. Sze et al. (2010) also measured cardiac activity in all subjects and found that in meditators this activity correlated most clearly with reported emotion experience (as measured by a rating dial). However, rather surprisingly, they did not find that reported visceral awareness in meditators correlated with cardiac activity—a result they attributed to the inadequacy of their self-report inventory for bodily awareness, which did not inquire about actual bodily feelings but only asked about bodily functioning more generally. More rigorous first- and second-person methods may help address these kinds of shortcomings.

21. Grewe et al. (2007) also measured actual physiological responses to music in the form of skin conductance and facial muscle activity. Throughout the paper, however, they conflate "physiological changes" with "reported (or experienced) physiological changes"; in addition, they confusingly distinguish reported physiological changes from "subjective feelings," as if to imply that feelings of physiological changes are not lived experiences. But see the more recent study by Grewe, Kopiez, and Altenmüller (2009) for a clearer distinction between subjective reports of chills, and changes in skin conductance and heart rate. This study interestingly found that skin conductance and heart rate both started rising about two seconds before self-reported chills.

22. In these experiments, subjects are asked to count their perceived heartbeats silently (without feeling for their pulse) or to evaluate whether their heartbeats are synchronous with tones triggered by the heartbeats themselves, with varying delays (see, e.g., Critchley et al. 2004).

23. Of course, a variety of ethical and practical considerations make this kind of inquiry particularly difficult. See also Topulos, Lansing, and Banzett (1993) for a study in which healthy, unsedated subjects (for ethical reasons, these were the experimenters themselves) willingly underwent a complete neuromuscular blockade. They reported experiencing emotions such as fear and panic, but it remains unclear from the paper whether the blockade interrupted visceral feedback and, again, whether the subjects experienced their emotions as "bodily" (and if so, in which sense).

24. In a recent book, Damasio (2010, 102) admits that the notion of the as-if body loop as he originally proposed it had only "circumstantial evidence." He claims, however, that such evidence has now been found; in particular, he refers to evidence for the existence of motor mirror neurons, which fire when one observes someone else perform a goal-oriented action "as if" the observer were herself performing that action: "So-called mirror neurons are, in effect, the ultimate as-if body device" (103). Yet note that evidence for the existence of mirror neurons is not evidence for the existence of brain systems that "bypass" one's own body and, as they do so, simulate an experience. There is no evidence of what human subjects experience when they see another's action or expression and their mirror system activates. Certainly when I see another person perform a goal-oriented action, I do not feel "as if" I were the one performing the action. See also the next chapter for a more detailed discussion and for references.

7 Feeling Others

1. For expository convenience, in this chapter I refer to the empathizing subject as "she" and to the empathized as "he."

2. For more details about Husserl's views on empathy, see Zahavi 2012.

3. Stein also discusses the empathy for what she calls "phenomena of life" such as sluggishness, vigor, health, aging, and so on. I come back to these later, in sec. 7.4.

4. Several videos of Kismet can be seen at http://www.iwaswondering.org/cynthia_video.html. A nice video titled "sad robot get scolded," showing how people react to Kismet, can be seen on YouTube at http://www.youtube.com/watch?v=3GkI374ZkM4 &feature=related.

5. As Stein ([1917] 1989, 89) notes, "empathic fulfillment" is possible even in relation to plants: "We not only see such vigor and sluggishness in people and animals, but also in plants. ... Of course, what I comprehend in this case is a considerable modification of my own life." Scheler ([1923] 1954, 239) argues that perceiving expressivity in the world is our most fundamental attitude, one that we gradually "unlearn" as we grow up. Development, in other words, involves learning that not everything is animated and conscious: "'Expression' is indeed the very first thing that man apprehends of what lies around him. ... Not only is there no question here of an analogical inference ... [but] what we call development ... is ... a continuous process of disenchantment. ... Learning ... is ... a continual '*de-animation*'" (italics in original).

6. The Buddhist meditative practice of *metta* (loving kindness) requires bringing to mind people toward whom one has different feelings. This includes, among other things, bringing to mind a "neutral" person, namely, someone toward whom one does not have particularly good or bad feelings, such as the postman or the casual acquaintance. Whenever I practice this meditation, I find it difficult to bring to mind such a person. I have never talked to my postman, but I definitely have a "positive" impression of her and of our encounters. I have tried with several other people (bus drivers, porters, hairdressers), but every time I conjure up their figure and our encounter, I find that my attitude toward them is never completely indifferent or neutral.

7. For Schmitz's original treatment of the phenomenon of atmosphere, see Schmitz 1969. See also Hauskeller 1995 for an introduction and further elaboration of the phenomenon in relation to various perceptual modalities. For a recent discussion, see Griffero 2010.

8. The German equivalent is *Mitfühlung* or *Mitgefühl* (*mit* = with), often translated as "fellow feeling." Yet it is not obvious that fellow feeling, as characterized in the phenomenological literature, requires compassion. Stein, for example, reserves the term *Mitfühlung* for cases in which one empathizes for a prolonged time with the other's feelings (including feelings of joy), and in addition the other is "really con-

scious" of his own feelings and their object: "Should empathy persist beside primordial joy over the joyful event (beside the comprehension of the joy of the other), and, moreover, should the other really be conscious of the event as joyful (possibly it is also joyful for me, for example, if this passed examination is the condition for a trip together so that I am happy for him as the means to it), we can designate this primordial act as joy-with-him or, more generally, as fellow feeling (*sympathy*)" (Stein [1917] 1989, 14). Here *Mitfühlung* is thus an intensified and deeper experience of closeness. As for the Italian language, it is interesting to note that the term *simpatia* is used quite differently nowadays. It mainly refers to a person's quality; to be *simpatico* is to be liked by others, to be considered friendly and often also funny. *Simpatia* is also something one feels toward someone who is *simpatico*. Likewise for the equivalent French terms.

9. I am grateful to Jenny Wilks for this quote.

10. Mimicry thus understood has also been characterized as "simple imitation," to differentiate it from "complex imitation," "imitative learning," or "true imitation," namely, the imitation of someone else's behavior for the purpose of achieving a specific goal (e.g., Tomasello 1999). The question of the relationship between these two forms of imitation, as well as the extent to which mimicry is mere "response priming," or rather "true imitation," is a highly debated one (complicated by the fact that the imitation of facial expressions, for example, is imitation neither of an object-directed action nor of a meaningless movement).

11. TMS consists in applying a magnetic field to some area of the brain. This magnetic stimulation induces a small electric current, which interferes with the electrical activity of the brain area underneath the magnet, in effect "knocking it out" for a short time. When applied to the motor cortex, TMS induces excitatory activity (known as "motor evoked potentials," or MEPs) in (contralateral) muscles.

12. This is all I shall say about mirror neurons in this chapter, as the debate about their possible function is increasingly complex, and an adequate treatment would require an extensive dedicated discussion. I simply point out here that the debate on the function of mirror neurons is primarily concerned with their role in mind reading, and in particular mirror neurons have often been interpreted as supporting ST versus TT, namely, as simulations of the other's state that enable one to understand his intentions and emotions (e.g., Gallese and Goldman 1998; Gallese 2001, 2005; Goldman and Sripada 2005). This interpretation, however, has been questioned, and alternative interpretations have been proposed (see, e.g., Csibra 2007; Gallagher 2007; Jacob 2009; Herschbach 2012; for some replies, see, e.g., Rizzolatti and Sinigaglia 2010). For present purposes, an important consideration is that if mirror neurons mediate mimicry (at least in some circumstances), and if mimicry, as I argue in the main text, plays an important role in social bonding, then mirror neurons themselves have such a role—which raises the further question of how to reconcile this function with already existing interpretations of mirror neurons.

13. In the nonreverse "generate and test" simulationist model, the observer first generates a hypothesis about the other's state of mind, then produces a corresponding facial expression, and then compares the generated expression against the one of the target (see Goldman and Sripada 2005; note that their aim in this paper is not to defend a simulationist model of mimicry but to distinguish different simulationist models).

14. This manipulation is different from the one of other studies that also asked subjects to hold a pen in their mouths, but for the purposes of inducing a smile (mentioned in chap. 4). In the latter studies, subjects were asked to hold a pen horizontally between their teeth and to contract the lips "backwards" to expose the teeth. In the study by Niedenthal and colleagues, subjects were asked to hold the pen horizontally between both teeth and lips (i.e., in this study, the lips were closed).

15. The same point applies to simulationist interpretations of so-called emotion mirror neurons that claim that understanding others' emotions involves sharing their feelings. Wicker et al. (2003, 655), e.g., write: "To understand the facial expression of disgust displayed by others, a feeling of disgust must occur also in the observer." For Adolphs (2006, 30), "The simulation mechanism through which we infer another person's emotion is empathic: it involves actually feeling (aspects of) the emotion of the other person." Carr et al. (2003, 5502) interpret their results on observation and imitation of emotional expressions along similar lines: "We ground our empathic resonance in the experience of our acting body and the emotions associated with specific movements. As Lipps (1907) noted, 'When I observe a circus performer on a hanging wire, I feel I am inside him.'"

16. We know that there are conditions, such as "imitative behavior" and "echopraxia," that involve a disruption of these inhibiting processes (or at least that are interpreted this way; see the discussion in Rizzolatti and Sinigaglia [2006] 2008, chap. 6).

17. For more recent work about affect attunement, see, e.g., Jonsson and Clinton 2006. Note also that the phenomenon has been studied mostly in mother-infant interactions (and is now often called "maternal affect attunement"). We know less about affect attunement in adults, although the studies on mimicry, contagion, and group emotion mentioned earlier are beginning to give us an idea of how adults attune to one another.

18. Tronick et al. (1978) showed that if the mother puts on a "blank face," the infant becomes distressed. More generally, if the mother intentionally "misattunes" to the child in situations where she would normally attune—for example, by responding with a jiggle that is apparently more or less intense than the movements and vocalizations of the child—the child appears surprised and stops his activity (Stern 1985).

References

Abraham, R. H., and C. D. Shaw. 1992. *Dynamics: The Geometry of Behavior*, 2nd ed. Redwood City, CA: Addison-Wesley.

Adelmann, P. K., and R. B. Zajonc. 1989. Facial efference and the experience of emotion. *Annual Review of Psychology* 40:249–280.

Adolphs, R. 2006. How do we know the minds of others? Domain-specificity, simulation, and enactive social cognition. *Brain Research* 1079:25–35.

Adolphs, R., and L. Pessoa. 2010. Emotion processing and the amygdala: From a "low road" to "many roads" of evaluating biological significance. *Nature Reviews Neuroscience* 11:773–782.

Arnold, M. B. 1960a. *Emotion and Personality*, vol. 1: *Psychological Aspects*. New York: Columbia University Press.

Arnold, M. B. 1960b. *Emotion and Personality*, vol. 2: *Neurological and Physiological Aspects*. New York: Columbia University Press.

Atkinson, A. P. 2007. Face processing and empathy. In *Empathy in Mental Illness*, ed. T. F. D. Farrow and P. W. R. Woodruff, 360–385. Cambridge: Cambridge University Press.

Ax, A. F. 1953. The physiological differentiation between fear and anger in humans. *Psychosomatic Medicine* 15:433–442.

Bar, M. 2007. The proactive brain: Using analogies and associations to generate predictions. *Trends in Cognitive Sciences* 11:280–289.

Barrett, L. F. 2006a. Are emotions natural kinds? *Perspectives on Psychological Science* 1:28–58.

Barrett, L. F. 2006b. Solving the emotion paradox: Categorization and the experience of emotion. *Personality and Social Psychology Review* 10:20–46.

Barrett, L. F. 2006c. Valence is a basic building block of emotional life. *Journal of Research in Personality* 40:35–55.

Barrett, L. F., and M. Bar. 2009. See it with feeling: Affective predictions during object perception. *Philosophical Transactions of the Royal Society of London, Series B: Biological Sciences* 364:1325–1334.

Barrett, L. F., and E. A. Kensinger. 2010. Context is routinely encoded during emotion perception. *Psychological Science* 21:595–599.

Barsade, S. G. 2002. The ripple effect: Emotional contagion and its influence on group behavior. *Administrative Science Quarterly* 47:644–675.

Bauby, J.-D. 1997. *The Diving Bell and the Butterfly.* New York: Vintage.

Bayne, T. 2004. Closing the gap? Some questions for neurophenomenology. *Phenomenology and the Cognitive Sciences* 3:349–364.

Bayne, T. 2007. Conscious states and conscious creatures: Explanation in the scientific study of consciousness. *Philosophical Perspectives* 21:1–22.

Beck, A. T., and R. A. Steer. 1993. *Manual for the Beck Depression Inventory.* San Antonio, TX: The Psychological Corporation.

Beebe-Center, J. G. 1932. *The Psychology of Pleasantness and Unpleasantness.* New York: Van Nostrand.

Beer, J. 2007. Neural systems for self-conscious emotions and their underlying appraisals. In *The Self-Conscious Emotions: Theory and Research*, ed. J. Tracy, R. Robins, and J. P. Tangney, 54–67. New York: Guilford Press.

Beer, R. D. 2000. Dynamical approaches to cognitive science. *Trends in Cognitive Sciences* 4:91–99.

Beer, R. D. 2003. The dynamics of active categorical perception in an evolved model agent. *Adaptive Behavior* 11:209–243.

Bejjani, B.-P., P. Damier, I. Arnulf, L. Thivard, A.-M. Bonnet, D. Dormont, P. Cornu, B. Pidoux, Y. Samson, and Y. Agid. 1999. Transient acute depression induced by high-frequency deep-brain stimulation. *New England Journal of Medicine* 340:1476–1480.

Ben-Ze'ev, A. 1990. Envy and jealousy. *Canadian Journal of Philosophy* 20:487–517.

Ben-Ze'ev, A. 2010. The thing called emotion. In *The Oxford Handbook of Philosophy of Emotion*, ed. P. Goldie, 41–62. New York: Oxford University Press.

Berger, S. M., and S. W. Hadley. 1975. Some effects of a model's performance of an observer's electromyographic activity. *American Journal of Psychology* 88:263–276.

Berkowitz, L., and B. T. Troccoli. 1990. Feelings, direction of attention, and expressed evaluations of others. *Cognition and Emotion* 4:305–325.

Berntson, G. G., and J. T. Cacioppo. 2009. Autonomic nervous system. In *The Oxford Companion to Emotion and the Affective Sciences*, ed. D. Sander and K. R. Scherer, 65–67. Oxford: Oxford University Press.

Bhadantacariya Buddhaghosa. 1999. *The Path of Purification*. Trans. Bhikkhu Nanamoli. Onalaska, WA: Buddhist Publication Society.

Birbaumer, N., and H. Kimmel. 1979. *Biofeedback and Self-Regulation*. Hillsdale, NJ: Erlbaum.

Bitbol, M. 2007. Ontology, matter, and emergence. *Phenomenology and the Cognitive Sciences* 6:293–307.

Blairy, S., P. Herrera, and U. Hess. 1999. Mimicry and the judgment of emotional facial expressions. *Journal of Nonverbal Behavior* 23:5–41.

Blood, A. J., and R. J. Zatorre. 2001. Intensely pleasurable responses to music correlate with activity in brain regions implicated in reward and emotion. *Proceedings of the National Academy of Sciences of the United States of America* 98:11818–11823.

Bogart, E. R., and D. Matsumoto. 2010. Facial mimicry is not necessary to recognize emotion: Facial expression recognition by people with Moebius syndrome. *Social Neuroscience* 5:241–251.

Boiten, F. A., N. H. Frijda, and C. J. E. Wientjes. 1994. Emotions and respiratory patterns: Review and critical analysis. *International Journal of Psychophysiology* 17:103–128.

Breazeal, C. L. 2002. *Designing Sociable Robots*. Cambridge, MA: MIT Press.

Brennan, T. 2003. Stoic moral psychology. In *The Cambridge Companion to the Stoics*, ed. B. Inwood, 257–294. Cambridge: Cambridge University Press.

Buccino, G., F. Binkofski, G. R. Fink, L. Fadiga, L. Fogassi, V. Gallese, R. J. Seitz, K. Zilles, G. Rizzolatti, and H.-J. Freund. 2001. Action observation activates premotor and parietal areas in a somatotopic manner: An fMRI study. *European Journal of Neuroscience* 13:400–404.

Cacioppo, J. T., G. G. Berntson, J. T. Larsen, K. M. Poehlmann, and T. A. Ito. 2000. The psychophysiology of emotion. In *Handbook of Emotions*, 2nd ed., ed. M. Lewis and J. M. Haviland-Jones, 173–191. New York: Guilford Press.

Calder, A. J., A. D. Lawrence, and A. W. Young. 2001. Neuropsychology of fear and loathing. *Nature Reviews Neuroscience* 2:352–363.

Caldwell, P. 2006. *Finding You Finding Me*. Philadelphia, PA: Jessica Kingsley.

Camras, L. A. 2000. Surprise! Facial expressions can be coordinative motor structures. In *Emotion, Development, and Self-Organization: Dynamic Systems Approaches to Emotional Development*, ed. M. D. Lewis and I. Granic, 100–124. Cambridge: Cambridge University Press.

Camras, L. A., L. Lambrecht, and G. Michel. 1996. Infant "surprise" expressions as coordinative motor structures. *Journal of Nonverbal Behavior* 20:183–195.

Camras, L. A., and D. C. Witherington. 2005. Dynamical systems approaches in emotional development. *Developmental Review* 25:328–350.

Cannon, W. B. 1914. The interrelations of emotions as suggested by recent physiological researchers. *American Journal of Psychology* 25:256–282.

Cannon, W. B. 1927. The James-Lange theory of emotions: A critical examination and an alternative theory. *American Journal of Psychology* 39:106–124.

Cannon, P. R., A. E. Hayes, and S. P. Tipper. 2009. An electromyographic investigation of the impact of task relevance on facial mimicry. *Cognition and Emotion* 23:918–929.

Cappella, J. N. 1991. The biological origins of automated patterns of human interaction. *Communication Theory* 1:4–35.

Carman, T. 1999. The body in Husserl and Merleau-Ponty. *Philosophical Topics* 27:205–226.

Carr, L., M. Iacoboni, M.-C. Dubeau, J. Mazziotta, and G. Lenzi. 2003. Neural mechanisms of empathy in humans: A relay from neural systems for imitation to limbic areas. *Proceedings of the National Academy of Sciences of the United States of America* 100:5497–5502.

Carroll, J. M., and J. A. Russell. 1996. Do facial expressions signal specific emotions? Judging emotion from the face in context. *Journal of Personality and Social Psychology* 70:205–218.

Catmur, C., V. Walsh, and C. M. Heyes. 2007. Sensorimotor learning configures the human mirror system. *Current Biology* 17:1527–1531.

Chalmers, D. J. 1996. *The Conscious Mind: In Search of a Fundamental Theory*. New York: Oxford University Press.

Chalmers, D. J. 2000. What is a neural correlate of consciousness? In *Neural Correlates of Consciousness*, ed. T. Metzinger, 18–39. Cambridge, MA: MIT Press.

Charland, L. C. 2010. Reinstating the passions: Arguments from the history of psychopathology. In *The Oxford Handbook of Philosophy of Emotion*, ed. P. Goldie, 237–259. New York: Oxford University Press.

Charney, E. J. 1966. Postural configuration in psychotherapy. *Psychosomatic Medicine* 28:305–315.

Chartrand, T. L., and J. A. Bargh. 1999. The chameleon effect: The perception-behavior link and social interaction. *Journal of Personality and Social Psychology* 76:893–910.

Chartrand, T. L., and R. van Baaren. 2009. Human mimicry. *Advances in Experimental Social Psychology* 41:219–274.

Chemero, A. 2009. *Radical Embodied Cognitive Science*. Cambridge, MA: MIT Press.

Chisholm, N., and G. Gillett. 2005. The patient's journey: Living with locked-in syndrome. *British Medical Journal* 331:94–97.

Christoff, K., A. M. Gordon, J. Smallwood, R. Smith, and J. W. Schooler. 2009. Experience sampling during fMRI reveals default network and executive system contributions to mind wandering. *Proceedings of the National Academy of Sciences of the United States of America* 106:8719–8724.

Chwalisz, K., E. Diener, and D. Gallagher. 1988. Autonomic arousal feedback and emotional experience: Evidence from the spinal cord injured. *Journal of Personality and Social Psychology* 54:820–828.

Clark, A. 1997. *Being There: Putting Brain, Body, and World Together Again.* Cambridge, MA: MIT Press.

Clark, A. 2001. *Mindware: An Introduction to the Philosophy of Cognitive Science.* New York: Oxford University Press.

Clark, J. 2010. Relations of homology between higher cognitive emotions and basic emotions. *Biology and Philosophy* 25:75–94.

Cobos, P., M. Sánchez, C. García, M. N. Vera, and J. Vila. 2002. Revisiting the James versus Cannon debate on emotion: Startle and autonomic modulation in patients with spinal cord injuries. *Biological Psychology* 61:251–269.

Colombetti, G. 2005. Appraising valence. *Journal of Consciousness Studies* 12:103–126.

Colombetti, G. 2007. Enactive appraisal. *Phenomenology and the Cognitive Sciences* 6:527–546.

Colombetti, G. 2008. The somatic marker hypotheses: What the Iowa gambling task does and does not show. *British Journal for the Philosophy of Science* 59:51–71.

Colombetti, G. 2009. What language does to feelings. *Journal of Consciousness Studies* 16:4–26.

Colombetti, G. 2010. Enaction, sense-making, and emotion. In *Enaction: Toward a New Paradigm for Cognitive Science*, ed. J. Stewart, O. Gapenne, and E. D. Di Paolo, 145–164. Cambridge, MA: MIT Press.

Colombetti, G. 2011. Varieties of pre-reflective self-awareness: Foreground and background bodily feelings in emotion experience. *Inquiry* 54:293–313.

Colombetti, G. 2013. Psychopathology and the enactive mind. In *The Oxford Handbook of Philosophy and Psychiatry*, ed. K. W. M. Fulford, M. Davies, G. Graham, et al., 1083–1102. Oxford: Oxford University Press.

Colombetti, G., and M. Ratcliffe. 2012. Bodily feeling in depersonalisation: A phenomenological account. *Emotion Review* 4:145–150.

Colombetti, G., and E. Thompson. 2008. The feeling body: Towards an enactive approach to emotion. In *Developmental Perspectives on Embodiment and Consciousness*, ed. W. F. Overton, U. Müller, and J. L. Newman, 45–68. New York: Erlbaum.

Cosmelli, D., O. David, J.-P. Lachaux, J. Martinerie, L. Garnero, B. Renault, and F. J. Varela. 2004. Waves of consciousness: Ongoing cortical patterns during binocular rivalry. *NeuroImage* 23:128–140.

Cosmelli, D., and E. Thompson. 2010. Embodiment or envatment? Reflections on the bodily basis of consciousness. *Enaction: Toward a New Paradigm for Cognitive Science*, ed. J. Stewart, O. Gapenne, and E. D. Di Paolo, 361–385. Cambridge, MA: MIT Press.

Cosmides, L., and J. Tooby. 2000. Evolutionary psychology and the emotions. In *Handbook of Emotions*, 2nd ed., ed. M. Lewis and J. M. Haviland-Jones, 91–115. New York: Guilford Press.

Craig, A. D. 2002. How do you feel? Interoception: The sense of the physiological condition of the body. *Nature Reviews Neuroscience* 3:655–666.

Craig, A. D. 2004. Human feelings: Why are some more aware than others? *Trends in Cognitive Sciences* 8:239–241.

Crane, R. 2009. *Mindfulness-Based Cognitive Therapy*. Hove, West Sussex: Routledge.

Critchley, H. D., C. J. Mathias, and R. J. Dolan. 2001. Neuroanatomical basis for first- and second-order representations of bodily states. *Nature Neuroscience* 4:207–212.

Critchley, H. D., S. Wiens, P. Rotshtein, A. Öhman, and R. J. Dolan. 2004. Neural systems supporting interoceptive awareness. *Nature Neuroscience* 7:189–195.

Csibra, G. 2007. Action mirroring and action interpretation: An alternative account. In *Sensorimotor Foundations of Higher Cognition: Attention and Performance XXII*, ed. P. Haggard, Y. Rosetti, and M. Kawato, 435–459. Oxford: Oxford University Press.

Csikszentmihalyi, M. 1992. *Flow: The Psychology of Happiness*. London: Rider.

Dael, N., M. Mortillaro, and K. R. Scherer. 2012. Emotion expression in body action and posture. *Emotion* 12:1085–1101.

Damasio, A. R. 1994. *Descartes' Error: Emotion, Reason, and the Human Brain*. New York: Putnam.

Damasio, A. R. 1999. *The Feeling of What Happens: Body, Emotion, and the Making of Consciousness*. London: Vintage.

Damasio, A. R. 2003. *Looking for Spinoza: Joy, Sorrow, and the Feeling Brain*. Orlando: Harcourt.

Damasio, A. R. 2010. *Self Comes to Mind: Constructing the Conscious Brain*. London: Heinemann.

Damasio, A. R., T. J. Grabowski, A. Bechara, H. Damasio, L. L. B. Ponto, J. Parvizi, and R. D. Hichwa. 2000. Subcortical and cortical brain activity during the feeling of self-generated emotions. *Nature Neuroscience* 3:1049–1056.

Dan Glauser, E. S., and K. R. Scherer. 2008. Neuronal processes involved in subjective feeling emergences: Oscillatory activity during an emotional monitoring task. *Brain Topography* 20:224–231.

Darwin, C. [1872] 2007. *The Expression of the Emotions in Man and Animals*. Mineola, NY: Dover.

Davidson, R. J. 1994. On emotion, mood, and related affective constructs. In *The Nature of Emotion: Fundamental Questions*, ed. P. Ekman and R. J. Davidson, 51–55. New York: Oxford University Press.

Davidson, R. J., D. Pizzagalli, J. B. Nitschke, and N. H. Kalin. 2003. Parsing the subcomponents of emotion and disorders of emotion: Perspectives from affective neuroscience. In *Handbook of Affective Sciences*, ed. R. J. Davidson, K. R. Scherer, and H. H. Goldsmith, 8–24. New York: Oxford University Press.

Davidson, R. J., K. R. Scherer, and H. H. Goldsmith, eds. 2003. *Handbook of Affective Sciences*. New York: Oxford University Press.

Davis, J. I., A. Senghas, F. Brandt, and K. N. Ochsner. 2010. The effects of Botox injections on emotional experience. *Emotion* 10:433–440.

deCharms, C. R. 2008. Applications of real time fMRI. *Nature Reviews Neuroscience* 9:720–729.

deCharms, C. R., F. Maeda, G. H. Glover, D. Ludlow, J. M. Pauly, D. Soneji, J. D. E. Gabrieli, and S. C. Mackey. 2005. Control over brain activation and pain learned by using real-time functional MRI. *Proceedings of the National Academy of Sciences of the United States of America* 102:18626–18631.

De Jaegher, H., and E. Di Paolo. 2007. Participatory sense-making: An enactive approach to social cognition. *Phenomenology and the Cognitive Sciences* 6:485–507.

Delahunty, R. J. 1985. *Spinoza*. London: Routledge & Kegan Paul.

Dennett, D. C. 1991. *Consciousness Explained*. Boston: Little, Brown.

Dennett, D. C. 2011. Shall we *Tango*? No, but thanks for asking. *Journal of Consciousness Studies* 18:23–34.

Depraz, N., F. Varela, and P. Vermersch. 2003. *On Becoming Aware: A Pragmatics of Experiencing*. Amsterdam: John Benjamins.

Descartes, R. [1641] 1996. *Meditations on First Philosophy: With Selections from the Objections and Replies*. Rev. ed. Trans. J. Cottingham. Cambridge: Cambridge University Press.

Descartes, R. [1649] 1989. *The Passions of the Soul*. Trans. S. H. Voss. Indianapolis: Hackett.

Descartes, R. [1664] 2003. *Treatise of Man*. Trans. T. S. Hall. Prometheus.

De Sousa, R. 1987. *The Rationality of Emotion*. Cambridge, MA: MIT Press.

Dewey, J. 1895. The theory of emotion. (II.) The significance of emotion. *Psychological Review* 2:13–32.

Dewey, J. [1934] 1980. *Art as Experience*. New York: Perigee Books.

D'Hondt, F., M. Lassonde, O. Collignon, A.-S. Dubarry, M. Robert, S. Rigoulot, J. Honoré, F. Lepore, and H. Sequeira. 2010. Early brain-body impact of emotional arousal. *Frontiers in Human Neuroscience* 4:1–10.

Dickerson, S. S., T. L. Gruenewald, and M. E. Kemeny. 2004. When the social self is threatened: Shame, physiology, and health. *Journal of Personality* 72:1191–1215.

Dimberg, U. 1982. Facial reactions to facial expressions. *Psychophysiology* 19:643–647.

Dimberg, U., M. Thunberg, and K. Elmehed. 2000. Unconscious facial reactions to emotional facial expressions. *Psychological Science* 11:86–89.

Di Paolo, E. A. 2005. Autopoiesis, adaptivity, teleology, agency. *Phenomenology and the Cognitive Sciences* 4:97–125.

Di Paolo, E. A. 2009. Extended life. *Topoi* 28:9–21.

Di Paolo, E. A., M. Rohde, and H. De Jaegher. 2010. Horizons for the enactive mind: Values, social interaction, and play. In *Enaction: Toward a New Paradigm for Cognitive Science*, ed. J. Stewart, O. Gapenne, and E. D. Di Paolo, 33–87. Cambridge, MA: MIT Press.

Dixon, T. 2003. *From Passions to Emotions: The Creation of a Secular Psychological Category*. Cambridge: Cambridge University Press.

Dondi, M., F. Simion, and G. Caltran. 1999. Can newborns discriminate between their own cry and the cry of another newborn infant? *Developmental Psychology* 2:418–426.

Dretske, F. 1981. *Knowledge and the Flow of Information*. Cambridge, MA: MIT Press.

Dreyfus, H. L. 1972. *What Computers Can't Do: A Critique of Artificial Reason*. New York: Harper & Row.

Duffy, E. 1941. An explanation of "emotional" phenomena without the use of the concept "emotion." *Journal of General Psychology* 25:283–293.

Dutton, D. G., and A. P. Aron. 1974. Some evidence for heightened sexual attraction under conditions of high anxiety. *Journal of Personality and Social Psychology* 30:510–517.

Edelman, G. M. 1987. *Neural Darwinism: The Theory of Neuronal Group Selection*. New York: Basic Books.

Ekman, P. 1971. Universals and cultural differences in facial expressions of emotion. In *Nebraska Symposium on Motivation* 19, ed. J. Cole, 207–282. Lincoln: University of Nebraska Press.

Ekman, P. 1980a. Biological and cultural contributions to body and facial movement in the expression of emotions. In *Explaining Emotions*, ed. A. O. Rorty, 73–102. Berkeley: University of California Press.

Ekman, P. 1980b. *The Face of Man*. New York: Garland.

Ekman, P. 1994. All emotions are basic. In *The Nature of Emotion*, ed. P. Ekman and R. Davidson, 15–19. Oxford: Oxford University Press.

Ekman, P. 1999. Basic emotions. In *Handbook of Cognition and Emotion*, ed. T. Dalgleish and M. Power, 45–60. Sussex, UK: John Wiley.

Ekman, P. 2003. *Emotions Revealed: Understanding Faces and Feelings*. London: Weidenfeld & Nicolson.

Ekman, P., and D. Cordaro. 2011. What is meant by calling emotions basic. *Emotion Review* 3:364–370.

Ekman, P., and W. V. Friesen. 1971. Constants across cultures in the face and emotion. *Journal of Personality and Social Psychology* 17:124–129.

Ekman, P., and W. V. Friesen. 1975. *Unmasking the Face: A Guide to Recognizing Emotions from Facial Clues*. Englewood Cliffs, NJ: Prentice-Hall.

Ekman, P., and W. V. Friesen. 1978. *Facial Action Coding System: A Technique for the Measurement of Facial Movement*. Palo Alto: Consulting Psychologists Press.

Ekman, P., and W. V. Friesen. 1986. A new pan-cultural facial expression of emotion. *Motivation and Emotion* 10:159–168.

Ekman, P., and K. G. Heider. 1988. The universality of contempt expression: A replication. *Motivation and Emotion* 12:303–308.

Ekman, P., R. W. Levenson, and W. V. Friesen. 1983. Autonomic nervous system activity distinguishes among emotions. *Science* 221:1208–1210.

Ekman, P., E. R. Sorenson, and W. V. Friesen. 1969. Pan-cultural elements in facial displays of emotions. *Science* 164:86–88.

Ephraim, G. 1986. *A Brief Introduction to Augmented Mothering*. Radlett: Harperbury Hospital School.

Fadiga, L., L. Fogassi, G. Pavesi, and G. Rizzolatti. 1995. Motor facilitation during action observation: A magnetic stimulation study. *Journal of Neurophysiology* 73:2608–2611.

Fehr, E., and J. A. Russell. 1984. Concept of emotion viewed from a prototype perspective. *Journal of Experimental Psychology: General* 113:464–486.

Feldman, C. 2005. *Compassion: Listening to the Cries of the World*. Berkeley, CA: Rodmell Press.

Fell, J. P., III. 1965. *Emotion in the Thought of Sartre*. New York: Columbia University Press.

Ferry, B., B. Roozendaal, and J. McGaugh. 1999. Role of norepinephrine in mediating stress hormone regulation of long-term memory storage: A critical involvement of the amygdala. *Biological Psychiatry* 46:1140–1152.

Fessler, D. 2007. From appeasement to conformity: Evolutionary and cultural perspectives on shame, competition, and cooperation. In *The Self-Conscious Emotions: Theory and Research*, ed. J. Tracy, R. Robins, and J. P. Tangney, 174–193. New York: Guilford Press.

Field, T., M. Diego, M. Hernandez-Reif, and M. Fernandez. 2007. Depressed mothers' newborns show less discrimination of other newborns' cry sounds. *Infant Behavior and Development* 30:431–435.

Fodor, J. A. 1983. *The Modularity of Mind*. Cambridge, MA: MIT Press.

Fogel, A., H.-C. Hsu, A. F. Shapiro, G. C. Nelson-Goens, and C. Secrist. 2006. Effects of normal and perturbed social play on the duration and amplitude of different types of infant smiles. *Developmental Psychology* 42:459–473.

Fogel, A., E. Nwokah, J. Y. Dedo, D. Messinger, K. L. Dickson, E. Matusov, and S. Holt. 1992. Social process theory of emotion: A dynamic systems approach. *Social Development* 1:122–142.

Fogel, A., and E. Thelen. 1987. Development of early expressive and communicative action: Reinterpreting the evidence from a dynamical systems perspective. *Developmental Psychology* 23:747–761.

Foglia, L., and R. Grush. 2011. The limitations of a purely enactive (non-representational) account of imagery. *Journal of Consciousness Studies* 18:35–43.

Fox, E. 2008. *Emotion Science: Cognitive and Neuroscientific Approaches to Understanding Human Emotions*. Basingstoke: Palgrave Macmillan.

Frank, M. G., P. E. Ekman, and W. V. Friesen. 1993. Behavioral markers and recognizability of the smile of enjoyment. *Journal of Personality and Social Psychology* 64:83–93.

Freeman, W. J. 1999. Consciousness, intentionality, and causality. *Journal of Consciousness Studies* 6:143–172.

Freeman, W. J. 2000. Emotion is essential to all intentional behavior. In *Emotion, Development, and Self-Organization: Dynamic Systems Approaches to Emotional Development*, ed. M. D. Lewis and I. Granic, 209–235. Cambridge: Cambridge University Press.

Frijda, N. H. 1953. The understanding of facial expression of emotion. *Acta Psychologica* 9:294–362.

Frijda, N. H. 1986. *The Emotions*. Cambridge: Cambridge University Press.

Frijda, N. H. 1993. The place of appraisal in emotion. *Cognition and Emotion* 7:357–387.

Friston, K. 2009. The free energy principle: A rough guide to the brain? *Trends in Cognitive Sciences* 13:293–301.

Fuchs, T. 2005. Corporealized and disembodied minds: A phenomenological view of the body in melancholia and schizophrenia. *Philosophy, Psychiatry, and Psychology* 12:95–107.

Funkenstein, D. H., S. H. King, and M. Drolette. 1954. The direction of answer during a laboratory stress-inducing situation. *Psychosomatic Medicine* 16:404–413.

Gabrielsson, A., and P. N. Juslin. 2003. Emotional expression in music. In *Handbook of Affective Sciences*, ed. R. J. Davidson, K. R. Scherer, and H. H. Goldsmith, 503–534. New York: Oxford University Press.

Gaines, J. J. 1990. Maine de Biran and the body-subject. *Philosophy Today* 34:67–79.

Gallagher, S. 2001. The practice of mind: Theory, simulation, or primary interaction? *Journal of Consciousness Studies* 8:83–108.

Gallagher, S. 2003. Phenomenology and experimental design: Toward a phenomenologically enlightened experimental science. *Journal of Consciousness Studies* 10:85–99.

Gallagher, S. 2005. *How the Body Shapes the Mind*. New York: Oxford University Press.

Gallagher, S. 2007. Simulation trouble. *Social Neuroscience* 2:353–365.

Gallagher, S., and D. Zahavi. 2008. *The Phenomenological Mind: An Introduction to Philosophy of Mind and Cognitive Science*. London: Routledge.

Gallese, V. 2001. The "shared manifold" hypothesis: From mirror neurons to empathy. *Journal of Consciousness Studies* 8:33–50.

Gallese, V. 2005. Embodied simulation: From neurons to phenomenal experience. *Phenomenology and the Cognitive Sciences* 4:23–48.

Gallese, V., L. Fadiga, L. Fogassi, and G. Rizzolatti. 1996. Action recognition in the premotor cortex. *Brain* 119:593–609.

Gallese, V., and A. Goldman. 1998. Mirror neurons and the simulation theory of mind-reading. *Trends in Cognitive Sciences* 2:493–501.

Gangitano, M., F. M. Mottaghy, and A. Pascual-Leone. 2001. Phase specific modulation of cortical motor output during movement observation. *Neuroreport* 12:1489–1492.

Gardstrom, S. C. 2007. *Music Therapy Improvisation for Groups: Essential Leadership Competences.* Gilsum, NH: Barcelona Publishers.

Gendlin, E. T. 1996. *Focusing-Oriented Psychotherapy: A Manual of the Experiential Method.* New York: Guilford Press.

Gibbs, R. W. 2006. *Embodiment and Cognitive Science.* Cambridge: Cambridge University Press.

Gilbert, P. 2007. The evolution of shame as a marker for relationship security. In *The Self-Conscious Emotions: Theory and Research,* ed. J. Tracy, R. Robins, and J. P. Tangney, 283–309. New York: Guilford Press.

Giunti, M. 1997. *Computation, Dynamics, and Cognition.* Oxford: Oxford University Press.

Goldie, P. 2000. *The Emotions: A Philosophical Exploration.* Oxford: Oxford University Press.

Goldie, P., ed. 2010. *The Oxford Handbook of Philosophy of Emotion.* New York: Oxford University Press.

Goldman, A. I., and C. S. Sripada. 2005. Simulationist models of face-based emotion recognition. *Cognition* 94:193–213.

Granic, I. 2000. The self-organization of parent-child relations: Beyond bidirectional models. In *Emotion, Development, and Self-Organization: Dynamic Systems Approaches to Emotional Development,* ed. M. D. Lewis and I. Granic, 267–297. Cambridge: Cambridge University Press.

Grewe, O., R. Kopiez, and E. Altenmüller. 2009. The chill parameter: Goose bumps and shivers as promising measures in emotion research. *Music Perception: An Interdisciplinary Journal* 27:61–74.

Grewe, O., F. Nagel, R. Kopiez, and E. Altenmüller. 2007. Emotions over time: Synchronicity and development of subjective, physiological, and facial affective reactions to music. *Emotion* 7:774–788.

Griffero, T. 2010. *Atmosferologia: Estetica degli spazi emozionali.* Bari: Gius, Laterza e Figli.

Griffiths, P. E. 1997. *What Emotions Really Are.* Chicago: University of Chicago Press.

Griffiths, P. E., and R. D. Gray. 1994. Developmental systems and evolutionary explanation. *Journal of Philosophy* 91:277–304.

Gruenewald, T., S. Dickerson, and M. E. Kemeny. 2007. A social function for self-conscious emotions: The social preservation theory. In *The Self-Conscious Emotions: Theory and Research,* ed. J. Tracy, R. Robins, and J. P. Tangney, 68–90. New York: Guilford Press.

Guignon, C. 2003. Moods in Heidegger's *Being and Time*. In *What Is an Emotion? Classic and Contemporary Readings*, ed. R. C. Solomon, 181–190. Oxford: Oxford University Press.

Gurwitsch, A. 1964. *The Field of Consciousness*. Pittsburgh, PA: Duquesne University Press.

Gurwitsch, A. 1985. *Marginal Consciousness*. Athens: Ohio University Press.

Haken, H. 1977. *Synergetics—an Introduction: Nonequilibrium Phase Transitions and Self-Organization in Physics, Chemistry, and Biology*. Berlin: Springer.

Hamilton, M. C. 1995. Hamilton anxiety scale. In *Sourcebook of Adult Assessment: Applied Clinical Psychology*, ed. N. S. Schutte and J. M. Malouff, 154–157. New York: Plenum Press.

Hampshire, S. 1951. *Spinoza*. New York: Penguin Books.

Hanson, J., and M. R. Kelly, eds. 2012. *Michel Henry: The Affects of Thought*. London: Continuum.

Hardcastle, V. G. 1999. It's OK to be complicated: The case of emotion. *Journal of Consciousness Studies* 6:237–249.

Harrison, N. A., M. A. Gray, P. J. Gianaros, and H. D. Critchley. 2010. The embodiment of emotional feelings in the brain. *Journal of Neuroscience* 30:12878–12884.

Harrison, N. A., T. Singer, P. Rotshtein, R. J. Dolan, and H. D. Critchley. 2006. Pupillary contagion: Central mechanisms engaged in sadness processing. *Social Cognitive and Affective Neuroscience* 1:5–17.

Hatfield, E., J. T. Cacioppo, and R. L. Rapson. 1994. *Emotional Contagion*. Cambridge: Cambridge University Press.

Hatfield, E., R. L. Rapson, and Y.-C. L. Le. 2009. Emotional contagion and mimicry. In *The Social Neuroscience of Empathy*, ed. J. Decety and W. Ickes, 19–30. Cambridge, MA: MIT Press.

Hatfield, G. 2007. Did Descartes have a Jamesian theory of the emotions? *Philosophical Psychology* 20:413–440.

Hauskeller, M. 1995. *Atmosphären Erleben: Philosophische Untersuchungen zur Sinneswahrnehmung*. Berlin: Akademie.

Heberlein, A. S., and A. P. Atkinson. 2009. Neuroscientific evidence for simulation and shared substrates in emotion recognition: Beyond faces. *Emotion Review* 1:162–177.

Heidegger, M. [1926] 1962. *Being and Time*. Trans. J. Macquarrie and E. Robinson. Oxford: Blackwell.

Heidegger, M. [1926] 1996. *Being and Time*. Trans. J. Stambaugh. Albany: SUNY Press.

Heiser, M., M. Iacoboni, F. Maeda, J. Marcus, and J. C. Mazziotta. 2003. The essential role of Broca's area in imitation. *European Journal of Neuroscience* 17:1123–1128.

Henry, M. 1965. *Philosophie et phénoménologie du corps: Essai sur l'ontologie biranienne*. Paris: Presses Universitaires de France.

Herschbach, M. 2012. Mirroring versus simulation: On the representational function of simulation. *Synthese* 189: 483–513.

Hess, U., and S. Blairy. 2001. Facial mimicry and emotional contagion to dynamic emotional facial expressions and their influence on decoding accuracy. *International Journal of Psychophysiology* 40:129–141.

Hess, U., S. Blairy, and P. Philippot. 1999. Facial mimicry. In *The Social Context of Nonverbal Behavior*, ed. P. Philippot, R. Feldman, and E. Coats, 213–241. New York: Cambridge University Press.

Hess, U., and P. Bourgeois. 2010. You smile—I smile: Emotion expression in social interaction. *Biological Psychology* 84:514–520.

Heyes, C. M. 2011. Automatic imitation. *Psychological Bulletin* 137:463–483.

Hobbes, T. [1651] 1991. *Leviathan*. Cambridge: Cambridge University Press.

Hobson, P. R. 2002. *The Cradle of Thought: Exploring the Origins of Thinking*. London: Macmillan.

Hobson, P. R. 2009. Wittgenstein and the developmental psychopathology of autism. *New Ideas in Psychology* 27:243–257.

Hohmann, G. W. 1966. Some effects of spinal cord lesions on experienced emotional feelings. *Psychophysiology* 3:143–156.

Hsu, H.-C., and A. Fogel. 2003. Stability and transitions in mother-infant face-to-face communication during the first six months: A microhistorical approach. *Developmental Psychology* 39:1061–1082.

Hurlburt, R. T. 2007. Can there be a satisfactory introspective method? In R. T. Hurlburt and E. Schwitzgebel, *Describing Inner Experience? Proponent Meets Skeptic*, 13–39. Cambridge, MA: MIT Press.

Hurlburt, R. T. 2009. Iteratively apprehending pristine experience. In *Ten Years of Viewing from Within: The Legacy of F. J. Varela*, ed. C. Petitmengin, 156–188. Thorverton, UK: Imprint Academic.

Hurlburt, R. T., and E. Schwitzgebel. 2007. *Describing Inner Experience? Proponent Meets Skeptic*. Cambridge, MA: MIT Press.

Hurley, S. L. 1998. *Consciousness in Action*. Cambridge, MA: Harvard University Press.

Husserl, E. [1952] 1989. *Ideas Pertaining to a Pure Phenomenology and to a Phenomenological Philosophy: Second Book.* Trans. R. Rojcewicz and A. Schuwer. Dordrecht: Kluwer.

Hutto, D. D. 2011. Philosophy of mind's new lease on life. *Journal of Consciousness Studies* 18:44–64.

Hutto, D. D. 2012. Truly enactive emotion. *Emotion Review* 4:176–181.

Iacoboni, M. 2009. Imitation, empathy, and mirror neurons. *Annual Review of Psychology* 60:653–670.

Izard, C. E. 1968. Cross-cultural research findings on development in recognition of facial behavior. In *Proceedings of the 76th Annual Convention of the American Psychological Association* 3:727.

Izard, C. E. 1969. The emotions and emotion constructs in personality and culture research. In *Handbook of Modern Personality Research,* ed. R. B. Cattell and R. M. Dreger, 496–510. New York: Wiley.

Izard, C. E. 1971. *The Face of Emotion.* New York: Appleton-Century-Crofts.

Izard, C. E. 1972. *Patterns of Emotions: A New Analysis of Anxiety and Depression.* New York: Academic Press.

Izard, C. E. 2011. Forms and functions of emotions: Matters of emotion-cognition interactions. *Emotion Review* 3:371–378.

Jack, A., and A. Roepstorff. 2003. *Trusting the Subject?,* vol. 1. Thorverton, UK: Imprint Academic.

Jack, A., and A. Roepstorff. 2004. *Trusting the Subject?,* vol. 2. Thorverton, UK: Imprint Academic.

Jacob, P. 2009. A tuning-fork model of human social cognition: A critique. *Consciousness and Cognition* 18:229–243.

James, W. 1884. What is an emotion? *Mind* 9:188–205.

James, W. [1890] 1950. *The Principles of Psychology (Volume One).* New York: Dover Publications.

Johnson, M. 2007. *The Meaning of the Body: Aesthetics of Human Understanding.* Chicago: University of Chicago Press.

Johnston, L. 2002. Behavioral mimicry and stigmatization. *Social Cognition* 20:18–35.

Johnston, S. J., S. G. Boehm, D. Healy, R. Goebel, and D. E. J. Linden. 2010. Neurofeedback: A promising tool for the self-regulation of emotion networks. *NeuroImage* 49:1066–1072.

Jonas, H. 1965. Spinoza and the theory of organism. *Journal of the History of Philosophy* 3:43–57.

Jonas, H. [1966] 2001. *The Phenomenon of Life: Toward a Philosophical Biology*. Evanston, IL: Northwestern University Press.

Jones, S. S. 2009. The development of imitation in infancy. *Philosophical Transactions of the Royal Society of London, Series B: Biological Sciences* 364:2325–2335.

Jonsson, C.-O., and D. Clinton. 2006. What do mothers attune to during interactions with their infants? *Infant and Child Development* 15:387–402.

Juarrero, A. 1999. *Dynamics in Action: Intentional Behavior as a Complex System*. Cambridge, MA: MIT Press.

Kahneman, D. 1999. Objective happiness. In *Well-Being: The Foundations of Hedonic Psychology*, ed. D. Kahneman, E. Diener, and N. Schwarz, 3–25. New York: Russell Sage.

Keijzer, F. 2001. *Representation and Behavior*. Cambridge, MA: MIT Press.

Kelso, J. A. S. 1995. *Dynamic Patterns: The Self-Organization of Brain and Behavior*. Cambridge, MA: MIT Press.

Kendon, A. 1970. Movement coordination in social interactions: Some examples described. *Acta Psychologica* 32:1–25.

Kövecses, Z. 2000. *Metaphor and Emotion: Culture, Language, and Body in Human Feeling*. Cambridge: Cambridge University Press.

Kreibig, S. 2010. Autonomic nervous system activity in emotion: A review. *Biological Psychology* 84:394–421.

Krueger, J. Forthcoming. Ontogenesis of the socially extended mind. *Cognitive Systems Research*.

Laible, D. J., and R. A. Thompson. 2000. Attachment and self-organization. In *Emotion, Development, and Self-Organization: Dynamic Systems Approaches to Emotional Development*, ed. M. D. Lewis and I. Granic, 298–323. Cambridge: Cambridge University Press.

Lakin, J. L., and T. L. Chartrand. 2003. Using nonconscious behavioral mimicry to create affiliation and rapport. *Psychological Science* 14:334–339.

Lakin, J. L., and T. L. Chartrand. 2013. Behavioral mimicry as an affiliative response to social exclusion. In *The Handbook of Social Exclusion*, ed. C. N. DeWall. New York: Oxford University Press.

Lakin, J. L., T. L. Chartrand, and R. M. Arkin. 2008. I am too just like you: Nonconscious mimicry as an automatic behavioral response to social exclusion. *Psychological Science* 19:816–822.

Lambie, J. A., and A. J. Marcel. 2002. Consciousness and the varieties of emotion experience: A theoretical framework. *Psychological Review* 109:219–259.

Lange, C. G. [1885] 1922. The emotions: A psychophysiological study. In *The Emotions*, ed. K. Dunlap, 33–90. Baltimore: Williams & Wilkins.

Larsen, R., M. Kasimatis, and K. Frey. 1992. Facilitating the furrowed brow: An unobtrusive test of the facial feedback hypothesis applied to unpleasant affect. *Cognition and Emotion* 6:321–338.

Lavelli, M., and A. Fogel. 2005. Developmental changes in the relationship between the infant's attention and emotion during early face-to-face communication: The two-month transition. *Developmental Psychology* 41:265–280.

Lazarus, R. S. 1966. *Psychological Stress and the Coping Process.* New York: McGraw-Hill.

Lazarus, R. S. 2001. Relational meaning and discrete emotions. In *Appraisal Processes in Emotion: Theory, Methods, Research*, ed. K. R. Scherer, A. Schorr, and T. Johnstone, 37–67. Oxford: Oxford University Press.

Lazarus, R. S., and E. Alfert. 1964. Short-circuiting of threat by experimentally altering cognitive appraisal. *Journal of Abnormal and Social Psychology* 69:195–205.

Leder, D. 1990. *The Absent Body.* Chicago: University of Chicago Press.

LeDoux, J. E. 1996. *The Emotional Brain.* New York: Simon & Schuster.

Lee, N.-I. 1998. Edmund Husserl's phenomenology of mood. In *Alterity and Facticity*, ed. N. Depraz and D. Zahavi, 103–120. Dordrecht: Kluwer.

Lee, T. W., O. Josephs, R. J. Dolan, and H. D. Critchley. 2006. Imitating expressions: Emotion-specific neural substrates in facial mimicry. *Social Cognitive and Affective Neuroscience* 1:122–135.

Legrand, D. 2005. Transparently oneself. *Psyche* 11 (5).

Legrand, D. 2007. Pre-reflective self-consciousness: On being bodily in the world. *Janus Head* 9:493–519.

Legrand, D., and S. Ravn. 2009. Perceiving subjectivity in bodily movement: The case of dancers. *Phenomenology and the Cognitive Sciences* 8:389–408.

Le Van Quyen, M., and C. Petitmengin. 2002. Neuronal dynamics and conscious experience: An example of reciprocal causation before epileptic seizures. *Phenomenology and the Cognitive Sciences* 1:169–180.

Levenson, R. W. 2003. Autonomic specificity and emotion. In *Handbook of Affective Sciences*, ed. R. J. Davidson, K. R. Scherer, and H. H. Goldsmith, 212–224. New York: Oxford University Press.

Levenson, R. W. 2011. Basic emotions questions. *Emotion Review* 3:379–386.

Levy, R. I. 1984. Emotion, knowing, and culture. In *Culture Theory: Essays on Mind, Self, and Emotion*, ed. R. A. Shweder and R. A. LeVine, 214–237. Cambridge: Cambridge University Press.

Lewis, M. D. 2000. Emotional organization at three time scales. In *Emotion, Development, and Self-Organization: Dynamic Systems Approaches to Emotional Development*, ed. M. D. Lewis and I. Granic, 37–69. Cambridge: Cambridge University Press.

Lewis, M. D. 2005. Bridging emotion theory and neurobiology through dynamical systems modeling. *Behavioral and Brain Sciences* 28:169–245.

Lewis, M. D., and I. Granic, eds. 2000. *Emotion, Development, and Self-Organization: Dynamic Systems Approaches to Emotional Development*. Cambridge: Cambridge University Press.

Lewis, M. D., and A. Liu. 2011. Three time scales of neural self-organization underlying basic and nonbasic emotions. *Emotion Review* 3:416–423.

Lewis, M. D., and R. M. Todd. 2005. Getting emotional: A neural perspective on emotion, intention, and consciousness. *Journal of Consciousness Studies* 12:210–235.

Likowski, K. U., A. Muhlberger, B. Seibt, P. Pauli, and P. Weyers. 2008. Modulation of facial mimicry by attitudes. *Journal of Experimental Social Psychology* 44:1065–1072.

Lindquist, K. A., L. F. Barrett, E. Feld-Moreau, and J. A. Russell. 2006. Language and the perception of emotion. *Emotion* 6:125–138.

Lindquist, K. A., T. D. Wager, H. Kober, E. Feld-Moreau, and L. F. Barrett. 2012. The brain basis of emotion: A meta-analytic review. *Behavioral and Brain Sciences* 35:121–143.

Lipps, T. 1907. Das Wissen von fremden Ichen. *Psychologische Untersuchungen* 1:694–722.

Lundqvist, L. O., and U. Dimberg. 1995. Facial expressions are contagious. *Journal of Psychophysiology* 9:203–211.

Lutz, A., J. Brefczynski-Lewis, T. Johnstone, and R. J. Davidson. 2008. Regulation of the neural circuitry of emotion by compassion meditation: Effects of meditative expertise. *PLOS One* 3:e1897.

Lutz, A., J.-P. Lachaux, J. Martinerie, and F. J. Varela. 2002. Guiding the study of brain dynamics by using first-person data: Synchrony patterns correlate with ongoing conscious states during a simple visual task. *Proceedings of the National Academy of Sciences of the United States of America* 99:1586–1591.

Maeda, F., G. Kleiner-Fisman, and A. Pascual-Leone. 2002. Motor facilitation while observing hand actions: Specificity of the effect and role of the observer's orientation. *Journal of Neurophysiology* 87:1329–1335.

Maine de Biran, F.-P.-G. 1841. De l'aperception immédiate. In *Oeuvres philosophiques III*, 3–137. Paris: Librairie de Ladrange.

Marshall, E. 2008. Spinoza's cognitive affects and their feel. *British Journal for the History of Philosophy* 16:1–23.

Marshall, G. D., and P. G. Zimbardo. 1979. Affective consequences of inadequately explained physiological arousal. *Journal of Personality and Social Psychology* 37:970–988.

Maslach, C. 1979. Negative emotional biasing of unexplained arousal. *Journal of Personality and Social Psychology* 37:953–969.

Matsumoto, D., and P. Ekman. 2009. Basic emotions. In *The Oxford Companion to Emotion and the Affective Sciences*, ed. D. Sander and K. R. Scherer, 69–72. Oxford: Oxford University Press.

Maturana, H. R., and F. J. Varela. 1980. *Autopoiesis and Cognition: The Realization of the Living*. Dordrecht: D. Reidel.

Mauss, I. B., R. B. Levenson, L. McCarter, F. H. Wilhelm, and J. J. Gross. 2005. The tie that binds? Coherence among emotion experience, behavior, and physiology. *Emotion* 5:175–190.

Mayr, E. 1974. Behavior programs and evolutionary strategies. *American Scientist* 62:650–659.

McIntosh, D. N. 1996. Facial feedback hypotheses: Evidence, implications, and directions. *Motivation and Emotion* 20:121–147.

McNeill, W. H. 1995. *Keeping Together in Time: Dance and Drill in Human History*. Cambridge, MA: Harvard University Press.

Meltzoff, A. N., and M. K. Moore. 1977. Imitation of facial and manual gestures by human neonates. *Science* 198:75–78.

Merleau-Ponty, M. [1945] 1962. *Phenomenology of Perception*. Trans. C. Smith. London: Routledge.

Merleau-Ponty, M. [1968] 2001. *The Incarnate Subject: Malebranche, Biran, and Bergson on the Union of Body and Soul*. Trans. P. B. Milan. Amherst, NY: Humanity Books.

Michel, G., L. Camras, and J. Sullivan. 1992. Infant interest expressions as coordinative motor structures. *Infant Behavior and Development* 15:347–358.

Mittelmann, B., and H. G. Wolff. 1943. Emotions and skin temperature: Observations on patients during psychotherapeutic (psychoanalytic) interviews. *Psychosomatic Medicine* 5:211–213.

Montoya, P., and R. Schandry. 1994. Emotional experience and heartbeat perception in patients with spinal cord injury and control subjects. *Journal of Psychophysiology* 8:289–296.

Morrison, I., D. Lloyd, G. di Pellegrino, and N. Roberts. 2004. Vicarious responses to pain in anterior cingulate cortex: Is empathy a multisensory issue? *Cognitive, Affective, and Behavioral Neuroscience* 4:270–278.

Mukamel, R., A. D. Ekstrom, J. Kaplan, M. Iacoboni, and I. Fried. 2010. Single-neuron responses in humans during execution and observation of actions. *Current Biology* 20:750–756.

Murphy, F. C., I. Nimmo-Smith, and A. D. Lawrence. 2003. Functional neuroanatomy of emotion: A meta-analysis. *Cognitive, Affective, and Behavioral Neuroscience* 3:207–233.

Murray, A. 2002. Philosophy and the "anteriority complex." *Phenomenology and the Cognitive Sciences* 1:27–47.

Nagel, F., R. Kopiez, O. Grewe, and E. Altenmüller. 2007. EMuJoy: Software for continuous measurement of perceived emotions in music. *Behavior Research Methods* 39:283–290.

Neal, D. T., and T. Chartrand. 2011. Embodied emotion perception: Amplifying and dampening facial feedback modulates emotion perception accuracy. *Social Psychology and Personality Science* 2:673–678.

Nemeroff, C. B. 1998. The neurobiology of depression. *Scientific American* 278:42–47.

Nicotra, A., H. D. Critchley, C. J. Mathias, and R. J. Dolan. 2006. Emotional and autonomic consequences of spinal cord injury explored using functional brain imaging. *Brain* 129:718–728.

Niedenthal, P. M. 2007. Embodying emotion. *Science* 316:1002–1005.

Niedenthal, P. M., and M. Brauer. 2012. Social functionality of human emotion. *Annual Review of Psychology* 63:259–285.

Niedenthal, P. M., M. Brauer, J. B. Halberstadt, and A. H. Inner-Ker. 2001. When did her smile drop? Facial mimicry and the influences of emotional state on the detection of change in emotional expression. *Cognition and Emotion* 15:853–864.

Niedenthal, P. M., M. Mermillod, M. Maringer, and U. Hess. 2010. The simulation of smiles (SIMS) model: Embodied simulation and the meaning of facial expression. *Behavioral and Brain Sciences* 33:417–433.

Niederhoffer, K. G., and J. W. Pennebaker. 2002. Linguistic style matching in social interaction. *Journal of Language and Social Psychology* 10:59–65.

Nieuwenhuyse, B., L. Offenberg, and N. H. Frijda. 1987. Subjective emotion and reported body experience. *Motivation and Emotion* 11:169–182.

Nisbett, R. E., and S. Schachter. 1966. Cognitive manipulation of pain. *Journal of Experimental Social Psychology* 2:227–236.

Nisbett, R. E., and T. D. Wilson. 1977. Telling more than we can know: Verbal reports on mental processes. *Psychological Review* 75:522–536.

Noë, A. 2004. *Action in Perception*. Cambridge, MA: MIT Press.

O'Carroll, R. E., R. Ayling, S. M. O'Reilly, and N. T. North. 2003. Alexithymia and sense of coherence in patients with total spinal cord transection. *Psychosomatic Medicine* 65:151–155.

Ogarkova, A. Forthcoming. Folk emotion concepts: Lexicalization of emotional experiences across languages and cultures. In *Components of Emotional Meaning: A Sourcebook*, ed. J. Fontaine, K. R. Scherer, and C. Soriano. Oxford: Oxford University Press.

Öhman, A., and S. Mineka. 2001. Fears, phobias, and preparedness: Toward an evolved module of fear and fear learning. *Psychological Review* 108:483–522.

O'Regan, K. J., and A. Noë. 2001. A sensorimotor account of vision and visual consciousness. *Behavioral and Brain Sciences* 24:883–917.

Ortony, A., and T. J. Turner. 1990. What's basic about basic emotions? *Psychological Review* 97:315–331.

Overgaard, S. 2004. Heidegger on embodiment. *Journal of the British Society for Phenomenology* 35:116–131.

Oyama, S. 2000. *The Ontogeny of Information: Developmental Systems and Evolution*. Durham, NC: Duke University Press.

Panksepp, J. 1998a. *Affective Neuroscience: The Foundations of Human and Animal Emotions*. New York: Oxford University Press.

Panksepp, J. 1998b. The periconscious substrates of consciousness: Affective states and the evolutionary strategies of the self. *Journal of Consciousness Studies* 5:566–582.

Panksepp, J. 2005. Affective consciousness: Core emotional feelings in animals and humans. *Consciousness and Cognition* 14:30–80.

Panksepp, J. 2007. Neurologizing the psychology of affects: How appraisal-based constructivism and basic emotion theory can coexist. *Perspectives on Psychological Science* 2:281–296.

Panksepp, J., and C. Trevarthen. 2009. The neuroscience of emotion in music. In *Communicative Musicality: Exploring the Basis of Human Companionship*, ed. S. Malloch and C. Trevarthen, 105–146. Oxford: Oxford University Press.

Panksepp, J., and D. Watt. 2011. What is basic about basic emotions? Lasting lessons from affective neuroscience. *Emotion Review* 3:387–396.

Parvizi, J., S. Anderson, C. Martin, H. Damasio, and A. R. Damasio. 2001. Pathological laughter and crying: a link to the cerebellum. *Brain* 124:1708–1719.

Parvizi, J., and A. R. Damasio. 2001. Consciousness and the brainstem. *Cognition* 79:135–160.

Patočka, J. [1995] 1998. *Body, Community, Language, World.* Trans. E. Kohák. Chicago: Open Court.

Patterson, G. R. 1982. *Coercive Family Processes.* Eugene, OR: Castalia.

Pert, C. B. 1997. *Molecules of Emotions.* London: Simon & Schuster.

Pessoa, L. 2008. On the relationship between emotion and cognition. *Nature Reviews Neuroscience* 9:148–158.

Pessoa, L. 2010. Emotion and cognition and the amygdala: From "what is it?" to "what's to be done?" *Neuropsychologia* 48:3416–3429.

Petitmengin, C. 2006. Describing one's subjective experience in the second person: An interview method for the science of consciousness. *Phenomenology and the Cognitive Sciences* 5:229–269.

Petitmengin, C. 2007. Towards the source of thoughts: The gestural and transmodal dimension of lived experience. *Journal of Consciousness Studies* 14:54–82.

Petitmengin, C., ed. 2009. *Ten Years of Viewing from Within: The Legacy of F. J. Varela.* Thorverton, UK: Imprint Academic.

Petitmengin-Peugeot, C. 1999. The intuitive experience. *Journal of Consciousness Studies* 6:43–77.

Petitmengin, C., and Bitbol, M. 2009. The validity of first-person descriptions as authenticity and coherence. In *Ten Years of Viewing from Within: The Legacy of F. J. Varela,* ed. C. Petitmengin, 363–404. Thorverton, UK: Imprint Academic.

Petitmengin, C., V. Navarro, and M. Le Van Quyen. 2007. Anticipating seizure: Prereflective experience at the center of neuro-phenomenology. *Consciousness and Cognition* 16:746–764.

Phan, K. L., T. D. Wager, S. F. Taylor, and I. Liberzon. 2002. Functional neuroanatomy of emotion: A meta-analysis of emotion activation studies in PET and fMRI. *NeuroImage* 16:331–348.

Philippot, P., G. Chapelle, and S. Blairy. 2002. Respiratory feedback in the generation of emotion. *Cognition and Emotion* 16:605–627.

Philippot, P., and B. Rimé. 1997. The perception of bodily sensations during emotion: A cross-cultural perspective. *Polish Psychological Bulletin* 28:175–188.

Philippot, P., and Segal, Z. 2009. Mindfulness based psychological interventions: Developing emotional awareness for better being. In *Ten Years of Viewing from Within: The Legacy of F. J. Varela,* ed. C. Petitmengin, 285–306. Thorverton, UK: Imprint Academic.

Pickering, A. 2010. *The Cybernetic Brain: Sketches of Another Future*. Chicago: University of Chicago Press.

Plutchik, R. 2001. The nature of emotions. *American Scientist* 89:334–350.

Plutchik, R., and A. F. Ax. 1967. A critique of *Determinants of Emotional State* by Schachter and Singer. *Psychophysiology* 4:79–82.

Polanyi, M. 1958. *Personal Knowledge: Towards a Post-critical Philosophy*. Chicago: University of Chicago Press.

Porges, S. 1993. *Body perception questionnaire*. University of Maryland, Laboratory of Developmental Assessment.

Port, R. F., and T. J. van Gelder, eds. 1995. *Mind as Motion*. Cambridge, MA: MIT Press.

Pourtois, G., D. Grandjean, D. Sander, and P. Vuilleumier. 2004. Electrophysiological correlates of rapid spatial orienting towards fearful faces. *Cerebral Cortex* 14:619–633.

Preston, S. D., and F. B. M. de Waal. 2002. Empathy: Its ultimate and proximate bases. *Behavioral and Brain Sciences* 25:1–19.

Price, D. D., and J. J. Barrell. 2012. *Inner Experience and Neuroscience: Merging Both Perspectives*. Cambridge, MA: MIT Press.

Price, C. J., T. D. Hoyda, and A. V. Ferguson. 2008. The area postrema: A brain monitor and integrator of systemic autonomic state. *Neuroscientist* 14:182–194.

Price, D. D., J. J. Barrell, and P. Rainville. 2002. Integrating experiential-phenomenological methods and neuroscience to study neural mechanisms of pain and consciousness. *Consciousness and Cognition* 11:593–608.

Prinz, J. J. 2004a. Embodied emotions. In *Thinking about Feeling*, ed. R. C. Solomon, 44–60. Oxford: Oxford University Press.

Prinz, J. J. 2004b. *Gut Reactions: A Perceptual Theory of Emotion*. New York: Oxford University Press.

Prinz, J. J. 2005. Are emotions feelings? *Journal of Consciousness Studies* 12:9–25.

Purves, D., G. J. Augustine, D. Fitzpatrick, W. C. Hall, A.-S. LaMantia, J. O. McNamara, and L. E. White, eds. 2008. *Neuroscience*. 4th ed. Sunderland, MA: Sinauer Associates.

Quartz, S. R., and T. J. Sejnowski. 2002. *Liars, Lovers, and Heroes: What the New Brain Science Reveals about How We Become Who We Are*. New York: Harper & Row.

Rainville, P., A. Bechara, N. Naqvi, and A. R. Damasio. 2006. Basic emotions are associated with distinct patterns of cardiorespiratory activity. *International Journal of Psychophysiology* 61:5–18.

Ratcliffe, M. 2007. *Rethinking Common Sense Psychology: A Critique of Folk Psychology, Theory of Mind, and Simulation.* New York: Palgrave Macmillan.

Ratcliffe, M. 2008. *Feelings of Being: Phenomenology, Psychiatry, and the Sense of Reality.* Oxford: Oxford University Press.

Ratcliffe, M. 2009. Understanding existential changes in psychiatric illness: The indispensability of phenomenology. In *Psychiatry as Cognitive Neuroscience*, ed. M. Broome and L. Bortolotti, 223–244. Oxford: Oxford University Press.

Ratcliffe, M. 2010. The phenomenology of mood and the meaning of life. In *The Oxford Handbook of Philosophy of Emotion*, ed. P. Goldie, 349–371. New York: Oxford University Press.

Ray, E., and C. Heyes. 2011. Imitation in infancy: The wealth of the stimulus. *Developmental Science* 14:92–105.

Reddy, V. 2008. *How Infants Know Minds.* Cambridge, MA: Harvard University Press.

Register, L., and T. Henley. 1992. The phenomenology of intimacy. *Journal of Social and Personal Relationships* 9:467–481.

Reisenzein, R. 1983. The Schachter theory of emotion: Two decades later. *Psychological Bulletin* 94:239–264.

Rizzolatti, G., and C. Sinigaglia. [2006] 2008. *Mirrors in the Brain: How Our Minds Share Actions and Emotions.* Oxford: Oxford University Press.

Rizzolatti, G., and C. Sinigaglia. 2010. The functional role of the parieto-frontal mirror circuit: Interpretations and misinterpretations. *Nature Reviews Neuroscience* 11:264–274.

Rorty, A. 1982. From passions to emotions and sentiments. *Philosophy* 57:175–188.

Roseman, I. J., and C. A. Smith. 2001. Appraisal theory: Overview, assumptions, varieties, controversies. In *Appraisal Processes in Emotion: Theory, Methods, Research*, ed. K. R. Scherer, A. Schorr, and T. Johnstone, 3–19. Oxford: Oxford University Press.

Roy, J.-M., J. Petitot, B. Pachoud, and F. J. Varela. 1999. Beyond the gap: An introduction to naturalizing phenomenology. In *Naturalizing Phenomenology: Issues in Contemporary Phenomenology and Cognitive Science*, ed. J.-M. Roy, J. Petitot, B. Pachoud, and F. J. Varela, 1–80. Stanford: Stanford University Press.

Rudrauf, D., J.-P. Lachaux, A. Damasio, S. Baillet, L. Hugueville, J. Martinerie, H. Damasio, and B. Renault. 2009. Enter feelings: Somatosensory responses following early stages of visual induction of emotion. *International Journal of Psychophysiology* 72:13–23.

Russell, J. A. 1991. Culture and the categorization of emotion. *Psychological Bulletin* 110:426–450.

Russell, J. A. 1994. Is there universal recognition of emotion from facial expression? A review of the cross-cultural studies. *Psychological Bulletin* 115:102–141.

Russell, J. A. 2003. Core affect and the psychological construction of emotion. *Psychological Review* 110:145–172.

Russell, J. A. 2005. Emotion in human consciousness is built on core affect. *Journal of Consciousness Studies* 12:26–42.

Ryle, G. 1949. *The Concept of Mind.* New York: Barnes & Noble.

Salimpoor, V. N., M. Benovoy, K. Larcher, A. Dagher, and B. Zatorre. 2011. Anatomically distinct dopamine release during anticipation and experience of peak emotion to music. *Nature Neuroscience* 14:257–262.

Sander, D. 2009. Amygdala. In *The Oxford Companion to Emotion and the Affective Sciences,* ed. D. Sander and K. R. Scherer, 28–32. Oxford: Oxford University Press.

Sander, D., J. Grafman, and T. Zalla. 2003. The human amygdala: An evolved system for relevance detection. *Reviews in the Neurosciences* 14:303–316.

Sander, D., and K. R. Scherer, eds. 2009. *The Oxford Companion to Emotion and the Affective Sciences.* Oxford: Oxford University Press.

Sartre, J.-P. [1939] 1962. *Sketch for a Theory of the Emotions.* Trans. P. Mairet. London: Methuen.

Sartre, J.-P. [1943] 1958. *Being and Nothingness: An Essay on Phenomenological Ontology.* Trans. H. E. Barnes. London: Methuen.

Sass, L. A. 2004. Affectivity in schizophrenia: A phenomenological view. *Journal of Consciousness Studies* 11:127–147.

Scarantino, A. 2012. Functional specialization does not require a one-to-one mapping between brain regions and emotions. *Behavioral and Brain Sciences* 35:161–162.

Scarantino, A., and P. Griffiths. 2011. Don't give up on basic emotions. *Emotion Review* 3:444–454.

Schachter, S., and J. E. Singer. 1962. Cognitive, social, and physiological determinants of emotional state. *Psychological Review* 69:379–399.

Scheler, M. [1913–1916] 1973. *Formalism in Ethics and Non-formal Ethics of Values.* Trans. M. S. Frings and R. L. Funk. Evanston, IL: Northwestern University Press.

Scheler, M. [1923] 1954. *The Nature of Sympathy.* Trans. P. Heath. London: Routledge & Kegan Paul.

Scherer, K. R. 2000. Emotions as episodes of subsystem synchronization driven by nonlinear appraisal processes. In *Emotion, Development, and Self-Organization: Dynamic Systems Approaches to Emotional Development,* ed. M. D. Lewis and I. Granic, 100–124. Cambridge: Cambridge University Press.

Scherer, K. R. 2009. The dynamic architecture of emotion: Evidence for the component process model. *Cognition and Emotion* 23:1307–1351.

Scherer, K. R., and H. Ellgring. 2007. Are facial expressions of emotion produced by categorical affect programs or dynamically driven by appraisal? *Emotion* 7:113–130.

Scherer, K. R., and P. C. Ellsworth. 2009. Appraisal theories. In *The Oxford Companion to Emotion and the Affective Sciences*, ed. D. Sander and K. R. Scherer, 45–49. Oxford: Oxford University Press.

Scherer, K. R., A. Schorr, and T. Johnstone, eds. 2001. *Appraisal Processes in Emotion: Theory, Methods, Research*. Oxford: Oxford University Press.

Scherer, K. R., and H. G. Wallbott. 1994. Evidence for universality and cultural variation of differential emotion response patterning. *Journal of Personality and Social Psychology* 66:310–328.

Schmitter, A. M. 2010. Seventeenth and eighteenth century theories of emotions. In *The Stanford Encyclopedia of Philosophy* (winter 2010 edition), ed. E. N. Zalta. http://plato.stanford.edu/archives/win2010/entries/emotions-17th18th.

Schmitz, H. 1969. *Der Gefühlsraum (System der Philosophie III:2)*. Bonn: Bouvier.

Schmitz, H., R. O. Müllan, and I. Slaby. 2011. Emotions outside the box: The new phenomenology of feeling and corporeality. *Phenomenology and the Cognitive Sciences* 10:241–259.

Schneidermann, N., J. Francis, L. D. Sampson, and J. S. Schwaber. 1974. CNS integration of learned cardiovascular behavior. In *Limbic and Autonomic Nervous System Research*, ed. V. C. DiCara, 277–309. New York: Plenum.

Schredl, M. 2010. Dream content analysis: Basic principles. *International Journal of Dream Research* 3:65–73.

Schubert, E. 2001. Continuous measurement of self-report emotional response to music. In *Music and Emotion: Theory and Research*, ed. P. N. Juslin and J. A. Sloboda, 393–414. New York: Oxford University Press.

Schwitzgebel, E. 2007. Eric's reflections. In R. T. Hurlburt and E. Schwitzgebel, *Describing Inner Experience? Proponent Meets Skeptic*, 221–250. Cambridge, MA: MIT Press.

Segal, G. 2000. Beyond subjectivity: Spinoza's cognitivism of the emotions. *British Journal for the History of Philosophy* 8:1–19.

Segal, Z. V., J. M. G. Williams, and J. D. Teasdale. 2002. *Mindfulness-Based Cognitive Therapy for Depression: A New Approach to Preventing Relapse*. New York: Guilford Press.

Segerstrom, S. C., ed. 2012. *The Oxford Handbook of Psycho-Neuro-Immunology*. Oxford: Oxford University Press.

Seigel, J. 2005. *The Idea of the Self: Thought and Experience in Western Europe since the Seventeenth Century*. Cambridge: Cambridge University Press.

Sergerie, K., C. Chocol, and J. L. Armony. 2008. The role of the amygdala in emotional processing: A quantitative meta-analysis of functional neuroimaging studies. *Neuroscience and Biobehavioral Reviews* 32:811–830.

Shapiro, L. 2011. *Embodied Cognition.* London: Routledge.

Shaw, P., E. J. Lawrence, C. Radbourne, J. Bramham, C. E. Polkey, and A. S. David. 2004. The impact of early and late damage to the human amygdala on "theory of mind" reasoning. *Brain* 127:1535–1548.

Sheets-Johnstone, M. 1999. Emotion and movement: A beginning empirical-phenomenological analysis of their relationship. *Journal of Consciousness Studies* 6:259–277.

Sheets-Johnstone, M. 2009. Animation: The fundamental, essential, and properly descriptive concept. *Continental Philosophy Review* 42:375–400.

Shusterman, R. 2008. *Body Consciousness: A Philosophy of Mindfulness and Somaesthetics.* Cambridge: Cambridge University Press.

Shusterman, R. 2011. Somatic style. *Journal of Aesthetics and Art Criticism* 69:147–159.

Simeon, D., and J. Abugel. 2006. *Feeling Unreal: Depersonalization Disorder and the Loss of the Self.* Oxford: Oxford University Press.

Singer, T., B. Seymur, J. P. O'Doherty, H. Kaube, R. J. Dolan, and C. D. Frith. 2004. Empathy for pain involves the affective but not the sensory components of pain. *Science* 303:1157–1162.

Sloboda, J. A. 1991. Music structure and emotional response: Some empirical findings. *Psychology of Music* 19:110–120.

Smith, J. A., ed. 2008. *Qualitative Psychology: A Practical Guide to Research Methods.* London: Sage.

Smith, J. A., and Osborn, M. 2008. Interpretative phenomenological analysis. In *Qualitative Psychology: A Practical Guide to Research Methods,* ed. J. A. Smith, 53–80. London: Sage.

Smuts, B. 2001. Encounter with animal minds. *Journal of Consciousness Studies* 8:293–309.

Solomon, R. C. 2007. *True to Our Feelings: What Our Emotions Are Really Telling Us.* Oxford: Oxford University Press.

Soussignan, R. 2002. Duchenne smile, emotional experience, and autonomic reactivity: A test of the facial feedback hypothesis. *Emotion* 2:52–74.

Speisman, J. C., R. S. Lazarus, A. Mordkoff, and L. Davison. 1964. Experimental reduction of stress based on ego-defense theory. *Journal of Abnormal and Social Psychology* 68:367–380.

Spinoza, B. [1677] 1894. *Ethics.* Trans. W. H. White; rev. trans. by A. Hutchinson Stirling. London: Fisher Unwin.

Stanghellini, G. 2004. *Disembodied Spirits and Deanimated Bodies: The Psychopathology of Common Sense*. Oxford: Oxford University Press.

Stein, E. [1917] 1989. *On the Problem of Empathy*, 3rd rev. ed. Trans. W. Stein. Washington, DC: ICS Publications.

Stel, M., R. B. van Baaren, and R. Vonk. 2008. Effects of mimicking: Acting prosocially by being emotionally moved. *European Journal of Social Psychology* 38:965–976.

Stel, M., and A. van Knippenberg. 2008. The role of facial mimicry in the recognition of affect. *Psychological Science* 19:984–985.

Stepper, S., and F. Strack. 1993. Proprioceptive determinants of emotional and nonemotional feelings. *Journal of Personality and Social Psychology* 64:211–220.

Sterman, M. B. 1993. Sensorimotor EEG feedback training in the study and treatment of epilepsy. In *Neurobehavioral Treatment of Epilepsy*, ed. D. J. Mostofsky and Y. Loyning, 1–17. Hillsdale, NJ: Erlbaum.

Stern, D. N. 1985. *The Interpersonal World of the Infant: A View from Psychoanalysis and Developmental Psychology*. New York: Basic Books.

Stewart, J., O. Gapenne, and E. D. Di Paolo, eds. 2010. *Enaction: Toward a New Paradigm for Cognitive Science*. Cambridge, MA: MIT Press.

Strack, F., L. L. Martin, and S. Stepper. 1988. Inhibiting and facilitating conditions of the human smile: A nonobtrusive test of the facial feedback hypothesis. *Journal of Personality and Social Psychology* 54:768–777.

Stueber, K. 2008. Empathy. In *The Stanford Encyclopedia of Philosophy* (fall 2008 edition), ed. E. N. Zalta. http://plato.stanford.edu/archives/fall2008/entries/empathy.

Sudnow, D. 1978. *Ways of the Hand: The Organization of Improvised Conduct*. London: Routledge.

Svenaeus, F. 2009. The phenomenology of falling ill: An explication, critique, and improvement of Sartre's theory of embodiment and alienation. *Human Studies* 32:53–66.

Sze, J. A., A. Gyruak, J. W. Yuan, and R. W. Levenson. 2010. Coherence between emotional experience and physiology: Does body awareness training have an impact? *Emotion* 10:803–814.

Teroni, F., and J. Deonna. 2008. Differentiating shame from guilt. *Consciousness and Cognition* 17:725–740.

Thayer, R. E. 1989. *The Biopsychology of Mood and Arousal*. New York: Oxford University Press.

Thelen, E., G. Schöner, C. Scheier, and L. B. Smith. 2001. The dynamics of embodiment: A field theory of infant perseverative reaching. *Behavioral and Brain Sciences* 24:1–86.

Thelen, E., and L. B. Smith. 1994. *A Dynamic Systems Approach to the Development of Cognition and Action*. Cambridge, MA: MIT Press.

Thompson, E. 2001. Empathy and consciousness. *Journal of Consciousness Studies* 8:1–32.

Thompson, E. 2007. *Mind in Life: Biology, Phenomenology, and the Sciences of Mind*. Cambridge, MA: Harvard University Press.

Thompson, E. 2011a. Précis of *Mind in Life: Biology, Phenomenology, and the Sciences of Mind*. *Journal of Consciousness Studies* 18:10–22.

Thompson, E. 2011b. Reply to commentaries. *Journal of Consciousness Studies* 18:176–223.

Thompson, E., and D. Cosmelli. Forthcoming. Brain in vat or body in a world? Brainbound versus enactive views of experience. *Philosophical Topics*.

Thompson, E., A. Lutz, and D. Cosmelli. 2005. Neurophenomenology: An introduction for neurophilosophy. In *Cognition and the Brain: The Philosophy and Neuroscience Movement*, ed. A. Brook and K. Akins, 40–97. New York: Cambridge University Press.

Thompson, E., and M. Stapleton. 2009. Making sense of sense-making: Reflections on enactive and extended mind theories. *Topoi* 28:23–30.

Thompson, E., and D. Zahavi. 2007. Philosophical issues: Continental phenomenology. In *The Cambridge Handbook of Consciousness*, ed. P. D. Zelazo, M. Moscovitch, and E. Thompson, 67–88. Cambridge: Cambridge University Press.

Tomasello, M. 1999. *The Cultural Origins of Human Cognition*. Cambridge, MA: Harvard University Press.

Tomkins, S. S. 1962. *Affect, Imagery, and Consciousness*, vol. 1. New York: Springer.

Tomkins, S. S. 1963. *Affect, Imagery, and Consciousness*, vol. 2. New York: Springer.

Topulos, G. P., R. W. Lansing, and R. B. Banzett. 1993. The experience of complete neuromuscular blockade in awake humans. *Journal of Clinical Anesthesia* 5:369–374.

Tracy, J. L., R. W. Robins, and K. H. Lagattuta. 2005. Can children recognize pride? *Emotion* 5:251–257.

Tracy, J., R. Robins, and J. P. Tangney, eds. 2007. *The Self-Conscious Emotions: Theory and Research*. New York: Guilford Press.

Trevarthen, C. 1979. Communication and cooperation in early infancy: A description of primary intersubjectivity. In *Before Speech: The Beginning of Interpersonal Communication*, ed. M. Bullowa, 321–347. Cambridge: Cambridge University Press.

Tronick, E., H. Als, L. Adamson, S. Wise, and T. Brazelton. 1978. The infant's response to entrapment between contradictory messages in face-to-face interaction. *Journal of the American Academy of Child and Adolescent Psychiatry* 17:1–13.

Trope, Y. 1986. Identification and inferential processes in dispositional attribution. *Psychological Review* 93:239–257.

Tucker, D. M. 2005. Mechanisms of the occasional self. *Behavioral and Brain Sciences* 28:219–220.

Tucker, D. M., D. Derryberry, and P. Luu. 2000. Anatomy and physiology of human emotion: Vertical integration of brainstem, limbic, and cortical systems. In *The Neuropsychology of Emotion*, ed. J. C. Borod, 56–79. Oxford: Oxford University Press.

Uexküll, J. von [1934] 2010. *A Foray into the Worlds of Animals and Humans. With a Theory of Meaning*. Trans. J. D. O'Neill. Minneapolis: University of Minnesota Press.

Valins, S. 1966. Cognitive effects of false heart-rate feedback. *Journal of Personality and Social Psychology* 4:400–408.

van der Gaag, C., R. B. Minderaa, and C. Keysers. 2007. Facial expressions: What the mirror neuron system can and cannot tell us. *Social Neuroscience* 2:179–222.

van Gelder, T. J. 1998. The dynamical hypothesis in cognitive science. *Behavioral and Brain Sciences* 21:1–14.

van Gelder, T. J., and R. F. Port. 1995. It's about time: An overview of the dynamical approach to cognition. In *Mind as Motion*, ed. R. F. Port and T. J. van Gelder, 1–43. Cambridge, MA: MIT Press.

Varela, F. J. 1979. *Principles of Biological Autonomy*. New York: Elsevier.

Varela, F. J. 1996. Neurophenomenology: A methodological remedy for the hard problem. *Journal of Consciousness Studies* 3:330–350.

Varela, F. J., and J. Shear. 1999. *The View from Within: First-Person Approaches to the Study of Consciousness*. Thorverton, UK: Imprint Academic.

Varela, F. J., E. Thompson, and E. Rosch. 1991. *The Embodied Mind: Cognitive Science and Human Experience*. Cambridge, MA: MIT Press.

Velmans, M., ed. 2000. *Investigating Phenomenal Consciousness: New Methodologies and Maps*. Amsterdam: John Benjamins.

Vermersch, P. 1999. Introspection as practice. *Journal of Consciousness Studies* 6:17–42.

Vuilleumier, P. 2005. How brains beware: Neural mechanisms of emotional attention. *Trends in Cognitive Sciences* 9:585–594.

Vytal, K., and S. Hamann. 2010. Neuroimaging support for discrete neural correlates of basic emotions: A voxel-based meta-analysis. *Journal of Cognitive Neuroscience* 22:2864–2885.

Wallace, A. 1999. The Buddhist tradition of *Samatha*: Methods for refining and examining consciousness. *Journal of Consciousness Studies* 6:175–187.

Walter, H. 2012. Social cognitive neuroscience of empathy: Concepts, circuits, and genes. *Emotion Review* 4:9–17.

Watson, D., and L. A. Clark. 1994. Emotions, moods, traits, and temperaments: Conceptual distinctions and empirical findings. In *The Nature of Emotion: Fundamental Questions*, ed. P. Ekman and R. J. Davidson, 89–93. New York: Oxford University Press.

Watson, D., L. A. Clark, and A. Tellegen. 1988. Development and validation of brief measures of positive and negative affect: The PANAS scales. *Journal of Personality and Social Psychology* 54:1063–1070.

Watson, J. B. 1919. *Psychology from the Standpoint of a Behaviorist.* Philadelphia: Lippincott.

Weber, A., and F. J. Varela. 2002. Life after Kant: Natural purposes and the autopoietic foundations of biological individuality. *Phenomenology and the Cognitive Sciences* 1:97–125.

Welton, D. 1999. Soft, smooth hands: Husserl's phenomenology of the lived body. In *The Body: Classic and Contemporary Readings*, ed. D. Welton, 38–56. Malden, MA: Blackwell.

Wheeler, M. W. 2005. *Reconstructing the Cognitive World: The Next Step.* Cambridge, MA: MIT Press.

Wheeler, M. W. 2011. Mind in life or life in mind? Making sense of deep continuity. *Journal of Consciousness Studies* 18:148–168.

Wicker, B., C. Keysers, J. Plailly, J. P. Rovet, V. Gallese, and G. Rizzolatti. 2003. Both of us disgusted in my insula: The common neural basis of seeing and feeling disgust. *Neuron* 40:655–664.

Wider, K. V. 1997. *The Bodily Nature of Consciousness: Sartre and Contemporary Philosophy of Mind.* Ithaca, NY: Cornell University Press.

Wierzbicka, A. 1995. Everyday conceptions of emotion: A semantic perspective. In *Everyday Conceptions of Emotion: An Introduction to the Psychology, Anthropology, and Linguistics of Emotion*, ed. J. A. Russell, J. M. Fernandez-Dols, A. S. Manstead, and J. C. Wellencamp, 17–48. Dordrecht: Kluwer.

Wierzbicka, A. 1999. *Emotions across Languages and Cultures.* Cambridge: Cambridge University Press.

Wild, B., M. Erb, and M. Bartels. 2001. Are emotions contagious? Evoked emotions while viewing emotionally expressive faces: Quality, quantity, time course, and gender differences. *Psychiatry Research* 102:109–124.

Wispé, L. 1987. History of the concept of empathy. In *Empathy and Its Development*, ed. N. Eisenberg and J. Strayer, 17–37. Cambridge: Cambridge University Press.

Wittgenstein, L. 1980. *Remarks on the Philosophy of Psychology*, vol. 2. Ed. G. H. von Wright. Trans. G. C. H. Nyman, C. G. Luckhart, and M. A. E. Aue. Oxford: Blackwell.

Wolff, P. H. 1967. The role of biological rhythms in early psychological development. *Bulletin of the Menninger Clinic* 31:197–218.

Wolff, P. H. 1987. *The Development of Behavioral States and the Expression of Emotions in Early Infancy*. Chicago: University of Chicago Press.

Wundt, W. 1907. *Outlines of Psychology*. Leipzig: Engelmann.

Zahavi, D. 1999. *Self-Awareness and Alterity: A Phenomenological Investigation*. Evanston, IL: Northwestern University Press.

Zahavi, D. 2004. Phenomenology and the project of naturalization. *Phenomenology and the Cognitive Sciences* 3:331–347.

Zahavi, D. 2005. *Subjectivity and Selfhood: Investigating the First-Person Perspective*. Cambridge, MA: MIT Press.

Zahavi, D. 2007. Killing the strawman: Dennett and phenomenology. *Phenomenology and the Cognitive Sciences* 6:21–43.

Zahavi, D. 2008. Simulation, projection, and empathy. *Consciousness and Cognition* 17:514–522.

Zahavi, D. 2010. Empathy, embodiment, and interpersonal understanding: From Lipps to Schutz. *Inquiry* 53:285–306.

Zahavi, D. 2011a. Empathy and direct social perception. *Review of Philosophy and Psychology* 2–3:541–558.

Zahavi, D. 2011b. Varieties of reflection. *Journal of Consciousness Studies* 18:9–19.

Zahavi, D. 2012. Empathy and mirroring: Husserl and Gallese. In *Life, Subjectivity, and Art: Essays in Honor of Rudolf Bernet*, ed. R. Breeur and U. Melle, 217–254. Dordrecht: Springer.

Zajonc, R. B. 1980. Feeling and thinking: Preferences need no inferences. *American Psychologist* 35:151–175.

Zeedyk, S. M. 2006. From intersubjectivity to subjectivity: The transformative roles of emotional intimacy and imitation. *Infant and Child Development* 15:321–344.

Zillmann, D., and J. Bryant. 1974. Effect of residual excitation on the emotional response to provocation and delayed aggressive behavior. *Journal of Personality and Social Psychology* 30:782–791.

Index

Absorption, experience of, 114, 122, 128–132

Action readiness, 108, 119, 165. *See also* Action tendencies

Action tendencies, 42, 47, 50, 65, 83, 95–96, 99–100, 119

Adaptivity, in autonomous systems, 15–17, 209n22

Adolphs, R., 42, 228n15

Affect attunement, 198–199, 228n17

Affective neuroscience
neglect of emotion experience in, 143–148

Affective science. *See also* Affective neuroscience; Dynamical affective science
disciplines of, xii
and primordial affectivity, 20–24

Affectivity
active and passive dimensions of, 10
as a broad and deep phenomenon, 1–4
and enactive sense making, 18–20 (*see also* Sense making)
primordial, 2–4, 15, 19–24, 81

Affect programs, 26–28, 30, 32–33, 36, 49, 75–76, 215n9
and dynamical approaches to emotions, 58, 62, 70–71
separate from higher cognitive emotions, 73

Amygdala, 99, 190, 211–212n6, 212n9, 218n8
damage to, 35, 46
and fear, 34–35, 41–42, 44, 98
as a hub, 45
modulates visual stimuli, 42
as a relevance detector, 103–104

A-not-B error, 97

Appraisal, 45, 47, 50. *See also* Component process model (CPM); Core relational themes
automatic, 28, 76, 85, 106, 109
deliberate, 85, 106
disembodied, 83, 96, 98, 111
as driving the emotional episode, 50, 52, 61, 71, 96, 217n2
embodied, 42, 109–111 (*see also* Prinz, J. J.)
enactive reconceptualization of, 101–106
influenced by facial expressions, 95–96
phenomenology of, 106–109
primary and secondary, 85

Arkin, R. N., 194

Arnold, M. B., 84–85, 87

Aron, A. P., 90

Arousal, physiological, 87, 210n2. *See also* Autonomic nervous system (ANS)
dimensions of, 94
and lived experience, 92–93
as separate from appraisal, 96, 98
viewed as undifferentiated, 83, 87–91, 94

Arousal transfer, 90–91

As-if body loops, 168–169, 225n24

Atkinson, A. P., 191, 196

Atmosphere, 179–180

Attachment theory, 69

Autonomic nervous system (ANS), 26, 210n2

  differentiation of, 35–36, 85, 87, 94

  and disgust, 36, 162, 168

  and music, 161

  and shame, 73–74

Autonomous systems, 15–19, 55, 102, 209n22

  adaptive, 16, 82, 218n4 (*see also* Adaptivity)

  autopoietic systems as, 16

Autonomy, 15, 18, 53, 106, 209n22. *See also* Autonomous systems

  adaptive, 101, 209n22 (*see also* Adaptivity)

  autopoietic, 16

  vs. heteronomy perspective, 57

  in Spinoza, 206n9

Autopoiesis, 208n21, 209n22, 218n4. *See also* Autopoietic systems

Autopoietic systems, 16

  and teleology, 209n23

Ax, A. F., 87, 90

Background

  bodily feelings, 14, 122–128, 131–132

  disappearance, 124

  emotions, 23, 123

  feelings, 81, 123, 210n29

Bar, M., 105–106

Bargh, J. A., 187–188, 194

Barrett, L. F., 32–35, 46, 48–49, 105–106, 211n6, 213n11

Barsade, S. G., 196

Bartels, M., 195

Basic emotions. *See also* Affect programs; Expression of Emotion; Primary affects

  arbitrariness of, 36–40

  biologically, 29

as building blocks, 26, 37–38, 40–42, 44, 72, 74, 212n10

  characteristics of, 28

  conceptually, 29

  and discreteness, 28, 75–77, 216n11

  and display rules, 28, 32, 70–71

  and language, 30–31

  misguided criticisms of, 29–36

  psychologically, 29

Basic emotion theory (BET). *See* Basic emotions

Basic empathy, 173–178

  and feelings of closeness, 181–184

  and impressions, 179–180

  and sympathy, 184–187

Bayne, T., 138, 140, 142

Beer, R. D., 58, 97–98

Bejjiani, B.-P., 92

Ben-Ze'ev, A., 79, 224n14

Berger, S. M., 188

Berkowitz, L., 95

Biofeedback, 138, 162–163, 166

Bitbol, M., 56, 147, 222n5

Blairy, S., 165, 191, 195

Blends of emotions, 33, 41–43, 72

Blood, A. J., 146

Bodily feelings

  and appraisal, 108–109

  background, 14, 122–128, 131–132

  conspicuous, 114, 118–122, 129–132

  and emotion experience, 113–133, 163–170

  foreground, 121–122, 129–132

  inconspicuous, 114, 122–128, 129, 132, 163

Body. *See also* Arousal, physiological; Autonomic nervous system (ANS); Bodily feelings; Lived body

  absent, 114, 116–118, 122, 124, 129, 131

  downplayed in emotion research, 87–91

  as an intentional object of awareness, 113–118, 120–122, 124, 130, 132–133, 220n2

marginal, 115, 122, 125–126, 131
as a medium, 114, 116, 123, 128, 221n9
as merely interacting with cognition, 94–98
performative, 117–118, 121
transparent, 114, 117–118, 121–124
Body perception questionnaire, 145
Bogart, E. R., 191
Botox, and emotion recognition, 191
Brain in a vat, thought experiment, 199–200
Brauer, M., 196
Breazeal, C. L., 178
Bryant, J., 90
Buccino, S., 189

Cacioppo, J. T., 33, 94, 190, 210n2
Caldwell, P., 102–103
Caltran, G., 188
Camras, L. A., 59–62
Cannon, P. R., 188
Cannon, W. B., 87–88
Cappella, J. N., 188
Carr, L., 189–190, 228n15
Cartesian
conception of mind, xiv, 96, 175, 208n17
mechanism, 206n9
Catmur, C., 189
Chalmers, D. J., 141
Chameleon effect, 187
Chapelle, G., 165
Charney, E. J., 194
Chartrand, T. L., 187–188, 191, 194
Chills, 146, 161, 165, 225n21
Circular causality, 56, 65, 104, 218n8
Clark, A., 55–57, 205n1, 213n1, 214n3
Clark, J. A., 73–74
Cognition
affective, xvii, 18, 205n2
in all living systems, 18, 101, 209n25
and core affect, 21
emergent, 97–98

and emotion, xvii, 23–24, 42, 65, 87, 98–101, 205n2
focus on, 205n2
as a module, 96–98
and representations, 57, 209n25
as sense-making, xvii, 18, 83, 101 (see also Sense making)
as separate from bodily arousal, 91, 217n1
social, 171–172, 194
and specific emotions, 83, 88–89, 94
temporal character of, 53, 57
traditional accounts of, 103
Cognitive approach to emotion. See Appraisal
Component process model (CPM), 46, 49–52, 84, 94–95, 100, 103, 217n2
contrasted with the dynamical approach, 60–62, 71, 96–98
Conatus, 4–6
Conceptual act
approach, 66
model, 48
Contagion
emotional, 182, 190, 196
and feelings of closeness, 196
phenomenal, 190, 192–193, 195
Coordinative muscular structures, 58–62
Cordaro, D., 33, 37, 211n4, 212n8
Core affect, 20–22, 47, 75
Core relational themes, 42, 85–86, 110–111
Cosmelli, D., 102–103, 136, 142, 149, 169
Cosmides, L., 37, 211n3
Craig, A. D., 166, 167, 221n7
Critchley, H. D., 145, 166–167, 223n9, 225n22
Crying
ANS activity in, 36
in infants, 58–60, 66
for joy, 32–33
pathological, 93
and sympathy, 186
Csikszentmihalyi, M., 131

Damasio, A. R., 22–24, 41–42, 44, 92, 123–124, 142, 154, 167–169, 210n27, 210n29, 222n7, 225n24

Darwin, C., 38–40, 72, 213n15

Dasein. *See* Heidegger, M.

Davidson, R. J., 12, 148

Deep continuity of life and mind, xvi, 19, 141, 170, 203

De Jaegher, H., xiv, 101, 110, 172

Dennett, D. C., 139

Depraz, N., 149

Derryberry, D., 45

Descartes, R., 29
  influence on Maine de Biran, 9
  influence on Spinoza 4, 7–8

De Sousa, R., 48, 79

Dewey, J., xiv, 107–108, 179–180, 219n10

Dimberg, U., 187

Dimensional models of emotion, 46, 75, 216n12. *See also* Psychological construction of emotion

Di Paolo, E., xiv, 16, 101, 110, 172

Direct perception of emotion, 175–178. *See also* Basic empathy

Disgust, 27, 30, 38, 41, 88, 151, 212n6
  bodily feelings in, 118, 120, 133
  different forms of, 35–36, 162, 168
  experience of, 43
  neuroimaging studies of, 34–35
  observation of others', 103, 192–193

Dondi, M., 188

Dutton, D. G., 90

Dynamical affective science, 53, 56–69
  and basic emotions, 70–74
  and moods, 77–79, 81–82

Dynamical cognitive science, 53, 57–58, 96–97

Dynamical emotional episodes, 69–71

Dynamical systems theory (DST)
  and autonomy, 53
  fundamental concepts of, 54–56

Ekman, P., 27–28, 30–31, 33, 36–40, 75, 177, 215n9, 216n12

Ellgring, H., 51, 61, 75

Ellsworth, P. C., 39

Elmehed, K., 187

Emergence, 56, 58–61, 65, 78, 214n3. *See also* Self-organization

Emotion. *See also* Emotion experience; Emotions; Expression of emotion
  and cognition, xvii, 23–24, 42, 65, 87, 98–101
  as a distinct faculty, 1
  and emotions, 1
  families of, 33
  folk psychological conception of, 25
  as a unified category, 41, 43

Emotional episodes. *See also* Emotion forms
  boundaries of, 77–78
  prototypical, 47
  in relation to emotions, 25
  as self-organizing, 57, 69–70

Emotional interpretation, 65

Emotional sharing, and feeling close, 182

Emotion experience
  and affective neuroscience, 143–148
  and appraisal, 92–93, 107–109
  and bodily feelings, 113–133, 163–170 (*see also* Bodily feelings)
  and first-person methods, 149–152, 155–158
  influenced by bodily attitude, 95–96
  and second-person methods, 152–158
  and third-person methods, 158–163

Emotion forms, 69–72, 76–79, 82, 151
  and mood forms (*see also* Moods), 78, 82

Emotions
  basic (*see* Basic emotions)
  and emotion, 1
  higher cognitive, 43, 45–46, 73–74, 215–216n10
  modal, 67

and moods, 1, 77–82
as occurrent events (*see also* Emotional
    episodes), 25
unity of basic and nonbasic emotions,
    72, 74 (*see also* Unity/disunity)
Empathy. *See* Basic empathy
Empfindnisse, 207n13
EMuJoy software, 160
Enactivism. *See* Enactive approach
Enactive approach, xiii
    and autonomy perspective, 53
    and deep continuity of life and mind,
        xvi
    and dynamical cognitive science, 53
    and dynamical emotional episodes, 77
    and embodiment, xiv–xv
    and neurophenomenology, 135, 142,
        170
    and phenomenology, xv–xvi, 140
    and sense making (*see* Sense making)
Ephraim, G., 199
Epilepsy, 138, 154, 160
Erb, M., 195
Existential feelings, 81–82, 128, 208n20
Expression of emotion, xv, 37, 40, 72
    and basic emotions, 26–28, 30, 38–39,
        70–71, 75
    bodily, 38–39, 62, 69, 72
    in the component process model
        (CPM), 50–51
    and coordinative muscular structures,
        58–62
    and emotion perception, 49, 176–179
    facial, 27–29, 31–34, 38–39, 49, 51,
        60, 75
    influence on appraisal, 95
    in interpersonal dynamics, 66–68 (*see
        also* Affect attunement)
    linguistic, 30, 119
    mimicry of, 187–188, 190–192 (*see
        also* Contagion)
    recognition of, 31–32
    and sympathy, 185–187
    vocal, 26, 39, 49, 59, 176, 178

Fadiga, L., 189
Feelings. *See* Basic empathy; Bodily feel-
    ings; Emotion Experience; Existen-
    tial feelings
Feldman, C., 186
Field, T., 188
First-order constraints, 56, 70
First-person data
    in affective neuroscience, 144–146
    and third-person data, 136–138,
        159–161
First-person methods, xvi, 135, 139,
    143, 147–152, 155–158, 225n20
    and bodily feelings, 163–164, 166
    integrated with third-person methods,
        159–163
    and others' emotions, 192–193
    vs. quick introspective remarks,
        212n10
    renewed interest in, 147
Flow, 131
Fogel, A., 59–60, 66–68
Freeman, W. J., 23, 63–64, 66, 104
Frey, K., 95
Friesen, W. V., 27–28, 37–39, 177
Frijda, N., 31, 108, 119, 163–165,
    219n11
Fuchs, T. 80, 121

Gallagher, S., 118, 137, 141, 156, 172,
    217n16, 222n4, 227n12
Gallese, V., 189, 227n12
Gardstrom, S. C., 195, 200
Gendlin, E. T., 163–164
Gestalt psychology, xiv
Goldie, P., 25, 113, 163, 176, 182,
    184–186
Goldman, A. I., 171, 190, 227n12,
    228n13
Granic, I., 68
Griffiths, P., 29, 43–45, 215–216n10
Guignon, C., 13, 208n17
Gurwitsch, A., 124–126, 221n10

Hadley, S. W., 188
Haken, H., 55–53
Hamann, S., 35
Hardcastle, V. G, 44
Harrison, N. A., 36, 162, 168, 188
Hatfield, E., 190, 192
Hayes, A. E., 188
Heidegger, M., 3, 11–15, 18, 81–82, 117, 128
Heiser, M., 189
Henry, M., 3, 9–11, 22, 117
Herrera, P., 191, 195
Hess, U., 191, 195
Heteronomy perspective, 57, 103
Heterophenomenology, 139
Heyes, C., 188–189
Hobbes, T., 4
Hobson, P. R., 176–177
Hurlburt, R. T., 156–157
Hurley, S. L., 64, 96, 100, 103
Husserl, E., xiv, 8, 81, 140, 174, 207n13, 220n2

Iacoboni, M., 189
Impressions, 173, 179–180
  physiognomic, 11, 14
Insula, 34–35, 167–168, 190, 193, 212n6
Intentionality
  of emotions and moods, 79–81
  as goal-orientation, 63, 66
  operative, 81
  and representations, 216–217n16
Interoception, 105, 120, 122, 164–167, 220n7
Intimacy, 183–184
Introspection, 140, 146–147, 212n10, 223n10, 223n12
Izard, C. E., 27, 31, 37, 144

James, W., xiv, 43, 84–85, 87, 113–114, 122, 163, 168, 219n1, 221n10
Johnston, L., 194
Jonas, H., xvi, 17, 18, 206n9, 209n24
Juarrero, A., 56, 214n2

Kasimatis, M., 95
Kelso, S. J. A., 53, 55, 213n1
Kendon, A., 188
Keysers, C., 189
Kinesthesia, 21–22, 118–122, 207n13, 220n6
Kismet, 178–179, 226n4
Kleiner-Fisman, G., 189
Körper, 8, 114–115, 173–174, 176, 220n3
Kövecses, Z., 119
Kreibig, S., 35, 94, 162
Krueger, J., 68

Lagattuta, K. H., 40
Laible, D. J., 69
Lakin, J. L., 194
Lambie, J. A., 156
Lange, C. G., 84–85, 87
Larsen, R. M., 95
Laughter, pathological, 92–93
Lawrence, A. D., 33–35, 211n5
Lazarus, R., 42, 85–87, 110
Le, Y.-C. L., 190, 192
Leder, D., 118, 124, 128–129
LeDoux, J. E., 41–42, 44, 212n9, 218n8
Lee, N., 81
Lee, T., 190
Legrand, D., 117–118, 121, 123–124, 164, 220n4
Leib, 8, 114–115, 121, 131, 173–175, 207n11, 220n3
Le Van Quyen, M., 136, 138, 154
Levenson, R. W., 27, 38, 76, 211n3
Levy, R. I., 30
Lewis, M. D., 42, 65–66, 99–100, 159, 216n14
Likowski, K. U., 195
Limbic system, 23, 41, 44, 63, 104, 158, 212n9
Lindquist, K. A., 49, 211n6
Lipps, T., 190, 228n15
Liu, A., 65–66
Lived body, 3, 7–9, 207n13, 220n3. See also Leib

experience of the other as a, 9,
173–176
as felt-through, 116, 122–123, 128
as an intentional object, 115–116
and living body, 164–170
and self-luminosity, 121–122
Locked-in syndrome, 167
Lutz, A., 136–138, 144, 149, 159, 221n2
Luu, P., 45

Maeda, F., 189
Maine de Biran, F.-P.-G., 3, 8–10, 13
Marcel, A. J., 156
Marshall, G. D., 92
Martin, L. L., 95
Maslach, C., 88, 92
Matsumoto, D., 75, 191, 212n7
McNeill, W. H., 197
Meltzoff, A. N., 187
Merleau-Ponty, M., xiv, 8, 81, 140,
207n13, 207n14, 220n3
Meta-analyses of emotion studies, 33–
36, 211n6
Mimicry
beyond strict, 198–201
empirical evidence of, 187–190
as simulation, 190–193
and social bonding, 194–198
Minderaa, R. B., 189
Mindfulness, xv, 149–150, 153
Mirror neurons, 189, 225n24, 227n12,
228n15
Moebius syndrome, 167, 191
Moods, xiii, 1–4, 20, 77–82
Heidegger on, 12–13
Husserl on, 81
Patočka on, 13–14
Moore, M. K., 187
Morrison, I., 193
Müllan, R. O., 179
Murphy, F. C., 33–35, 211n5
Murray, A., 140
Muscular bonding, 197
Music

bodily feelings while playing, 129–131
and continuous measurement of emotion, 160–161
emotional character of, 120
responses to, 49, 146, 161, 166,
225n21
therapy, 195, 200

Neal, D. T., 191
Neurofeedback, 162. See also
Biofeedback
Neurophenomenology, 135–136
and deep continuity of life and mind,
141
and dynamical neural signatures, 137–
138, 142, 222n3
experiment, 136–137
and the explanatory gap, 141
and heterophenomenology, 139
and introspection, 140–141
and naturalizing phenomenology,
139–140
and neural correlates of consciousness
(NCC), 141–143
Niedenthal, P. M., 96, 190–191, 196
Niederhoffer, K. J., 188
Nimmo-Smith, I., 33–35, 211n5
Nisbett, R. E., 146–147
Noë, A., 64

Ogarkova, A., 30
O'Regan, K. J., 64
Ortony, A., 29, 32, 213n15

Panksepp, J., 23, 30–31, 35, 38, 44, 76,
210n27, 223n7
Paradigm scenarios, 48
Parvizi, J., 93, 142, 169
Pascual-Leone, A., 189
Patočka, J., 13–14, 22, 127
Patterson, G. R., 68
Pennebaker, J. W., 188
Pert, C. B., 169, 218n5
Pessoa, L., 42, 45, 98–100

Petitmengin, C., 136, 138, 147, 154,
    156, 164, 221n2, 222n5
Phan, Luan K., 33–34, 211n5
Philippot, P., 158, 164–165
Plutchik, R., 41–42, 90
Polanyi, M., 129
Port, R. F., 53
Primary affects, 38–39
Primary intersubjectivity, 172
Prinz, J. J., 41–43, 109–111, 151
Proactive brain, 105
Proprioception, 21–22, 104, 115–116,
    118, 121–122, 130, 164, 167, 220n7
Psychological construction of emotion,
    20, 46–47, 66, 71, 213n14. *See also*
    Conceptual act; Core affect
Purves, D., 169

Quartz, S. R., 46

Rapson, R. L., 190, 192
Ravn, S., 164, 220n2, 220n4
Rayleigh-Bénard instability, 55–56, 70,
    214n3
Reflection, 107–108, 155–156, 209n26,
    219n10. *See also* Self-awareness,
    reflective
Reflexivity
    contrasted with reflectivity, 116
Reisenzein, R., 88, 93
Representations
    in dynamical cognitive science, 57
    emotions as, 42, 110 (*see also* Prinz,
    J. J.)
    and enactivism, 18, 64, 214n5,
    216n16
Rimé, B., 164
Rizzolatti, G., 189, 227n12, 228n16
Robins, R. W., 40
Rohde, M., xiv, 101, 110
Rosch, E., xiv–xv, 136, 214n5
Roseman, I. J., 96, 106–107
Russell, J. A., 20, 29–32, 46–49, 75,
    213n11, 213n13, 219n12

Salimpoor, V. N., 161
Sander, D., 21, 103, 218n8
Sartre, J.-P., 117, 126–127, 207n13,
    221n11
Sass, L. A., 121, 221n9
Scales for measuring emotion, 144–145
Scarantino, A., 29
Schachter, S., 88–89, 91–93, 217n1
Scheler, M., 176, 183–185, 207n11,
    220n3, 226n5
Scherer, K. R., 49–51, 61–62, 75, 94–97,
    148, 159, 164–165, 224n19
Schmitz, H. 179
Schneidermann, N., 44
Schwitzgebel, E., 147, 155
Second-order constraints, 59, 69
Second-person methods, xvi, 137, 148,
    152–158, 225n20
    and bodily feelings, 163–164, 166
    and others' emotions, 192–193
    vs. quick introspective remarks,
    212n10
    renewed interest in, 147
Seigel, J., 116
Sejnowski, T. J., 46
Self-awareness
    prereflective, 114, 116–118, 121,
    221n8
    reflective, 114, 116–117, 129–130, 156
Self-intimation. *See* Self-luminosity
Self-luminosity, 9, 121, 129, 131–132
Self-observation. *See* First-person
    methods
Self-organization, xvii, 52, 55, 61, 70,
    76, 101, 104
    first- and second-order constraints in,
    56, 69–70
    neural, 58, 63–66
Sense making, xvii, 2–3, 15–19, 22, 24,
    77, 81–82, 102, 111
    and appraisal, 83–84, 101
    participatory, 172
Sensing-in, 174, 176, 183

Sensorimotor approach to perception, 64
Sensory circumventricular organs, and as-if body loops, 169
Shame, 40, 73–74, 151, 224n12
Sheets-Johnstone, M., 21, 119, 220n6
Shusterman, R., 179, 207n13, 220n4
Simion, F., 188
Simulation, 171–173, 175, 227n12, 228n13, 228n15
   critique of, 190–193
   embodied, 190
   reverse, 190
Simulationist interpretation. *See* Simulation
Singer, J. E., 49–51, 61–62, 75, 94–97, 148, 159, 164–165
Singer, T., 193
Sinigaglia, C., 189, 227n12, 228n16
Slaby, J., 179
Smile, 32, 78, 177
   and coordinative muscular structures, 58–59
   and display rules, 29
   forms of, 67
   in a group, 196
   induced by holding a pen in the lips, 95, 228n14
   in infants, 66–68
Smith, C. A., 96, 106–107
Smith, L. D., 53, 62
Smuts, B., 200
Social cognition, 171–172, 194
Solomon, R. C. 79
Spinal cord injuries, 166–167
Spinoza, B., 4–7, 22, 29
Sripada, C. S., 171, 190, 227n12, 228n13
Stanghellini, G., 121
Stapleton, M., 17, 205n2, 209n21
Stein, E., 173–176, 180–183, 226n5, 226n8
Stel, M., 191, 195
Stepper, S., 95–96

Stern, D. N., 21–22, 198–199
Stimulus evaluation checks (SECs), 50–52, 61, 94–95
Stoics, 29
Strack, F., 95–96
Sudnow, D., 130–131
Sympathy, 184–187
Sze, J. A., 160, 164, 225n20

Thelen, E., 58–60, 62, 66, 97
Third-person methods, 135, 139, 143, 148, 158–159
   integrated with first-person methods, 159–163
Thompson, E., xiv–xvi, 15–19, 53–54, 56–57, 66, 69, 81, 102–104, 136, 139–142, 149, 169, 172, 205n2, 208n21, 209n22, 209n23, 210n27, 213n2, 214n5, 215n10, 216n16, 218n4, 222n6
Thompson, R. A., 69
Thunberg, M., 187
Tipper, S. P., 188
Tomkins, S., 26, 38–39, 75
Tooby, J., 37, 211n3
Tracy, J. L., 40
Trevarthen, C., 172
Troccoli, B. T., 95
Tucker, D. M., 45, 100
Turner, T. J., 29, 32, 213n15
Two-factor theory, 88, 90, 94
   phenomenological implausibility of, 92–93

Uexküll, J. v., 17
Umwelt, 17–19, 21, 101, 218n4
Unity/disunity, of emotion, 26, 40–46, 72

Valence, 20, 47–48, 75, 144, 210n28
Valins, S., 91
van Baaren, R. B., 194–5
van der Gaag, C., 189
van Gelder, T. J., 53

van Knippenberg, A., 191
Varela, F. J., xiv–xv, 15–18, 57, 103,
    135–136, 140–141, 149, 209n23,
    214n5, 222n6
Vermersch, P., 147, 149
Vertical integration, 45
Vertical modules, 100
Vitality affects, 21–22
Vonk, R., 195
Vytal, K., 35

Wallbott, H. G., 165
Walsh, V., 189
Watt, D. F., 38, 44, 211n3
Weber, A., 17–18, 209n23
Wheeler, M., 53, 57, 222n1, 209n22,
    231n1
Wicker, B., 193, 228n15
Wierzbicka, A., 30, 210n1
Wild, B., 195
Wilson, T. D. 146–147
Witherington, D. C., 59, 61–62
Wittgenstein, L., 176
Wolff, P. H., 58–59

Zahavi, D., 116–117, 121, 140–141, 156,
    171–172, 175–176, 190, 192, 217n16
Zatorre, R. J., 146
Zillmann, D., 90
Zimbardo, P. G., 92